Music Therapy for Premature and Newborn Infants

Edited by
Monika Nöcker-Ribaupierre

Barcelona
PUBLISHERS

Music Therapy for Premature and Newborn Infants

Copyright © 2004 by Barcelona Publishers

ISBN 1-891278-20-7

2 4 6 8 9 7 5 3 1

Distributed throughout the world by:
Barcelona Publishers
4 White Brook Road
Gilsum NH 03448
Tel: 603-357-0236 Fax: 603-357-2073
Website: www.barcelonapublishers.com
SAN 298-6299

Cover illustration and design:
© 2004 Frank McShane

DEDICATION

To Cathi

This book is the result of a long part of my life with my daughter, a former very small premature infant.

I deeply thank her for teaching me the value of fighting for life and love.

ACKNOWLEDGEMENTS

With deepest gratitude and respect to all the infants and their parents in neonatal intensive care units who allowed us to help them, learn from them and develop this work, and to all the international authors who supported this interdisciplinary book by sharing their know-how and love for these small, vulnerable babies.

My thanks also to those who were interested in the idea, the process and realization of this book: to *Jan Van Camp*, who inspired me in developing the concept; to *Sibylle Baumannn*, who helped in mapping it out; to *Stefan Lullies* whose friendship and interest always have been a constant support; to *Susan Weber* for her valuable editing and translating, and *Angelika M. Findgott* for editing the English edition.

TABLE OF CONTENTS

LIST OF CONTRIBUTORS

Robert Abrams, Ph.D.
> Professor Emeritus, Obstetrics and Gynecology, University of Florida, Gainesville /USA

Heidelise Als, Ph.D.
> Associate Professor of Psychology, Department of Psychiatry, Harvard Medical School; Senior Associate in Psychiatry and Director of Neurobehavioral Infant and Child Studies, Children's Hospital Boston, Boston, Massachusetts, USA. Dr. Als is a researcher and clinician with focus on the behavioral functioning of the high risk and preterm newborn, parent–infant interaction, and new methods of neurodevelopmental assessment and intervention from newborn period into early school years. She is author of the APIB (Assessment of Preterm Infants' Behavior) and originator of individualized, behaviorally-based NICU care (NIDCAP: Newborn Individualized Developmental Care and Assessment Program) and has published widely on her theoretical and empirical work.

Elisabeth Dardart
> Music therapist, trained in Écoute Musicale Analytique, and physical therapist. Ms. Dadart is working at the Centre Hospitalier Sud Francilien, Evry/France, specializing in neonatology and the development of the initial relationship between parents and infants, including baby massage.

Christine B. Fischer, M.D.
> Research Associate in the Neurobehavioral Infant and Child Studies Laboratory at Children's Hospital Boston, Boston, Massachusetts, USA. Dr. Fischer works in research and education in the field of individualized developmental care in the NICU.

Kenneth J. Gerhardt, Ph.D.
> Professor, Communication Sciences & Disorders and Associate Dean of the Graduate School, Department of Communication Sciences & Disorders, University of Florida, Gainesville/USA

Tina Gutbrod, Ph.D.
> Development Psychologist at the University of Hertfordshire/UK, currently involved in longitudinal research on the social–emotional development of very preterm infants; particularly interested in the formation of attachment in at-risk groups.

Deanna Hanson Abromeit, M.A., MT-BC

> Music therapist specializing in music therapy in neonatology. She designed and implemented the clinical music therapy program in the NICU at the University of Iowa Hospitals and Clinic/Children's Hospital of Iowa/USA. She is currently pursuing her Ph.D. at the University of Kansas.

Gisela M. Lenz

> Music therapist and trainer, working with the effects of music therapy on interactional disorders with infants and their mothers. In her private practice in Munich/Germany, Ms. Lenz deals with mother–infant dyads, and adult psychiatric, psychosomatic, and borderline patients as well.

Joanne V. Loewy, DA, MT-BC

> Music therapist, instituted the Armstrong Music Therapy Program at Beth Israel Medical Center in NYC, where she has been the director over ten years. She received her doctorate from New York University and currently teaches in the Hahnemann's Creative Arts in Therapy Program at Drexel University in Philadelphia. Consults in the USA and internationally developing music therapy programs in medical institutions. Her work has been published by the American Academy of Pediatrics and the American Academy of Physician and Patient. Dr. Loewy chaired the first symposium on Neonatal Music Therapy in the USA and edited the texts, *Music Therapy and Pediatric Pain* (Jeffrey Books), *Music Therapy in the NICU* (Satchnote-Armstrong Press), and other texts and articles related to music psychotherapy.

Suzanne Maiello, Ph.D.

> Psychoanalytic practice for children and adults in Rome/Italy. Dr. Maiello is a founding member and past President of A.I.P.P.I. (Italian Association of Psychoanalytic Child Psychotherapy) and coordinator of the A.I.P.P.I. Parent–Infant Consultation Center. She has lectured and published worldwide. Her special field of interest lies in prenatal auditory experience, proto-mental activity and the relation between trauma and severe psychopathology.

Dorothee von Moreau, Dipl. Psych.

> Psychological psychotherapist, music therapist and training music therapist, working at the Frankfurt University for Infant and Adolescent Psychiatry, Frankfurt/Germany. Her main area of research is in music therapy documentation systems. Ms. von Moreau currently teaches at the postgraduate MT Training Courses in Munich/Germany and is a

member of the editorial board of "Musiktherapeutische Umschau."

Monika Nöcker-Ribaupierre, Ph.D.

Music therapist, specializes in auditory stimulation after premature birth, (NICU, University Children's Hospital and Harlaching Hospital, Munich/Germany), and music therapy with developmentally disabled children. Dr. Nöcker-Ribaupierre is chairperson of the postgraduate Music Therapy Training in Munich/Germany, lecturer at Ludwig-Maximilian University in Munich, member of the Scientific Board of "Musiktherapeutische Umschau" and General Secretary of the EMTC (European Music Therapy Confederation).

Mechthild Papoušek, M.D.

Associate Professor of Developmental Psychobiology at Ludwig-Maximilian University in Munich, Germany; Psychiatrist, Parent-Infant Psychotherapist.

Fred J. Schwartz, M.D.

Board-certified anesthesiologist, practicing at Piedmont Hospital in Atlanta, Georgia/USA. Dr. Schwartz has used music in the operating room and delivery suite for over 20 years, and, for the last 10 years, he has also produced music for pregnancy, childbirth, and babies.

Helen Shoemark, MME, RMT

Music therapist, clinician at the Royal Children's Hospital, Melbourne, Australia. Helen Shoemark's clinical specialization is in neonatology focusing on infants with complex surgical conditions. Her work at RHM has been a model for clinical programs in Australia and in the United States. She is an honorary life member and Past President of the Australian Music Therapy Association and is currently the Chair of Publications. She is also an honorary research fellow with the Murdoch Children's Research Institute, Melbourne, Australia.

Dieter Wolke, Ph.D.

Professor of Lifespan Psychology at the University of Bristol/UK, Department of Community Based Medicine. Professor Wolke is Deputy Director of the Avalon Longitudinal Study of Parents and Children (ALSPAC) (until 2004) and Scientific Director/CEO of the Jacobs Foundation, Zurich/Switzerland (from 2004). He researches the development of children and adolescents.

Marie-Luise Zimmer

Music teacher, music therapist and trainer. Ms. Zimmer is working in Oncology and NICU at the Zentrum für Kinderheilkunde und Jugendmedizin, Bremen/Germany. She is a lecturer at the

Internationale Gesellschaft für Tiefenpsychologie, Stuttgart/Germany. She works with adult patients in her private practice (development disorders, eating disorders, sexual and drug abuse, psychosis and cancer).

PREFACE

During a joint International Music Therapy and Music Medicine Congress in Melbourne, Australia, a small group of music therapists and doctors, working with music in Neonatal Intensive Care Units—Rosalie R. Pratt, Jayne Standley, Helen Shoemark, Fred Schwartz, and myself—presented our own research results. This personal exchange was a wonderful experience, listening to and comparing each other's approaches, ideas, and goals.

Each of us uses distinct types of music or musical elements following diverse music therapy techniques. All of this experience and research has been published. However in this increasingly important field, it is still difficult to obtain a broad based body of information in a single volume. Thus, the idea was born to put together a book on the effect of music and music therapy in neonatal care. I wanted to include these different approaches in research and clinical practice, based on basic, interdisciplinary knowledge, and updated to include current research. In addition, I elected to stress the benefits of music and music therapy as an early intervention for the long term development of hospitalized infants and as a support for their parents.

The content is presented in two parts. The first part deals with basic theories—current research on auditive development, the meaning of the mother's voice from the onset of prenatal life and attachment formation with these very low birth weight infants. The treatment concept, NIDCAP, which is also based on the infant's development and the significance of the auditory system, leads to the second part of the book on music therapy. This presents an overview of individual music therapy approaches in research and clinical practice, qualitative and quantitative research with functional and psychotherapeutical aspects, using a wide palette of music and/or musical elements.

It is my objective to present these various approaches which support the clientele and current research methodology: music therapy approaches focused on the development of the infant, relationships and bonding and the infant's unfolding ability to communicate. Each chapter contains research as well as clinical practice and experience, offering practical advice for implementing music therapy in NICUs.

This book will hopefully meet the needs of various professionals in obtaining theoretical and practice–oriented information, support music therapists working in NICUs and encourage doctors, nurses, and parents to use the benefits of music in these professional modes.

Munich, January 2004   *Monika Nöcker-Ribaupierre*

FOREWORD

The human newborn enters the extra-uterine environment with amazing predispositions to perceive, process and memorize music in its basic elements. External sounds and music and the more intimate sensations of the mother's speaking or singing voice already reach the fetus' inner ear 3 to 4 months prior to birth, contributing to the structural and functional maturation of central auditory pathways. The natural perceptual world of the fetus is enriched even earlier with bodily sensations of various vital rhythms produced by the mother's breathing, speaking, walking, or dancing.

A growing number of scientific studies continue to demonstrate one of the miracles of neonatal perception, the ability to remember and recognize the unique prosodic melody, dynamics, and rhythm of both the mother's individual speech and native language in general. Equally amazing is the well documented evidence that the newborn's perceptual predispositions are met by a natural counterpart in social environment: parents and other caregivers are endowed with complementary predispositions and genuine propensities to speak, hum or sing to the newborn, and to provide body contact with a wealth of intuitive rhythmic stimulation. The mother's rhythms and speech are also unique in as much as they provide some perceptual continuity from prenatal to postnatal experience. The newborn's early preference for the melody, rhythm and dynamics of maternal speech is met again by the mother's unconscious tendency to simplify, expand and repeat melodic contours in her speech, a tendency that has been universally reported in mothers, fathers, non-parents, children and in a variety of cultures.

Preverbal parent–infant communication has often been characterized by musical metaphors such as "mutual dance" or "singing in unison." Forms and functions of vocal communication have been extensively studied. Both infant-directed speech and infant vocalizations share a richness of fundamental musical elements, closely interrelated with a variety of adaptive functions. Melodies in motherese facilitate identification of infant-directed speech and draw the infant's attention to its musical elements. Musical elements modulate arousal and attention, communicate positive hedonic affect and deliver biologically rooted messages. As in music, the rhythmic bodily and vocal interchanges are physiologically related to the regulation of the emotional state, to arousing and soothing interventions in parental care, and to the moment–to–moment build-up or release of affective tension and arousal.

Musical elements soon become a shared alphabet for preverbal communication, and a common mode for mutual entrainment, affective attunement and sharing of emotional experience. At the same time, they also serve multiple linguistic functions, thus preparing the ground for language acquisition.

Preterm infants with extremely precocious delivery are simply deprived of natural auditory and rhythmic stimulation and adaptive functions associated with the last trimester of pregnancy. Similarly, full-term newborns in neonatal intensive care and their parents have often been deprived of mutual bodily and vocal exchanges for long periods. Moreover, fears, depression and loss of perspective in the parents resulting from facing their baby's extreme prematurity, life-threatening crises, a serious illness or congenital malformation may also seriously inhibit the parents' intuitive abilities, particularly when they fail to elicit any positive response.

Current psychobiological evidence clearly suggests that basic elements of music serve a variety of adaptive functions in intuitive parenting and preverbal communication. Accordingly, music therapy in neonatal care may mean much more than a program of mere compensatory stimulation. It may as well serve important adaptive functions particularly in the realm of early intensive care. Stimulation with rhythmic touch or massage, or with a record of the mother's voice has positive effects by itself. It may directly affect regulation of the infant's physiological state and attention and perhaps even compensate for missing intrauterine stimulation, positively affecting the processes of brain maturation.

Recently, however, early intervention programs seem to follow a general trend from mere stimulation to dialogic framing. As demonstrated with the introduction of waterbeds, even the simplest form of contingency. allowing the neonate to control the timing, intensity and tempo of rhythmic stimulation through his/her own movements, will be more effective than non-contingent stimulation of a similar kind. Dialogic framing of compensatory stimulation, particularly by means of musical elements, offers at least two advantages. On the one hand, they allow for moment–to–moment adjustments to the newborn's state and feedback signals. On the other hand, music therapy directly involving the parent, may have a strong impact on the parent's distress or depression, stimulating the parent's intuitive propensities and possibly helping them to break their silence and begin communicating with their baby through vocalizing, humming or singing. Once the infant responds to one of the parent's melodies with a moment of attention or eye opening, the parent will experience emotional closeness to the baby and growing trust in his/her genuine competence as a parent.

Many years ago, Hanuš Papoušek proposed offering early intervention programs in forms of dialogic or communication–centered therapies, and used the concept of intuitive parenting as a model for therapeutic communication. Best results may be obtained when the therapist lets himself/herself be guided by the infant's cues of perceptual or interactional readiness and begins to rely on his/her own intuitive competence.

Music therapy lends itself particularly well to dialogic forms of intervention in neonatal care. It provides a basis for the infant to self-regulate the therapist's or parent's stimulation, and enables the therapist or parent to adjust what kind of musical stimulation is used at which time, in what amount, for how long, and with or without simultaneous tactile stimulation. The Kangaroo frame may offer good opportunities for communication-centered music therapy with both parent and infant. Right from the troubled beginnings of the developing parent–infant relationships, music therapy may thus provide a dyad with the potent means of communication, mutual relaxation, enjoyment, and playfulness.

The chapters in the present book provide a lively account of the small, but rapidly growing field of basic clinical research and exploration in the area of music therapy as applied in neonatal care. The book presents a wealth of creative approaches, new insight, clinical experience, psychodynamic reasoning, and research. Individual chapters describe, review and discuss physiological and psychological effects of various forms of music therapy in neonatal care. The book offers appealing perspectives to professionals in neonatal care, perspectives that add something more "natural" to the necessary, but often-abounding technology involved in neonatal care.

Mechthild Papoušek

PART 1

THE BASICS

Chapter 1

TRUSTING BEHAVIORAL COMMUNICATION:

INDIVIDUALIZED RELATIONSHIP-BASED DEVELOPMENTAL CARE IN THE NEWBORN INTENSIVE CARE UNIT—A WAY OF MEETING THE NEURODEVELOPMENTAL EXPECTATIONS OF THE PRETERM INFANT

Christine B. Fischer and Heidelise Als

Dramatic advances in neonatal medicine in the last 20 years are assuring the survival of more and smaller preterm infants. Thus, the goal of neonatal care has recently shifted from merely survival and avoidance of major disability to the preservation of normal brain development. Long-term studies show that prematurely born infants have a significantly higher risk of later neurodevelopmental problems than their full-term peers, even when they are spared medical complications of prematurity during their stay in a Newborn Intensive Care Unit (NICU). Beyond the continued efforts to improve technology and medical care in neonatology, there are two other areas of research investigating ways of improving the neurodevelopmental outcome of preterm infants.

The first is the question of whether some of the long-term developmental problems are a by-product of modern intensive care handling and high-tech environment (Gottfried, 1985; Wolke, 1987). How much and what kind of stimulation a preterm infant needs to foster healthy development remains controversial (Klaus & Fanaroff, 1976; Linn, et al., 1985; Feldman & Eidelman, 1998). Since Spitz' work (1945) about "hospitalism," there is concern that infants in hospitals receive too little and too monotonous stimulation. They are deprived of the usual environmental sensory and social stimuli, and therefore, are at a higher risk for delayed emotional and developmental problems. The clinical response to this was the introduction of increased sensory stimulation, such as massage or exposure to different sounds. Unfortunately, many of these interventions were poorly investigated with a variety of methodological flaws, which prevented a full interpretation of the results. On the other hand, there is also concern about stimulus overload. There are warnings that the high intensive care environment exposes the preterm infant to a constant bombardment of unexpected and stressful touch, light, sound, smell, taste and motion stimuli. Hands-off programs like the "Minitouch treatment" (Jacobsen, et al. 1993), or the introduction of "rest hours" in NICUs emphasize the need of protection from these harmful stimuli (Linn, et al., 1985; Wolke, 1987; Philbin, 2000a).

The second line of research concentrates on finding explanations for why some preterm infants fare better than others. What are the risk factors that threaten healthy development, and what are the protective factors that may dampen or neutralize these risk factors and ameliorate the infant's neurodevelopmental outcome? Why do some infants seem to be so vulnerable to biological and psychosocial risks, while others have a much greater resilience even to multiple biological and psychosocial insults, and seem almost invincible? What are effective interventions that change the balance between risk and protection and vulnerability and resilience? How can we improve the delivery of care and the care environment for prematurely born infants, in order to shift the odds in favor of a good neurodevelopmental outcome (Sticker, et al., 1999)?

The National Research Council and Institute of Medicine claims that "early environments that facilitate competence and a sense of efficacy are more likely to foster children who do well" (Shonkoff & Philipps, 2000). This also appears valid for the prematurely born infant in the NICU. The concept of individualized relationship–based developmental care in the NICU, as developed, described and tested by Als and colleagues (Als, 1982; Als, et al., 1986; 1994) in the form of the NIDCAP (Newborn Individualized Developmental Care and Assessment Program) model, provides a brain based framework for NICU environment and NICU care, facilitating this competence and a sense of efficacy for the preterm infant and its family.

PRENATAL DEVELOPMENT OF THE BRAIN

The goal underlying the Individualized Developmental Care and Assessment Program is a better understanding of the mechanisms involved in normal brain development. In addition, the consequences of the disruption of normal development in prematurely born infants are examined in order to find successful solutions. For an understanding of the influence of early experience on brain development in the preterm infant, it is essential to first understand the undisturbed development of the nervous system in the womb in a full-term infant.

Neural Components of Embryogenesis: Building the Essential Form of the Central Nervous System

About 18 days after the fusion of sperm and ovum, a set of cells on the back of the developing embryo form the so–called neural plate. The lateral margins of this plate fold over forming the neural tube, giving rise to the central nervous system. The head end of the neural tube develops into the various parts of the brain, while the remainder becomes the spinal cord, peripheral nerves, and certain glands in the body (Volpe, 2000). This process, which is genetically controlled for the most part, defines the greater structure of the central nervous system.

Neural Components of Fetal and Perinatal Development: Building the Intrinsic Structure of the Central Nervous System

• Neurogenesis—The Making of the Brain Cells

As early as 6 weeks of gestation, the first neurons originate from the germinal lining of the ventricular system of the brain. The rate of neuronal production at its peak time between the 3rd and 4th month is tremendous: every minute about 200,000 new neurons are generated, and by the expected time of delivery, there will be some 100 billion. At 18 weeks of gestation, the production of new neurons slows down considerably (Marin-Padilla, 1993).

• Neuronal Migration—Getting the Brain Cells to their Specific Locations

Beginning at around 8 weeks after conception, the neurons migrate from the location of their production to their specific locations in the cerebral cortex to form the cortical plate (Grey Matter). The first neurons that arrive in the cortex take the deepest position. Those who travel later, pass them and travel to more superficial positions, thus forming an inside-out pattern. At around 24 weeks of gestation, the greater percentage of neurons have reached their destined place in the cortex (Marin-Padilla, 1993; Volpe, 2000).

• Neuronal Maturation and Organization

At 24 weeks of gestation, the time when the youngest premature infants with a chance of survival are admitted to Newborn Intensive Care Units, the brain is growing rapidly. A massive increase in cortical cell growth and differentiation changes the brain surface from a smooth surface with few major enfolds to the multifold gyri and sulci formation of the brain at the expected time of birth (see figure 1; Cowan). The peak time of neuronal maturation and organization, the elaboration of synaptic connections with other cortical and subcortical regions of the developing brain, is beginning. As soon as a neuron has migrated and reached its final destination in the different layers of the cortex, it grows axons and dendrites, which are the structures used to connect with other nerve cells. In order to give rise to the amazing achievements of the human brain, each of the billions of neurons has to organize and communicate with an average 1,000 other neurons through synapses. Thus, meaningful neuronal networks develop, building the intricate circuitry of the human brain.

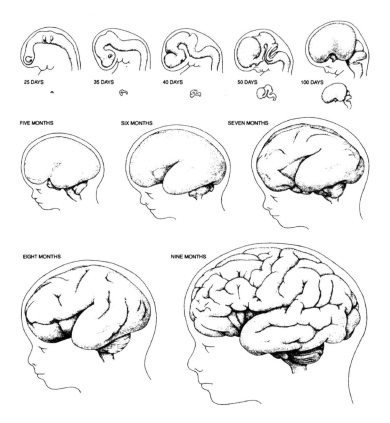

Figure 1: DEVELOPING HUMAN BRAIN is viewed from the side in this sequence of drawings, which show a succession of embryonic and fetal stages. The three main parts of the brain (the forebrain, the midbrain, and the hindbrain) originate as prominent swellings at the head end of the early neural tube. In human beings the cerebral hemispheres eventually overgrow the midbrain and also partly obscure the cerebellum. The characteristic convolutions and invaginations of the brain's surface do not begin to appear until about the middle of pregnancy (from Cowan, 1979; reprinted with permission from Nelson Prentiss).

Animal studies show that not the genetic code, but experience assumes the role of controlling and regulating which neurons connect with each other, and what circuitries are set up and established. Thus, the nervous system is designed to dynamically recruit and incorporate experience into its developing architecture and neurochemistry. Synapses that are used become stronger. Those that are not used or are redundant, are eliminated. It is estimated that about half of the neurons die in programmed cell death (apoptosis) before final maturation, and 40% of all synapses are subsequently "pruned back" as cortical development progresses (Volpe, 2000). The process of overproduction of neurons and synapses and subsequent neuron and synapse elimination plays a major role in the so-called plasticity of the developing human brain. The period of supernumerary synapses is considered the stage of "maximal opportunity and minimal commitments," providing enormous capacity for the generation of cortical diversity beyond genes (Rakic, 1995). The process of organizing and refining the neural connections is at its maximum during the perinatal period. It then proceeds rapidly throughout early childhood, continuing throughout life—however, far more slowly and less extensively than in these early pre- and post-natal months.

• Myelination—Forming the Supportive Tissue that Surrounds Nerve Cells
In order to speed up the transmission of neural impulses over sometimes quite large distances, a fatty sheath like insulation called myelin is deposited around axons. This process of myelination depends on the integrity of the neural network, and increases considerably between 31 and 40 weeks of gestation (Hüppi, et al., 1996). Myelination extends well into the postnatal period, and while most of the myelinated pathways are laid down in the early years, for some, as in the frontal cortex, myelination continues into the third decade of life. The rate and extent of myelination is also affected by experience.

• Neurochemistry of Early Brain Development
Chemical messengers in the brain play a crucial role for sending and receiving messages between neurons. These operate through receptors, most of which are located in the dendrites and synapses of neurons. The messengers and their receptors are intimately involved in growth and development of the nervous system and in neural plasticity. Input from the environment as well as events occurring in the body other than the brain influence and regulate aspects of brain neurochemistry (Rakic, 1995).

THE WORLD IN THE WOMB EXPERIENCED
THROUGHOUT THE NINE MONTHS OF PREGNANCY

The maternal womb ensures the normal environment for the growth and maturation of the developing brain. From earliest gestation on, the fetus not only takes in the various stimuli the maternal environment provides, but actively seeks them out, interacting with the environment. This uterine environment is rich and diverse, as well as highly controlled in respect to type, intensity, and timing of fetal stimuli.

• Development of Skin Sensitivity

At around 6 weeks post-conception, when the human embryo measures about 15mm, the skin area around the mouth becomes sensitive to stimulation. Over the next 2 weeks, sensitivity spreads to the nose, chin, eyelids, and palms of the hands. This is followed by sensitivity of genitalia and soles of the feet. At around 10 weeks post-conception, the entire face is sensitive, and at around 15 weeks, the whole body. (Humphrey, 1964, as quoted in: Als, 1999).

• Motion and Position

At approximately 6 weeks after conception, the formation of muscles is also rapidly advancing. The first movements, which can be observed through ultrasound imaging technology, are generalized flexion and extension, startles, hiccoughs, or head movements. During the next 8 weeks, movement patterns and repertory become more sophisticated. Arms and legs move in isolation. Hands start to explore face and body, first the same side, then crossing the midline. Neck flexion precedes forearm movement, thereby facilitating hand–face contact. Exploratory-type hand–face contact appears to become increasingly intentional, often associated with typical suckling movements of the lips, tongue, and jaw. Breathing movements start, the hands grasp and release, one hand holds onto the other and feet step along the uterine wall. The fetus yawns, sucks, swallows the amniotic fluid and frowns. A broad range of these individual physical movements are present relatively early, and their execution becomes smoother, as with time they are coordinated into integrated patterns. (Birnholz, 1988; Hepper & Shahidullah, 1992, review in: Als, 1999).

All fetal movement is closely connected to perception. Maternal movements such as walking or breathing add a second inseparable source of stimulation to the fetal tactile and vestibular system. From early on, feedback loops develop between movement, cutaneous sensitivity and cortical development. Thus, very early in brain development, when the first neurons have just reached their distinct places in the human cortex, dendritic branching, synaptogenesis, cytoarchitecture, and microorganization of the central nervous system are already guided by experience (Als, 1999).

• Odor and Taste

The environment of the fetus is replete with varied potential odor and taste stimuli. The amniotic fluid carries a large number of fragrances, which the fetus experiences through taste buds, ciliated neuroceptors of the olfactory nerve, trigeminal nerve endings and the vomeronasal subsystem, which is an accessory olfactive system especially functional in the fetus and regressing in later life (Lecanuet & Schaal, 1996). The dominant odor quality of the amniotic fluid is influenced by what the mother has ingested. There is evidence that the fetus learns, and remembers after birth flavors experienced prenatally, and seems to show a liking for these flavors as a young infant (Mennella, 2001).

• Auditory System

The human fetus has a fully functional auditory system in the last trimester of pregnancy. The intrauterine environment is also acoustically very rich. The constant rhythm of the maternal heartbeat is accompanied by maternal intestinal sounds from digestion. Sounds from the outside environment are altered by the transmission through the amniotic fluid, uterine wall and maternal tissues: higher frequencies are progressively filtered out, and the sound reaching the fetus predominantly consists of the low frequency spectrum. The prominent intrauterine sound however, dominating vascular, digestive and extra-maternal sounds is the maternal voice. The fetus clearly hears the characteristics of the maternal voice such as intonation, rhythm, and stress. This setting of low frequency background sounds with the salient and distinct features of the maternal voice makes the auditory environment in the womb an ideal learning situation. Several human studies demonstrate that the fetus not only can habituate to a recurrent sound experience, but also apply things prenatally learned after birth ("transnatal learning"). This may influence the newborn's postnatal preferences for particular stimulation. These studies show that newborns prefer their own mother's voice over other female voices (DeCasper & Fifer, 1980). Newborns recognize and prefer complex auditory stimuli they experienced repeatedly during pregnancy, i.e., their mother's language, a lullaby their mother repeatedly sang in the last weeks of pregnancy, a specific musical sequence, the theme music of a soap opera their mother watched regularly during pregnancy, or a specific story read to them (for a review, see: Lecanuet & Schaal, 1996; Moon & Fifer, 2000).

The maternal voice exemplifies another specific feature of the intrauterine learning environment. As the mother speaks, an auditory sensation reaches the fetus. At the same time, the fetus takes in the rhythmical movements of her diaphragmatic muscle. Depending on the current emotional status of the mother, not only her voice may change, but also her heart rate, her breathing, and the hormones rushing through her blood. The body position of the mother, i.e., lying in bed versus sitting or walking, may be accompanied with increased or reduced likelihood of being able to hear her voice. This connection of multiple different sensations is called multimodal perception and is in contrast to unimodal perception, when only one sensory organ is stimulated (Moon & Fifer, 2000).

• Vision

Light stimuli in the womb are extremely limited, with an estimated light transmission into the amniotic cavity of about 2%. The fetal brain neither expects nor needs external visual stimulation for the development of visual pathways. There is growing evidence that waves of internal retinal stimulation, as experienced in REM sleep, play an organizing role in the development of the visual neurosensory system (Graven, 2001).

• The Sequence of Development of the Neurosensory System

The development of the human neurosensory systems always occurs in a specific sequence: The first system that becomes functional is the tactile system, followed by the maturation of motion and position. Smell and taste are the next to develop. The development of hearing precedes the visual system, which is the last to mature (Lickliter, 2000). All sensory stimulation are characterized by the factors of timing, intensity and duration of stimulation. Prenatally incoming sensory stimulation may serve to uphold anatomic and functional integrity of the neurosensory systems during prenatal maturation, as well as playing a crucial role during the microorganization of neural networks. There is increasing evidence from animal studies, that unexpected stimuli or a change in the sequence of stimuli may lead to sensory developmental interference. For example, unusually early visual experience may compete with the development of earlier developing systems such as the auditory or olfactory system, and may alter auditory responsiveness and organization (Lickliter, 2000).

• The Full-term Infant

In the full-term infant, the massive increase in cortical cell growth and differentiation develops in an environment formed and shaped by the mother. The mother protects the fetus from environmental disturbances, provides constant temperature and regulates fetal physiology. A two-way transfer of oxygen and carbon dioxide, a steady supply of nutrients, amino acids, enzymes, vitamins, neuroactive peptides, antibodies and hormones are essential for the maternal–fetal unit. The fetus is in constant interaction with the environment, and actively shapes and competently uses the multifold possibilities the dynamic environment provides. Thus, the fetus is vitally involved in its own development (Als, 1995; Smotherman & Robinson, 1988).

THE CONTRASTING SENSORY EXPERIENCE
OF THE PRETERM INFANT EX-UTERO

The Preterm Infant—A "Displaced Fetus"

In the case of a preterm birth, this well equipped fetus suddenly moves from the manifold possibilities and characteristics of the womb environment into a very different world. Als calls the premature infant a "displaced fetus," who develops in the extrauterine setting of a high technology Newborn Intensive Care Unit at a time when the brain is growing more rapidly than at any other time in life (Als, 1999). As in the womb, the premature infant continues interacting with the environment, taking in stimuli the environment provides, and striving to go on with the developmental trajectories begun in the womb. Suddenly, however, there is a stark sensory mismatch, a world of difference between the stimuli and environment of the NICU, and what the brain expects to receive (Als, 1995).

• Disconnected from Maternal Regulation and Protection

The premature birth process causes huge physiological changes in the preterm infant in its attempt to survive outside the womb. Immature systems have to assume their tasks far too early, such as fetal circulation which suddenly must change its path, lungs must unfold to provide the infant with oxygen, the highly innervated digestive tract must work on digesting and extracting outside nutrition.

Besides these internal body changes, preterm infants suddenly experience the world without the regulating and shaping presence of the mother. As members of the human species, they expect the security of three evolutionary promised environments to promote appropriate development: the maternal womb, the mother's breast and their parents' bodies, and their family's and community's social group (Hofer, 1988). Infants born prematurely, having lost the security of the uterine environment, are deprived of the expected constant contact with their mothers. In most NICUs, infants experience the security of their parents' bodies at best for only a few hours every day. Without the regulation of the mother, physiological imbalances such as sudden changes in temperature in hormone levels and nutrient levels are the most common experiences for the prematurely born infant. Furthermore, the rhythmicity of the mother's activity and rest cycles as well as of her own nourishment replenishing and diminishing, hormonal fluctuations from calm, serene, content, happy to upset, aroused and sad, possibly angry are replaced by the artificial rhythm of the NICU's shift schedule, rigid feeding and care plans. The infant's chronobiology is left without the multifaceted individualized maternal internal biological and chronological rhythm which the infant would have experienced before maturing its own biological clock.

• Motion and Touch Experience of the Preterm Infant

Preterm birth brings an abrupt premature exchange of the aquatic environment of the womb with the terrestrial air and gravity environment of the NICU. This changes all aspects of physiology and function, making the execution of smooth movements much harder. The amniotic fluid filled sac and uterus touched the fetus constantly and assured return to softly flexed positions after all extension and activity. In air, the highly sensitive, densely innervated skin of the fetus experiences unexpected and continuous sensations of materials such as bed sheets, diapers, tubes, and tape. Blood sampling, removing of tape, inserting an i.v. tube and other invasive procedures are painful stimuli, which these especially fragile and smallest preterm infants experience on a daily, sometimes hourly basis (Murdoch & Darlow, 1984; Barker & Rutter, 1995). The misconception that preterm infants are less sensitive to pain than adults has given way to the knowledge that even the earliest born preterm infants have well functioning pain pathways and are frequently overwhelmed by physiologic stress responses to pain. The immature nervous system appears to be much more sensitive to tissue injury than the adult nervous system. Additionally, there is growing evidence that early pain and stressful experiences, besides causing acute changes, may also lead to permanent structural and functional changes, such as neuronal cell death, altered stress hormone circuits, altered pain thresholds, and abnormal pain related behaviors, and therefore altered behavioral cognitive function (Anand & Scalzo, 2000). The absence of support by the familiar person, the parent, in the face of frequent and repeated experience of pain appears to place the immature nervous system in double jeopardy for long-term sequaelae.

• Smell and Taste Experience of the Preterm Infant

At delivery, the preterm infant abruptly loses the familiar olfactory and gustatory environment and experience. Yet when held by the familiar parent, the mother's unique odor as well as that of her milk establishes a secure olfactory envelope for the infant, promoting suckling and relaxation, along with hormone release in the infant and mother (Uvnäs-Moberg, 1997). At all other times, odors and tastes from the intensive care environment and treatment dominate, such as the taste and smell of medications like antibiotics or caffeine, as well as disinfection solutions for hands and equipment. A number of NICUs have resorted to providing fragrance free environments in recognition of the infant's low threshold to olfactory activity.

• A Different World of Sounds

In a traditionally designed NICU many plexiglass incubators and metal cribs are lined up along the walls of one or several big rooms. The infant misses the attenuating effect of the maternal body. Not only the low frequency sounds such as the constant motor sounds of the incubator, but also high frequency sounds like monitor alarms abruptly and unmuted enter the infant's ear. In addition, staff voices, announcements through the overhead system, other infants crying, telephones ringing, housekeeping chores, equipment being moved, even radios playing, build a constant sound field, making the extraction and distinction of the mother's voice almost impossible. Typical sound patterns in NICUs have been reported to be loud and chaotic, devoid of predictable rhythm or pattern. They range from a low 38dB in a quiet Swedish NICU up to 75dB (which is equivalent to the sound level of a vacuum cleaner or heavy traffic) in a large US NICU (Long, et al., 1980; Philbin, 2000b). The infant experiences the mother's voice only during the hours when held closely by her. Inside a closed incubator, sounds become accentuated rather than, as is often assured, diminished. The levels of sound inside the incubator reported from different NICUs reaches between 50 and 109dB (Gottfried, 1985; Philbin, 2000b). The infant inside the incubator perceives tapping with fingers on the incubator like heavy traffic (80dB), and standard closing of the solid plastic portholes like a power mower (100dB). The dropping of the head end of the mattress produces 120dB, which is at the painful level of sound (AAP Committee on Environmental Health, 1997). The loudness of earphones and other devices that deliver music or speech directly to the infant's ear, is easily underestimated and difficult to monitor, and therefore considered potentially harmful (Graven, 2000). The American Academy of Pediatrics rates sound levels of greater than 45dB in a NICU a concern and to be avoided (AAP Committee on Environmental Health, 1997). The newest recommendations call for setting the sound levels in a unit so that the infant, when held by his mother, easily hears and recognizes her voice (Graven, 2000). Several studies showed that sound exposure in prematurely born infants may lead to short and long-term behavioral and physiological responses, such as changes in heart rate, blood pressure, intracranial pressure, potentiation of the effect of ototoxic drugs, and constant sleep disturbance, leading to sleep deprivation. Additionally, the increased frequencies in speech delay and language related problems may well be related at least in part to iatrogenic auditory and auditory processing dysfunction (Long, 1980; Gorski, et al., 1990; Graven, 2000).

• Unexpected Visual Stimuli

NICUs vary widely in regards to light exposure of preterm infants. Typically, units are illuminated 24 hours a day with a mixture of daylight and fluorescent artificial lighting. Levels reported range from 400–1000 lux during the day (sunlight shining through a south window is about 500–800 lux), and are reduced in some units during the night (Fiedler, 2000). In addition, preterm infants are often exposed to light as part of their treatment, and during special procedures. Thus, the preterm infant exchanges the dark environment of the uterus with an environment that is abruptly brighter than experienced at any other time in life. The effect of light and visual patterns on the development of the visual neurosensory system of premature infants is not known. Evidence is also lacking in humans about possible interference of this premature visual experience and the development of the other neurosensory systems, as found in animals (Lickliter, 2000).

• Interrupted Sleep
   Through the environmental stressors and Intensive Care Unit specific rhythms, the sleep of the preterm infant is repeatedly interrupted, and the developing state regulation compromised.

IMPACT OF PRETERM BIRTH ON THE NEUROBEHAVIORAL DEVELOPMENT

Cortical systems that provide buffering and differential inhibitory controls are still immature in the preterm infant. Thus, the preterm infant appears to be extremely sensitive and vulnerable to all kinds of environmental stressors in the NICU. Preterm birth threatens normal brain development in two ways. On the one hand, it makes the infant susceptible to circumstances that directly injure the brain, such as hypoxia, ischemia, intraventricular hemorrhage and infections, all correlated with long-term consequences on neurodevelopment. But even for prematurely born infants who are spared these complications, the premature birth and its consequent stay in the NICU interrupts the normal process of brain development by providing unexpected and differently timed stimuli, in the absence of evolutionary prepared, promised and expected stimuli. This leads to unexpected challenges that in turn lead to changes in brain development, appearing to result in less differentiated and modulated function, especially in complex mental processing and attentional regulation (Duffy, et al., 1984; 1990; Als, 1995; 1999).

   In comparison to their full-term peers, preterm infants have a significant increased risk for neurodevelopmental problems, i.e., attention deficit disorders, language comprehension and speech problems, emotional vulnerability, specific learning disabilities, consistently lower IQ, visual–motor impairments, which all may lead to the need for special school support (Hack, et al., 1995; Huddy, et al., 2001; McCormick, et al., 1996; Peterson, et al., 2000; Pharoah, et al., 1994a,b; Stjernqvist & Svenningsen, 1999; Wolke, 1998).

   A recent body of research links these neurodevelopmental problems to microstructural changes in brain development. Healthy preterm infants at their expected date of delivery show significantly delayed gray–white matter differentiation and myelination, as well as differences in fiber bundle thickness and orientation, including shorter fiber lengths, thinner fiber bundles and less well organized fiber bundles compared with those of infants born at term (Hüppi, 1996; 1998). Electrophysiological brain function studies in prematurely born infants 2 weeks after their expected date of delivery showed a delay in information transmission (longer latencies), as well as consistent amplitude suppression, especially in the frontal area of the brain, where complex mental processing and attention regulation is coordinated (Duffy, et al., 1990). Structural and electrophysiological differences and the corollary psychological findings continue into childhood and adolescence, underscoring that these are differences in brain development rather than delays, and making the concept of catching up irrelevant. Intervention programs, which start after discharge from the NICU and try to repair damage and shift this difference are expectedly limited in their effectiveness (McCormick, et al., 1998).

THE CONCEPT OF NEWBORN INDIVIDUALIZED DEVELOPMENTAL CARE

There is increasing evidence that the earliest possible intervention in NICU, in an individualized developmental framework, as developed by Als and her colleagues (see: Als, 1982; 1999; Als & Gilkerson, 1995; Als, et al., 1986; 1994), may be a feasible way to prevent some of the lasting effects of prematurity.

The concept of individualized developmental care is based on knowledge of the rapid and dynamic development of the human brain. The infant's behavior is seen as presenting reliable and continuous available information about the infant's current brain development and functioning. Thus, behavior serves as a guide and source of information about whether the infant is using and integrating current environmental sensory information in a productive way. The infant's behavior tells the caregiver about the infant's current goals and efforts. The behavior also indicates the infant's individual strategies to regulate and regain balance, and to forge the next steps of development.

The Synactive Theory

Als' "Model of Synactive Organization of Behavioral Development" (Als, 1982; see figure 2) is a formula for testing a framework for observation and assessment of behavioral functioning. During development, various subsystems of the functioning continuously act together ("syn–act") and are in mutual dynamic support of and regulation with one another, and in turn with the environment the organism currently finds him or herself in. These include the autonomic system, the motor system and the state organizational system, with the increasingly differentiating attentional–interactive system.

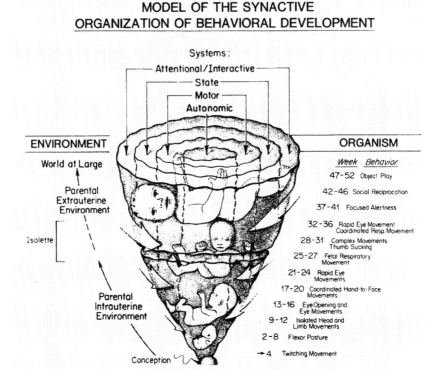

Figure 2: Model of the synactive organization of behavioral development (from: Als, 1982, reprinted with permission)

Development proceeds through continuous balancing of approach and avoidance behaviors into increasing differentiation and modulation. Thus, if timing, duration, complexity and intensity of a stimulus are currently appropriate for the current neurobehavioral balance of the infant, the infant has strategies available to approach this stimulus, seek it out and make it productive for its own development. The infant's behavior will communicate: "This is a stimulus I like, I can handle, I want to explore and come to know better." However, if timing, duration, complexity and intensity of the stimulus are currently too intense, too complex or poorly timed, the infant has strategies available to actively avoid the stimulus and move away from it. The infant's behavioral messages then relate, "Stop, this is too much, I am becoming overwhelmed, I am attempting to shut out, I am attempting to protect myself." (Als, 1982).

The behavioral subsystems thus serve as communication channels, through which the infant either signals stress and disorganization, or balance, self-regulation and competence. Observable behaviors in the autonomic system are the infant's breathing pattern, color fluctuations, visceral stability or instability and autonomic movements, such as twitches or tremors. The motor system communicates through movement patterns, fluctuation of body and facial tone, and the postural repertoire. The range of states from sleep to awake and alert, to upset and crying, the robustness and modulation of each of the states as well as the transition patterns from one state to another communicate the infant's current functioning. Generally, diffuse behaviors and extension (away) behaviors indicate strain and stress, whereas well-modulated behaviors and flexion (towards) behaviors indicate self-regulatory competence. (Als, 1982; Als, et al., 1982). Thus, an infant who takes a breathing pause, or breathes too fast and labored, or becomes very pale or dark, or very red or mottled; an infant who trembles, is startled, twitches its face, arms or legs; gags, spits up, or gasps, shows by these autonomic behaviors, that she/he is experiencing the current circumstances as a great challenge, is sensitive and stressed by them. Motor behaviors, which reflect stress and avoidance include losing all tone (flaccidity) of arms, legs and trunk and/or face, or excessive extending of arms and legs, arching and splaying of fingers and toes. An infant may use the motor system in an effort to regain balance, such as attempts to bring the hand to the mouth, bracing the legs against the incubator wall or against the hands of the caregiver, grasping and holding on to an offered finger. Through observation of these self-regulatory strategies and efforts, the infant indicates his or her competencies. An infant who is disorganized may sleep restlessly, when awake may look panicked and wide eyed, or strained and heavy lidded. He may quickly avert his eyes when looking; may stare into space, abruptly go from sleep to crying and just as abruptly fall back into a diffuse sleep, may appear frantic and inconsolable; may cry with a strained voice or silently with contorted facial expression. Thus, the infant behaviorally indicates, that he or she is stressed, out of balance and overwhelmed. Heart rate and smooth, regular breathing, good color and a stable digestive tract, relaxed posture and smooth well-regulated movements, restful sleep and animated alertness with shiny eyes, soft cheeks and a gently forward shaped mouth are all signals that the infant is doing well, regulating him- or herself competently, and perhaps even reaching out and initiating more interaction.

From Task–Oriented to Relationship–Based Care

The individualized developmental approach postulates that the infant's behavior provides the best information from which to design care (Als, 1982). The observation and interpretation of the behavior of the infant serves as a base to adjust and continuously readjust delivery of care and the environment in order to enhance the individual infant's strengths and reduce the infant's vulnerabilities.

The infant is seen as a competent and active participant. The caregiver enters into a dialogue with the infant, and always collaborating with the infant, performs all necessary medical interventions and care giving tasks. The caregiver listens to what the infant says, notices each touch, each change in the environment, each change of position, listens to what the infant communicates as to what the infant needs, and supports and adjusts delivery of care accordingly. Thus, an ongoing dialogue between infant and caregiver takes place.

Gilkerson and Als (1995) describe how the developmental approach to care shifted a nurse's thinking:

> *"I used to think, 'I am going to go in. Put a suction catheter down the endotracheal tube. I'm going to change the diaper, I am going to flip him, I'm going to close the door, and I'm going on to my next job and I'm not going to look in again until I have more tasks to do on him.' I knew what I had to do that day but I really didn't have a sense of who the little person was I was relating to.*
>
> *My mindset is different now. Now I think when I go into the isolette, it is almost like a visit. I'm coming in to communicate with you (baby) and the baby's going to communicate back with me. I'm going to observe and assess the infant and there are some things I have to do, but I'm going to watch what he's telling me and adjust what I have to do given the cues that he's giving me... I feel connected, so much more in tune."*

The traditional task-oriented approach of care grows into a relationship-based approach. The implementation requires "the processes of 'feeling,' 'seeing,' and 'noticing' what it is you are doing; then learning from what you feel, see and notice; and finally, intelligently, even intuitively adjusting your practice" (Tremmel, 1993, quoted in: Als & Gilkerson, 1995). Thus, developmental care is based on reflection. The developmental care approach builds on the strengths and competencies of the infant and family. It explores supportive opportunities in terms of the environment and delivery of care itself in order to enhance the infant's and the infant's family's sense of well-being, competence and effectiveness. The key to promoting such well-being is taking seriously, including the importance of the evolutionary promised environment of the maternal breast and the parents' bodies for the infant's development. When the NICU succeeds in organizing all care to promote the essential connection of the infant-parent system, and structures itself to safeguard its continuous bond, the family regains the assurance as primary nurturers and co-regulators of their infant (Als & Gilkerson, 1995), and the infant will thrive.

Guidelines for Developmentally Supportive NICU Care

Als and her colleagues have outlined guidelines for developmentally supportive NICU care (Als & Gilkerson, 1995; Als & McAnulty, 2000). In the approach to developmental care as described, the design and layout of the NICU puts the focus on creating a space and atmosphere where the infant and the family may heal, grow and thrive. The area is kept *calm and quiet*, in order that the infant may hear the parent's soft voice clearly, and parent and infant may sleep restfully. The *lighting is muted* and offers the possibility for individually adjusting to different levels for each infant. NICU activity unrelated to the infant's care and wellness is actively kept away from the bed space. The structure and ambience of the NICU reflects the key role of the *parents as the infant's most important nurturers and co-regulators*. The NICU provides physical and psychological space for peaceful closeness and intimacy of the whole family, including provision for parents to be with their infant 24 hours a day throughout hospitalization.

Individualized bedding and clothing, such as boundaries, buntings, "nesting," water pillow, sheepskin, and soft appropriately sized clothing is provided, adjusted to the infant's preferences and needs. From early on, the parent's body is seen as the most well adapted and nurturing bed for the infant. Opportunity for *Kangaroo care* is provided to assure emotional closeness, mutual regulation and expected neurosensory stimulation.

A primary care team is assigned to each infant and family to provide *consistency of care giving*, in order to create a sense of security and trust for the infant and family. The primary care team organizes interventions into individually appropriate clusters timed in accordance with the infant's sleep-wake cycles, states of alertness, medical needs and feeding competence. This assures times for undisturbed rest and supports growth. All special examinations, procedures and assessments including x-rays and eye examination, are performed in *collaboration* between the primary care nurse and the respective specialist, or another nurse and the parent. This assures that the infant is supported during all stressful procedures by a person who knows to read the infant and knows what best comforts and supports the infant. A specially trained *developmental support* person has a full staff position and serves as a resource for caregivers and families.

The implementation of all care takes place in this thoughtful and sensitive manner of *finely attuned dialogue between infant and caregiver*. It begins with the preparation and organization of the environment and includes introspection of the caregiver, to be emotionally and consciously available and open to the infant and family. Before hands–on interaction, the caregiver takes a moment to observe the infant, and then introduces herself with a soft voice and gentle nurturing touch. This approach helps the infant and caregiver to tune into the dialogue. The *pace of care* is consistently directed by the infant's cues. Periods of supported rest and recovery are provided, such as containment through gentle holding, and hand cradling, finger-holding or sucking. *Careful consideration is given to transition periods*, such as at the beginning and end of care, and between different care giving activities. Before moving on to another activity or leaving the infant, the caregiver makes sure that the infant is restful and comfortable.

Sometimes an infant who appears very quiet during or after caregiving procedures may likely be exhausted rather than restfully asleep. Special attention is paid to remain and gently support this infant until the infant has regained energy and self-regulation. During all necessary procedures, the infant is supported into a *softly flexed, comfortable aligned position*. The dialogue between caregiver and infant continues during feeding. The schedule and method of *feeding is individually adjusted* to the infant's rhythm and competencies. Feeding is turned into a pleasurable and nurturing experience. Over time, the infant is encouraged in taking more and more control regarding timing and duration. *Experiences of pleasure and joy* for the infant and family are important goals of everyday developmental NICU care. Individual support and encouragement of the infant and the family to take over and regulate one area of functioning after the other fosters increasing developmental competency.

RESEARCH EVIDENCE

Several studies have tested the individualized family-centered developmental care model of NICU care. An increasing body of evidence shows that very low birth weight preterm infants who are cared for in a family-centered developmentally supportive framework of NICU care, when compared with a control group receiving standard conventional NICU care, show improved medical outcome such as faster weaning from the respirator, less supplemental O_2 requirement, earlier weaning from feeding tube, and faster weight gain. Complications of prematurity such as bronchopulmonary dysplasia or intraventricular hemorrhage have been shown to be significantly less severe in the developmental care group. Infants in the developmental care group were discharged from the hospital at an earlier age, and their hospital charges were significantly reduced.

In a neurobehavioral assessment two weeks after the expected date of delivery, infants cared for in the individualized developmental care approach were significantly more well organized and showed improved self-regulatory capacities. Long-term neuropsychological outcome studies at 9 and 18 months, and 3 and 7 years show that these developmental advantages remain consistent for the group of infants cared for with the developmental care approach (Als, et al., 1986; 1994, and unpublished data; Becker, et al., 1991; Fleisher, et al., 1995; Parker, et al., 1992; Stevens, et al., 1996; Westrup, et al., 2000). A study of healthy low-risk preterm infants cared for with the individualized developmental approach showed at 2 weeks after expected time of delivery more well modulated behavioral organization autonomically, motorically, in terms of state organization and attentional functioning compared to a group of low-risk preterm infants cared for the conventional way. The preterm infants in the developmental care group were behaviorally comparable to healthy full-term infants. Electrophysiological findings indicate improved frontal lobe function (Buehler, et al., 1995).

CONCLUSION

In trusting the communication of the preterm infant, care providers in the NICU find a reliable continuously available source of information, about what a preterm infant currently expects, seeks, and attempts to accomplish. The question of how much and what stimulation the preterm infant expects for healthy development may be answered for each infant in an individualized and continuously attuned manner. Thus, the application of generalized standardized stimulation programs which disregard the behavioral signals and guidance of the individual infant may, while well intended, prove rather harmful to the individual infant. By contrast, approaching and interacting with an infant in a continuous, mutual connectedness and regulation, provides experiences that foster the strengths and a sense of competence and efficacy in the preterm infant. Thus, individualized relationship-based developmental care in the NICU may be seen as a protective factor, which increases the odds for the individual infant of favorable development and outcome.

Chapter 2

FETAL HEARING:
IMPLICATIONS FOR THE NEONATE

Kenneth J. Gerhardt and Robert M. Abrams

A wonderful story about the king of France, Henry IVth (1553), quoted by Jean-Pierre Lecanuet (1996) serves as an appropriate introduction to fetal hearing. "It is reported that whilst she was pregnant with the future King Henry IVth, Jeanne d'Albret had a woman play music for her every morning. This was in accord with the belief at the time that the fetus was able to hear the music in the womb and that listening to music would mould the temperament of the baby, thus preventing him from having a dark disposition. According to historians, Henry IVth never lost his joviality…" (Castarede, 1987).

Reports of fetal perception and response to sounds continue to be reported in today's lay literature. Obstetricians have been interested in using responses as a measure of fetal health. Psychobiologists, on the other hand, have been exploring the consequences of the prenatal function of the auditory system. Critical to any discussion on the meaning of sounds, particularly sounds organized into what we know as music, is a knowledge of what it is the fetus is truly hearing.

Based upon what we now understand of the transmission characteristics of sound into and through the body, it is clear that the perception of music by the fetus is quite different than it would be if "heard" outside of the womb. Thus, a quantification of those components of intrauterine sound—the frequency, intensity, and time—are deemed necessary before an interpretation of these effects on the fetus can justifiably be attempted.

SOUND TRANSMISSION TO THE FETAL HEAD

Specifications of the amplitudes and frequency distributions of sounds reaching the fetal head have implications for our understanding of fetal responses. The fetal sound environment is composed of a variety of internally generated noises, as well as many sounds originating in the environment of its mother (Gerhardt, Abrams, & Oliver, 1990). The stimulus used to produce a fetal response is altered as it passes through the abdominal wall and uterus and into the amniotic fluid.

As a general reference for the reader, the *frequency* of a sound relates to *pitch*; the *level in decibels* (dB) of a sound relates to *loudness*. The dB, a measurement of amplitude, uses a logarithmic scale typically referenced to a known sound pressure level (dB SPL, re: 20 microPascals. A Pascal [Pa] is a unit of pressure equal to a force of one Newton [N] acting over an area of a square meter). Frequency is expressed in cycles per second or Hertz (Hz). For example, 125Hz is the average fundamental frequency (or pitch) of an adult male's voice, or approximately one octave below middle C on the piano keyboard. The average fundamental frequency of a female's voice is 220Hz.

Speech produced during normal conversation is approximately 75dB SPL and is comprised of acoustical energy primarily between 200 and 3000Hz. Speech becomes unintelligible when the background noise in the speech-frequency range exceeds the level of the message by approximately 10dB.

There are many factors that determine how well a fetus will hear speech as well as music from outside its mother. These factors include the frequency content and level of the internal noise floor; the attenuation of external signals provided by the tissues and fluids surrounding the fetal head; sound transmission into the fetal inner ear and the sensitivity of the hearing mechanism at the time of sound stimulation.

The acoustical characteristics of external sounds that penetrate the uterus have been described in humans (Walker, Grimwade, & Wood, 1971; Querleu, Renard, Versyp, Paris-Delrue, & Crepin, 1988; Richards, Frentzen, Gerhardt, & McCann, 1992). An underwater microphone, referred to as a hydrophone, positioned inside the cervix or inside the uterine body after amniotomy has been used by many scientists to measure the sound pressure levels produced by a loudspeaker located near the abdomen. Recorded levels are then compared to levels detected with a standard microphone positioned between the loudspeaker and abdomen. Intrauterine levels in humans (Gagnon, Benzaquen, & Hunse, 1992) are very similar to those recorded in pregnant sheep via a chronically implanted hydrophone on the fetal head inside the intact uterus (Vince, Armitage, Baldwin, & Toner, 1982; Vince, Billing, Baldwin, Toner, & Weller 1985; Gerhardt, 1989).

Sounds generated inside the mother and present in the uterus are associated with maternal respiratory, cardiovascular and intestinal activity and with body movements (Armitage, Baldwin, & Vince, 1980; Querleu, Renard, & Crepin, 1989; Gerhardt, et al., 1990). These sounds provide a background or "noise floor" above which maternal vocalizations and externally generated sounds emerge. Internal sounds of sheep have a predominately low frequency (<100Hz) and reach 90dB SPL (Gerhardt, et al., 1990). Spectral levels decrease as frequency increases and are as low as 40dB for higher frequencies. Gagnon, et al. (1992) positioned a hydrophone in a pocket of fluid near the human fetal neck and measured sound pressure levels of 60dB for 100Hz and less than 40dB for 200Hz and above. Thus, for both humans and sheep, the noise floor tends to be dominated by low-frequency energy less that 100Hz and can reach levels as high as 90dB.

Exogenous low-frequency sounds, less than 200Hz, penetrate the uterus with very little reduction in sound pressure (<5dB). Some enhancement of low-frequency sound pressures has been reported in both humans (Richards, et al,. 1992) and sheep (Vince, et al., 1982; Vince, et al., 1985; Gerhardt, et al., 1990). In other words, sound pressures can be greater inside the abdomen than outside. Higher frequencies up to 4000Hz are attenuated by approximately 20dB. These general findings have been refined and extended by Peters, Gerhardt, Abrams, & Longmate, (1993) who evaluated the transfer of airborne sounds across the abdominal wall of sheep as a function of frequency and intraabdominal location.

Above the frequency range of 125–2000Hz, the abdomen can be characterized as a low-pass filter with high-frequency energy rejected at a rate of approximately 6dB/octave (Gerhardt, et al., 1990). Thus, the tissues and fluids of pregnancy shape external stimuli before reaching the fetal head.

DEVELOPMENT OF FETAL HEARING

Human fetal auditory responsiveness begins about the 24th week of gestation (Birnholz & Benacerraf, 1983; Crade & Lovett, 1988). During the next 15 weeks, exogenous sounds may have an effect on fetal behavior and central nervous system development. It is during the latter stages of fetal development, when the hearing mechanism is intact, that the human fetus may be most influenced by the sound environment inside and outside its mother (Spence & DeCasper, 1987).

The auditory system of the fetus does not just begin to function uniformly across frequencies. Low frequencies are coded at the apex; high frequencies are coded at the base of the cochlea. The development follows a consistent pattern. While the adult range of audibility is from 20–20,000Hz with greatest sensitivity in the 300–3000Hz range, the fetus hears a much more limited range. Hepper and Shahidullah (1994) examined the range of frequencies and intensity levels required to elicit human fetal movements as assessed with ultrasonography. Only one of 450 fetuses involved in the study demonstrated a response to a 500Hz tone at 19 weeks gestation. By 27 weeks, 96% of the fetuses responded to tones at 250 and 500Hz, while no responses were recorded from any of the fetuses for 1000 and 3000Hz. It was not until weeks 29 and 31 that the fetuses responded to tones at 1000 and 3000Hz, respectively. Between 33 and 35 weeks gestation, the fetuses were responding all of the time to presentations of 1000 and 3000Hz. As gestation progressed from 19–37 weeks, the fetuses responded to frequencies over a progressively wider range. During this period, there was a significant decrease in the intensity level of stimulus required to elicit a response for all frequencies. This finding suggests that fetal hearing to pure tones becomes more sensitive as gestation proceeds.

FETAL SOUND ISOLATION

Our understanding of the influences of sounds during prenatal life, as well as the possible adverse effects of intense sound exposures, is not complete. We have a fair idea about how much sound pressure is present around the fetal head and now have information about how much sound actually reaches the fetal inner ear. Gerhardt, et al. (1992) reported a procedure used to evaluate the extent to which exogenous sounds of different frequencies stimulate fetal hearing *in utero*. Inferences regarding sound transmission to the inner ear were made from cochlear microphonic (CM) input–output functions to stimuli with different frequency content. The CM, an alternating current generated by the hair cells of the inner ear, mimics the input signal in frequency and amplitude over a fairly wide range. Thus, the CM functions much like a microphone. Cochlear microphonics are sensitive indications of transmission characteristics of the middle ear. Changes in the condition of the middle ear influence the amplitude of the CM. Comparisons of CM recorded from fetuses *in utero* in response to sound field stimulation and CM recorded from young lambs after birth in the same sound field provided estimates of fetal sound isolation.

Assessment of fetal sound isolation was conducted in two stages. First, the fetuses of anesthetized pregnant ewes were surgically prepared for CM recordings. The fetuses were returned to the uterus and the uterus and abdomen of the ewes were closed. The CM electrodes were tunneled under the skin of the ewe, passing through a small incision on the flank and stored there in a pouch. After surgical recovery, the ewe was positioned two meters from a loudspeaker and sounds were played. The SPLs at which these stimuli produced CM fetal outputs were recorded.

Secondly, after fetal CMs recordings were completed *in utero*, the animal was anesthetized and the fetus was delivered. During the first few days after birth, the fluid in the middle ear cavities drains through the eustachian tubes. After drainage, improved mechanical function of the tympanic membrane and ossicles results in improved hearing sensitivity. CM input–output functions produced by the same stimuli were repeated for the lambs. The difference between the SPL necessary to generate pre-determined CM amplitudes from the fetus *in utero* and the SPL necessary to produce the same CM amplitudes from the lamb after delivery served as an index of fetal sound isolation.

The magnitude of fetal sound isolation was dependent upon stimulus frequency. For 125Hz, sound isolation ranged from 6–17dB, whereas for 2000Hz fetal sound isolation ranged from 27–56dB. Thus, the fetus appears well isolated from intense sounds at and above 500Hz. However, for 125Hz, fetal sound isolation averaged only 11dB.

At least two factors influence stimuli that evoke responses from the fetus. First, the amount of attenuation for different frequencies that is provided by the tissues and fluids surrounding the fetal head determines the spectral shaping of the signal. For frequencies with wavelengths larger than the dimension of the ewe's abdomen, pressure variations within the uterus are fairly uniform and in some instances the pressures are greater inside the uterus than outside. Secondly, the way in which airborne stimuli affects the fetus relates to the transmission of sound pressure from the fluid at the fetal head into the inner ear. The sound pressures reaches the inner ear through the skull (bone conduction) rather than through the outer and middle ears (air conduction) (Gerhardt, et al., 1996).

MODEL OF FETAL HEARING

It is intriguing to consider what sounds are present in the fetal environment and the extent to which the fetus can detect them. The data presented in the preceding sections have been integrated into a model of fetal sound transmission and are recorded in Figure 3. The model includes information regarding sound transmission through the tissues and fluids associated with pregnancy and sound transmission via bone conduction into the inner ear.

The ambient sound level *in utero* or noise floor is indicated in Figure 3 by a dashed line. In order for the fetus to detect it, extrinsic sounds have to exceed these levels. The internal noise floor of the mother is dominated by low-frequency energy produced by respiration, intestinal function, cardiovascular system and maternal movements. Presumably, the ability of the fetus to detect exogenous sounds will be dependent in part on the spectrum level of the noise floor due to masking. The thin solid line at the top of the figure represents a broadband noise in air. For sake of illustration, a spectral level of 90dB was considered. The dotted line represents the sound pressure that this noise level would produce in the uterus. As expected, high-frequency sound pressures would be reduced by about 20dB. The attenuation of low–frequency sounds by the abdominal wall, uterus and fluids surrounding the fetal head is quite small and in some cases sound enhancement pressure of about 5dB has been noted. Between 250 and 4000Hz, sound pressure levels drop at a rate of 6dB/octave.

Sound pressures at the fetal head create compressional forces through bone conduction that result in displacements of the basilar membrane thereby producing a CM. As explained above, by evaluating the CM (bold, solid line), it is possible to determine the extent to which the fetus is isolated from the external milieu. For 125 and 250Hz, a 90dB airborne signal would be reduced by 10–20dB in its passage to the fetal inner ear over what would be expected to reach the inner ear of the organism outside of the fetus. For 500 through 2000Hz, a 90dB signal would be reduced by 40–45dB. For frequencies in this range, the fetus is buffered from sounds in the environment surrounding its mother probably because of limited function of the ossicular chain. However, for low-frequency sounds, the fetus is not well isolated. It is interesting to note that low-frequency stimuli that reach the inner ear coincides with the development of the inner ear which first begins for low–frequency sounds.

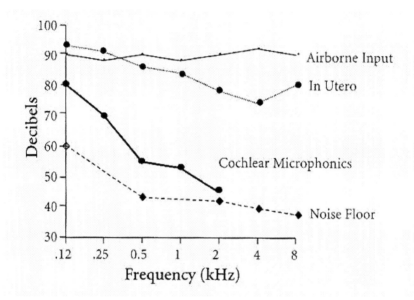

Figure 3: A model of sound transmission to the fetal inner ear. The noise floor is produced by internally generated sounds from digestion, maternal movements and perhaps the cardiovascular system. Sound levels (y–axis on the left) in the uterus are produced by airborne white noise. The parameter labeled cochlear microphone (y–axis on the right) comes from data described as fetal sound isolation. The cochlear microphone parameter describes the level of the exogenous noise that would stimulate the fetal cochlea. A 90dB noise in the sound field surrounding the mother would result in fetal stimulation at levels in excess of the internal noise floor from 125 through 2000Hz.

The fetus *in utero* will detect speech, but probably only the low-frequency components, below 500Hz, and only when the airborne signal exceeds about 60dB. If it is less that that, the signal may be masked by internal noises. It is assumed that the human fetus may be able to detect speech at conversational levels but only the low-frequency components.

Likewise, when music is played for the mother at comfortable listening levels, the fetus could sense rhythms, but the high-frequency overtones would not be of sufficient amplitude to be detected (Abrams, et al.,1998). Simply put, the fetus would be stimulated by music with the "bass" register turned up and the "treble" register turned down. How this information relates to *in utero* development of speech and language, to musical preferences and to subsequent cognitive development are topics of considerable speculation.

INTELLIGIBILITY OF SPEECH SOUNDS RECORDED AT THE HEAD OF THE FETUS

Fetal identification of its mother's voice and its ability to form memories of early exposure to speech are in part dependent on the intelligibility of the speech message. In a study conducted by Griffiths, Brown, Gerhardt, Abrams, and Morris (1994), a panel of over 100 untrained individuals judged the intelligibility of speech recorded *in utero* from a pregnant ewe. Intelligibility was influenced by three factors: transducer site (maternal flank or *in utero*); gender of the speaker (male vs. female); and intensity level (65, 75 or 85dB). For recordings made at the maternal flank, there was no significant difference between male and female speakers. Intelligibility scores increased with increased stimulus level for speakers and at both recording sites. However, intelligibility scores were significantly lower for females than for males when the recordings were made *in utero*.

An analysis of relevant information from recordings inside and outside the uterus showed that voicing information is better transmitted *in utero* than place or type of information. "Voicing" refers to the presence or absence of vocal fold vibrations (e.g., s vs. z). "Place" of articulation refers to the location of the major air-flow constriction during production (e.g., bilabial vs. alveolar). "Manner" refers to the way the speech sound is produced (e.g., plosive vs. glide).

Voicing information from the male speaker, which is carried by low-frequency energy, was largely preserved *in utero*. The participants evaluated the male speaker's voice equally well regardless of transducer site. The female's speech was not transmitted as well into the uterus. The fundamental frequency of the female speaker was higher than that of the male. Thus, it is understandable that vocal information from the male would carry better into the uterus than that from the female.

The maternal voice is a prominent stimulus. It is present during a crucial part of fetal development at a time in which several biological systems, including the auditory system, are developing. The immediate effects on the fetus of maternal vocal exposure may provide a way of tracking auditory system development, as well as measuring fetal ability to process sensory information (Fifer & Moon, 1988). Fetal auditory discrimination has also led to the hypothesis that prenatal experience with auditory stimulation is the precursor to postnatal linguistic development.

FETAL AUDITORY DISCRIMINATION

The fetal auditory system is functional by the start of the third trimester (Birnholz & Benacerraf, 1983). Although quantification of fetal hearing cannot be made using standard audiometric equipment, researchers have found methods to measure fetal responsiveness to exogenous stimuli. The most common approaches used to measure responsiveness to sound include the monitoring of fetal pulse rate (Johansson, Wedenberg, & Westen, 1964) and gross body activity or inactivity (Shahidullah & Hepper, 1994). Fetal movements in response to sound and/or vibroacoustic stimuli relate closely to the development of fetal audition (Gelman, Wood, Spellacy, & Abrams, 1982).

In 1983, Birnholz and Benacerraf measured fetal responsiveness to an electronic artificial larynx applied to the maternal abdomen. An ultrasonic imager monitored eye blinks in response to the stimulus. Blink responses were observed for fetuses from 16–32 weeks of gestation. Reflexive eye movements increased in frequency after the 26th week of gestation. Between weeks 28 and 36, eight of 236 fetuses demonstrated no observable response to EAL stimulation. Two of these fetuses were diagnosed later with severe sensorineural hearing loss and the other 6 suffered from a range of non-auditory anomalies.

The fetus has the capability to respond to tonal stimuli of varying frequencies as early as 19 weeks. Yet, can fetuses discriminate frequencies? By evaluating movement responses of human fetuses to paired pure tones, Shahidullah and Hepper (1994) reported that 35 week old fetuses were capable of distinguishing between two pure tones of 250 and 500Hz. However, fetuses at 27 weeks were not as likely to demonstrate the same abilities.

Shahidullah and Hepper (1994) also evaluated fetuses' abilities to differentiate between speech sounds. Fetuses at 27 and 35 weeks were exposed to a pair of pre-recorded syllables through an earphone placed on the maternal abdomen. It was found that 35 weeks old fetuses possessed the ability to discriminate among different phonemes, whereas younger fetuses did not.

MUSIC AND THE FETUS

Tones, noise, and speech are not the only externally generated forms of aural stimuli that may have a behavioral effect on the developing fetus. Male and female singing voices have the ability to penetrate the uterus, as documented by fetal movements (Woodward & Guidozzi, 1992). Fetal movements have also been shown to become livelier during exposure to music (Lind, 1980). The reaction of the fetus, which is typically an alteration in fetal heart rate, depends on volume, sudden crescendos, frequencies and the state of the fetus (Lind, 1980).

USE OF SOUND DURING MEDICAL EXAMINATIONS: FETAL ACOUSTIC STIMULATION TESTING

Acoustic energy can be delivered to the head of the fetus either by an airborne stimulus in the maternal environment or by a sound source, mechanically coupled to the mother's abdomen. The latter results in what is called vibroacoustic stimulation (VAS). Airborne acoustic stimulation from a loudspeaker or a noisy piece of machinery penetrates the uterus and can stimulate the fetus. VAS results from physical contact of the mother to vibrating sources such as a lawn mower, tractor or washing machine. These vibrations more easily penetrate the uterus with little loss in energy (Peters, Abrams, Gerhardt, & Longmate, 1991). The fetus may detect the sub–audible components of the vibration through the proprioceptive system or may hear the audible harmonics.

Obstetricians often use an electronic artificial larynx (EAL) as a sound source to elicit a response from the fetus to assess fetal health. The EAL is a small, hand-held device that was originally designed for use by alaryngeal speakers. It produces a vibrating signal with a fundamental frequency between 75–175Hz and multiple harmonics over 10,000Hz when recorded in air (Abrams, Gerhardt, Rosa, & Peters, 1995). The physician places the EAL diaphragm on the abdomen of the pregnant woman. When activated it produces an acoustical signal in the uterus that has peak energy from 500–1000 Hz and may reach over 129dB SPL at the fetal head (Nyman, et al., 1991). The level of the EAL recorded directly over the fetal head in sheep has been recorded as high as 135dB (Gerhardt, Abrams, Kovas, & Gomez, 1988).

Not only are there physical differences between acoustical stimulation and vibro-acoustical stimulation, but the responses of the fetus are also different. Greater pulse acceleration and more vigorous changes in fetal movements are obtained with VAS (Hepper & Shahidullah, 1994). Higher stimulus levels at the fetal head during VAS that during acoustical stimulation may account for these differences.

ADVERSE EFFECTS OF NOISE

The detrimental effects of exposures to noise on human hearing have been documented for at least 150 years. According to a 1990 U.S. Public Health Document, overexposure to noise is responsible for the hearing loss suffered by about half of the over 21 million Americans affected by this disorder. More than 20 million American workers are exposed on a routine basis to noise levels that are capable of inducing permanent hearing loss (National Institutes of Health Consensus Report, 1990).

Increased participation rates of women in the labor force has led to concern that possible guidelines are needed for pregnant women. In 1994, approximately 75% of women in the prime childbearing years of 24–35 were in the work force (Shehan, 1996). While hearing loss is documented in persons overexposed to intense noise, the effects of these exposures on the hearing of unborn children are unknown.

Important questions regarding noise effects on the fetus remain to be answered. Is noise exposure to a pregnant woman capable of producing damage to the hearing of her fetus? If so, are there reasonable safety limits that will protect the fetus?

Intense sound may act on the unborn through the direct effects of noise on the developing fetus and the mother with indirect neuroendocrine effects on the fetus. If the effect of noise is direct, then protecting the hearing of the mother does little for the hearing of the fetus. However, if it is indirect, ear protection for the mother may protect the fetus as well by altering the function of the mother's neuroendocrine system in an unspecified manner.

HEARING LOSS PRODUCED
DURING HUMAN FETAL LIFE

Two studies document an increased risk of hearing loss in children whose mothers were exposed to noise during pregnancy. Lalande, Hetu, and Lambert (1986) reported that noise exposure of 65–95dBA for 8 hours per day increased the risk of having a hearing impaired child by a factor of three. The children whose mothers worked during pregnancy in noise levels over 85dBA suffered greater hearing loss as compared to children whose mothers worked in conditions from 65–85dBA. In an earlier report, Daniel and Laciak (1982) documented hearing loss in children whose mothers worked in weaving industries where noise exposures were up to 100dB. While the studies suggested an increased likelihood of hearing loss as a consequence of noise exposures *in utero*, both reports have been criticized because of methodological problems including a lack of adequate control groups (Henderson, Subramaniam, & Boettcher, 1993).

Recent studies using pregnant sheep provide evidence that noise exposures to the ewe can induce changes in hearing sensitivity of the fetus. This is assessed by auditory brainstem response and can produce morphologic changes of the fetal inner ear as determined by scanning electron microscopy (Griffiths, et al., 1994; Huang, Gerhardt, Abrams, & Antonelli, 1997; Gerhardt, Pierson, Huang, Abrams, & Rarey, 1999). In all studies, extreme noise exposures of 120dB for 16 hours, repeated in some instances, were used. Pregnant women do not normally experience these noise conditions. Following noise exposure, there appeared to be a marked difference between the manner in which the auditory system of the immature fetus responded to noise exposure when compared to that of a more mature fetus. This finding relates to the period of increased susceptibility to noise damage in the immature ear, a finding also reported by others (Pujol & Uziel, 1989).

Valuable information about hearing loss can be gained by visual inspection of hair cell damage using high–magnification from scanning electron microscopy. The sensory hair cells from fetal sheep exposed to noise appeared different in a number of respects. Following exposure, hair cell damage of both inner and outer hair cells was noted primarily in the apical and middle turns of the cochlear. These regions of the inner ear respond to low frequency sounds. In contrast, adults exposed to noise suffer damage to the region of the inner ear that responds best to high frequency sounds.

It is highly unlikely that a pregnant woman would experience the magnitude of exposures used in the above reported studies. Moreover, the difference in susceptibility to noise between humans and sheep has not been determined. Thus, while these findings are of potential interest to the understanding of human fetuses exposed to noise, these results may only be specific to fetal sheep and not applicable to humans.

IMPLICATIONS OF FETAL HEARING OF INFANTS IN AN INTENSIVE CARE UNIT

The contrast of the sound environment in the uterus compared to that of the NICU is rather dramatic. Consider a child's situation born at 24 weeks gestation rather than 40 weeks. There are two major issues that affect the neonate in this stressful sound environment. First, its auditory system is not prepared to respond to high-frequency stimuli commonly found in the NICU, caused by equipment and people. As stated, the human fetus responses first to low frequency sounds that permeate the in utero environment. High frequency sounds are markedly filtered out during passage through uterine tissues and fluids. The second major issue involves the extraordinary developmental change to hearing that occurs immediately after birth; the neonate's middle ear begins to function.

The resonant features of the outer ear and the mechanical amplification provided by the middle ear are rendered inoperative because of the fluids that fill these cavities. Thus, the fetus hears through bone conduction. Resonance of the outer ear can increase the intensity of airborne sounds to the eardrum by up to 20dB for high frequency energy. Moreover, the mechanical advantage of the eardrum and the associated ossicular chain amplify sounds by an additional 30dB. Consequently, the immature neonate is now bombarded with sounds that are out of sequence and at levels that it has not yet experienced. Its immature inner ear and central auditory system are probably not equipped to interpret or appropriately integrate these sounds in a manner that it has in the uterine environment.

From a purely biological perspective, the sound environment that best simulates the uterine condition might provide the greatest opportunity for optimal development of the central auditory system. Once the neonate reaches a gestational age of 40 weeks, then its peripheral and central auditory systems are fully capable of interpreting and integrating a wide range of frequencies, be it voice or music. It can also compensate for the added sound levels that accompany the resolution of fluids in the outer and middle ears.

Two conditions are recommended for the NICU environment. First, it is important for sound levels to be low enough for the neonate to rest without interruption. Philbin, Robertson and Hall (1999) recommended that sound levels in an occupied bed or patient care area should not exceed an hourly average of 50dBA and peaks should not exceed 70dBA. While most scientists are not concerned that noise levels in the NICU may contribute to hearing loss, they are concerned about noise levels that disrupt behavior and that preclude a favorable signal–to–noise ratio. Any artificial sounds, including music, that cause care givers to speak with a raised voice, result in an unfavorable sound environment and inappropriately reduce the signal–to–noise ratio.

When music is played in the NICU, we recommend small speakers located near the neonate's head rather than being broadcast throughout the NICU. Also, the music needs to be produced so that the bass is emphasized and the treble diminished. Research is still needed on the impact of the neonate's sound environment, particularly as it relates to sleep and perceptual organization.

Chapter 3

ATTACHMENT FORMATION IN VERY PREMATURE INFANTS—A NEW GENERATION

Tina Gutbrod and Dieter Wolke

Improvements in perinatal medical care in the last twenty years have led to the increased survival of very preterm or very low birth weight infants (Hack, et al., 1995). As a consequence, a new population of infants have been born at risk which would not have survived thirty years ago. Concern has been expressed regarding the consequences of more frequent survival of ever smaller infants. The average duration of hospitalization has increased and readmission to hospital during the first several years has been reported to be as high as 38% in VLBW infants today. VLBW infants (and especially extremely low birth weight ELBW infants <1000g) are more likely to have major disabilities (i.e. cerebral palsy, learning disabilities, visual impairment) (Sternquist, 1996; Wolke & Meyer, 1999) as well as minor disabilities (learning difficulties, speech and language disorders, persistent neuromotor abnormalities, Attention and Hyperactivity Disorder (ADHD), etc.) than earlier generations of larger preterm infants (Bennett & Scott, 1997; Wolke, 1998). Approximately 25% of VLBW children suffer severe or multiple cognitive, learning and behavioral problems and a further 25% have moderate to mild psychological problems (Wolke, 1998, Wolke & Meyer, 1999). More specifically, hyperactivity problems (i.e. ADHD) are more commonly associated with very preterm birth (Botting, et al., 1997; Sykes, et al., 1997). Thus, many families have to adjust to the fact that while their child's life has been saved by neonatal intensive care, the child continues to have chronic medical conditions and display more difficult behavior that may take months or years to resolve or in some cases may never be diminished (Dusick, 1997). Most previous research on VLBW infants has focused on outcomes such as severe neurological or cognitive impairment (Aylward, et al., 1989; McCormick, 1997; Skuse, 1999; Wolke, 1998). There is a paucity of studies on the long-term socio–emotional development of these recently surviving VLBW infants. Parenthood is considered to be one of the primary developmental transitions occurring during the course of the lifespan, and the birth of a premature infant may pose a particular challenge for sensitive parenting and the development of a successful mother–child relationship.

This chapter will review the findings on the development and quality of attachment relationships between preterm infants and their mothers. Controversies in recent findings and theories on the development of attachment relationship will be highlighted and critically discussed. The implications for future research and intervention strategies will be put forward.

THE IMPORTANCE OF ATTACHMENT

Attachment refers to the affectional bonds that infants form with their caregivers and that endure across time and situations. According to Bowlby (1969) the infant's attachment system becomes particularly salient in situations of ambiguity, stress, illness or separation. In these situations, individual differences in attachment security determine the extent to which infants use their caretaker both as a haven for protection, as well as a secure base from which to explore their environment (Ainsworth, et al., 1978). The *"Strange Situation,"* a brief, 8–episode laboratory procedure, was specifically designed by Ainsworth (Ainsworth & Wittig, 1969) to activate infants' attachment systems by exposing them to separations from their caregivers, within the context of unfamiliar people and environment. Initially it was assumed that the extent to which infants became distressed during separation from their caregivers would give insight into the quality of their relationship. Ainsworth however revealed that infants' response to reunion with their mothers was principally reflective of their emotional tie to their mother. In the Strange Situation, infants are classified as *secure* (B pattern) if they use the mother as a secure base from which to explore, may be distressed in her absence but greet her positively on her return and resume exploration. Infants classified as *insecure–avoidant* (A) explore with little reference to the mother, are minimally distressed by her absence, and seem to ignore or avoid her upon return. Infants classified as *insecure–anxious/resistant* (C) fail to move away from mother and therefore explore minimally, are highly distressed by separations and are often difficult to settle on reunions. A further classification (D) has been designated to infants that show contradictory, misplaced or stereotypical behavior in response to the caregiver's absence. *Contradictory behavior,* for example, can be observed when the infant shows indifference upon mother's return after excessive distress during separation. Whereas infants rated as secure, avoidant, or resistant (A, B, or C) have been suggested to display "organized" strategies in dealing with parental reunion, disorganized attachment has been described as the breakdown of an organized strategy of emotion regulation (Main & Solomon, 1986).

These patterns are believed to provide insight into children's mental expectations ("internal working models of attachment") about caregiver behavior based on mother–infant interactions during the first year of life. According to attachment theory, these mental representations guide and influence children's emotional well-being and social interactions beyond the relationship with their primary caregiver. Securely attached infants have been found to be more competent and more self-confident in social and cognitive skills in later childhood (Main, Kaplan, & Cassidy, 1985; van Ijzendoorn, et al., 1995; Messer, 1999; Troy & Sroufe, 1987), whereas insecure (and especially disorganized) attachment has been associated with an increased risk of difficulties in peer relationships, emotional adjustment and behavior in later childhood (Bates & Bayles, 1988; Carlson, 1998; Main, et al., 1985; Suess, Grossmann, & Sroufe, 1992; van Ijzendoorn, et al., 1999; Wartner, et al., 1994).

THE IMPACT OF PREMATURITY ON SECURITY OF ATTACHMENT

Early "Mother–to–Infant Attachment" or "Bonding" in Mothers of Preterm Infants

Beginning in the 1940s attachment theory was applied to understanding toddlers' immediate and long-term responses to extended separations from caregivers, as well as to institutional care (Bowlby, 1988). As a result changes in policy guidelines were implemented in order to minimize stress caused by children's separations from parents during hospital stays. Decades later research on the development of attachment in preterm infants was initiated due to the concern that early separation due to the infant's long hospital stay could have adverse effects on the mother-infant relationship. Mothers of preterm infants often report a lack of attachment feelings toward their infant after birth and during their stay in hospital, due to lower physical proximity, less involvement in the care of their infant, and feeling "it's not really my child, it's more the nurses" (Minde, et al., 1983). Researchers have postulated that prolonged hospitalization in the NICU denies the mother a close relationship with her infant, and that this may thus impair the formation of a secure attachment relationship. Specifically the work of Klaus and Kennel (1970; 1982) emphasized the notion of a critical period after birth for successful bonding, which promoted the belief that preterm infants and their parents were at risk for attachment problems. This notion was later revoked, as most mothers of preterm infants reported being able to "bond" or become attached to their infants after overcoming the initial shock and emotional experience of premature birth (Richards, 1985; Sluckin, et al., 1984).

It is necessary at this point to clarify the difference between the terms *"mother–to–infant attachment"* (also referred to as "bonding") and *"infant-mother attachment."* The former has been described as a bond parents form with their infants, beginning during pregnancy and continuing in the period after birth, that is generally achieved by most parents within the first weeks or months of life. However, in a small percentage of mothers this bond, for example, is not achieved due to maternal mental illness (Hipwell & Kumar, 1997). In contrast, "attachment" describes the type of relationship an infant develops with his/her caregiver. Attachment behaviors, such as protesting separation and actively seeking proximity (usually manifested by the end of the first year) are believed to reflect the quality of the infant–mother relationship.

Despite recent efforts of NICU policies to promote maternal involvement in caring for their infant and to encourage physical proximity (e.g. kangarooing, breastfeeding, infant massage) (Anderson, 1991) as early as possible, infants are born smaller, with more medical complications and have longer hospitalizations, which may delay or impact on attachment formation. Little is known about the consequences of delayed or problematic maternal bonding or attachment after extensive post-natal separation, and in particular whether mothers' bonding or attachment difficulties have an influence on their infants' security of attachment.

Attachment in Preterm Infants

In the 1970s and 1980s researchers showed a wide interest in mother–infant interaction and attachment differences between preterm and full-term infants (for review see: Field, 1987). Studies that investigated attachment behavior at 12–18 months in the Strange Situation in preterm infants generally found no differences in attachment classifications compared to full-term infants (Brown & Bakeman, 1980; Easterbrooks, 1989; Macey, et al., 1987; Minde, Corter, & Goldberg, 1984; Rode, et al., 1981). The majority of these studies, however, focused on small samples of larger (>32 weeks gestation; >1500g birth weight) preterm infants from mostly middle-class families, that are known to be at low risk for long-term developmental problems (Wolke & Meier, 1999, 2000). For an overview of studies on preterm infants and attachment see Table 1.

A meta-analysis of attachment studies examined the relative effects of maternal and child problems on security of attachment in clinical samples and found that child problems did not lead to a significant decrease of secure attachment compared to the normal population (van Ijzendoorn, et al., 1992). Among child problems associated with problematic relationships, prematurity was found to be most intensively studied. Generally attachment differences were not found between preterm infants and full-term infants. However it is important to note that all studies on preterm infants included in the meta-analysis were published in the 1980s and focused on infants of relatively low medical risk (mean birth weight >1500g; mean gestation >30 wks).

Different conclusions were offered for the absence of higher insecurity of attachment in preterm infants. Van Ijzendoorn, et al. (1992) concluded that mothers of preterm infants are capable of adapting to and compensating for their infants' more difficult behavior and are able to promote sensitive interaction and secure attachment. Similarly, Macey, et al. (1987) suggested that the mother–infant relationship may be relatively insensitive to the disruptions of illness and prematurity. Other alternative explanations for the lack of attachment differences in preterm and full-term infants have focused on methodological limitations: i.e., the samples were too small to detect group differences, they were poorly matched or had no control groups, studies used different attachment assessments (Strange Situation, Attachment Q–Sort) and solely focused on intact white middle-class families. Wille, et al. (1991) compared samples of lower socio–economic class preterm and full-term infants and found a higher proportion of preterm infants to be insecurely attached. Although their sample consisted of relatively large low-risk preterms, Wille, et al. concluded that the combination of preterm birth and low socioeconomic status may have an adverse effect on the development of secure attachment relationships.

Recent cohorts of preterm infants include infants born at increasingly lower birth weight and gestation (Marlow 1993). They have experienced more medical complications and are at higher risk for long-term developmental sequelae than earlier cohorts. Thus differences between very preterm and full-term children in attachment have to be re-examined in light of an increasingly high-risk population of very preterm infants.

Surprisingly, only one study published since the last decade investigated attachment relationships of more recently born very preterm infants. In comparison to full-term infants Mangelsdorf, et al. (1996) found more than half of VLBW infants (<1250g) were classified as insecurely attached at 18 months corrected age (see Table 1). Although the sample size was small (N=34), the group of very preterm infants in this study was representative of the more recently surviving very preterm infants in length of hospitalization, medical complications, and intensity of care. In addition, more preterms changed from the secure to insecure classification in the Strange Situation from 14 to 18 months, compared to full-terms, who more commonly display a change toward secure attachment. This suggests that the adverse effects of very preterm birth on the mother–infant relationship may become more pronounced over time.

Disorganized Attachment

Behavioral indices of disorganized attachment classified in the Strange Situation include contradictory, misdirected or stereotypical behavior, freezing or stilling for a substantial amount of time, or direct apprehension or fear of the parent (Main & Solomon, 1990). Generally disorganized attachment behaviors are considered to be indicators of an experience of stress and anxiety that the child cannot resolve because the parent is the source of fright as well as being at the same time the only potential haven of safety. The incompatible behaviors of flight and proximity seeking are proposed to lead to a breakdown of organized attachment behaviors. Disorganized attachment has been associated with maltreating parents or parents struggling with unresolved loss of an attachment figure or other traumatic experiences (Van Ijzendoorn, 1995). In contrast to the other attachment classifications (A, B, C) disorganized attachment is considered to be a major risk factor in the development of child psychopathology (Carlson,

1998; Zeanah, et al., 1997).

Disorganized Attachment in High-Risk Samples

Only a few studies have investigated the prevalence of disorganized attachment in preterm infants. Due to small sample sizes, it is difficult to ascertain whether these preterm infants show a higher incidence of disorganized attachment than full-terms. Although previously suggested, there is little evidence to suggest that caregivers of preterms are more likely to abuse or neglect their children (Minde, 1980).

However, an interesting debate has recently been sparked regarding the meaning of behavioral indices of disorganized attachment, which may pertain to preterm infants in particular. Pipp-Siegel, et al. (1999), in a special edition of the Monographs of Child Development on the topic of Atypical Attachment in Children at Developmental Risk, suggested that neurological abnormalities can lead to similar behaviors specified in the disorganized attachment classification. For example, stress related symptoms, including repetitious, self-stimulating behavior or spontaneous extended stilling are not uncommon in children diagnosed with Down Syndrome or autism. Asymmetry of movement or jerky, mistimed movements may represent cerebral palsy or dyspraxia. Particular efforts need to be made to avoid misclassifications of behaviors, which would lead to overestimating the rate of disorganized attachment in neurologically impaired children. For example, in a sample of autistic and learning disabled infants, all autistic children were initially assigned a primary classification of D (Capps, et al., 1994). The authors decided to modify the criteria for disorganization in their study, by regarding stereotypical behaviors as a symptom of autism, rather than an indicator of disorganized attachment. Generally in classifying disorganized attachment in high-risk samples it is advised a) to rule out behaviors that may reflect neurological impairment, b) to observe whether behaviors occur exclusively toward the caregiver and thus reflect attachment rather than general behavior, and c) to obtain extensive information on the medical background of infants.

These are important considerations in determining the rate of disorganized attachment in very preterm infants, as the rate of neurological impairment (i.e. cerebral palsy, autism) is significantly higher in this at–risk group than in full-terms (Paneth, 1992). However, it is often impossible to determine the level of neurological insult in at–risk infants (i.e. very preterm infants) in the first year of life. It therefore remains challenging to distinguish true disorganized behavior from behaviors reflecting neurological insult. In addition, it has been proposed that interactions between infants and their parents may be influenced by the neurological condition of the infant (Pipp-Siegel, et al., 1999). It may thus be difficult to disentangle contributions of relational history and neurological impairment on attachment in very preterm samples.

Van Ijzendoorn, et al. (1999), based on a meta-analysis of studies on disorganized attachment, found that 15% of "normal" infants in middle-class, non-clinical studies were classified as disorganized, while in clinical groups with neurological abnormalities 35% were classified as disorganized. Only 3 studies included in the meta-analysis focused on preterm infants, and even though these samples were small and low in medical risk, 24% of preterm infants were classified as disorganized. Large studies on high-risk preterm infants are needed to disentangle disorganized attachment behaviors as true indicators of the infant–parent relationship from behaviors due to neurological insult.

To conclude, research on whether very preterm infants are at increased risk for insecure or disorganized attachment is still inconclusive due to small samples studied and methodological problems related to determining attachment quality in neurologically impaired infants. Theoretically most interesting is the question whether the same mechanisms that are involved in the formation of attachment in full-term infants are associated with the formation of secure attachment in very preterm infants. For example, attachment theory emphasizes the role of mothers (particularly the importance of sensitivity) in explaining infant attachment classifications. Unclear is whether mothers of very preterm infants have the same influence over how securely attached their infants will become to them. In addition, studies have provided controversial evidence on the extent to which infant characteristics (e.g. temperament) and medical complications account for individual differences in attachment classifications. Whether very preterm infants, who are found to be more irritable and who experience more medical complications make it more difficult for their caregivers to parent sensitively will be the focus of the following sections.

FACTORS ASSOCIATED WITH SECURITY OF ATTACHMENT

Maternal Sensitivity and Interaction Patterns

Full-Term Infants

According to attachment theory interaction quality is the main determinant for the developing infant-mother attachment relationship and is primarily driven by caregiver behavior toward the child. Specifically maternal sensitivity has been postulated to be the strongest predictor of attachment classifications in full-term infants. Sensitivity has been defined as the mother's ability and willingness to perceive her infant's communications as reflected in his or her behavior, emotional expression, and vocalizations. Can the mother see and interpret her infant's signals from the infant's point of view, and respond to them appropriately according to the infant's developmental and emotional needs (Ainsworth, et al. 1978)? Ainsworth described mothers of secure infants as being able to respond to their infants' crying in a timely manner and comforting manner, and being neither intrusive or ignoring of the infant's needs. Mothers of avoidant babies would often show high levels of rejection, especially when infants sought physical contact, whereas mothers of anxious-resistant children were found to be inconsistent in their care giving, sometimes being responsive, but frequently being unavailable. In accordance with Ainsworth's observations, other studies also found similar maternal care giving styles associated with infant attachment. Appropriate levels of maternal interactive behavior in early infancy predicted secure attachment, whereas intrusive and overbearing behavior was linked with avoidant, and understimulating behavior with anxious-resistant attachment classifications (Isabella & Belsky, 1991; Malatesta, et al., 1989; Smith & Pederson, 1988). In addition, infants classified as secure at 12–18 months displayed more synchronous and harmonious interactions, characterized by reciprocal turn-taking and lack of conflict with their caregivers within the first year of life than insecurely classified infants (Isabella & Belsky, 1991; Schoelmerich, et al., 1995).

Notwithstanding the importance of the caregiver role, it needs to be pointed out that the majority of studies investigating the impact of maternal sensitivity and care taking on attachment have generally focused on middle-class mothers with healthy full-term infants. In addition, a meta-analysis on the association between maternal sensitivity and infant attachment classification revealed only a small to moderate effect size for maternal sensitivity (r=.24) (de Wolff & van Ijzendoorn, 1997). This may in part be due to studies emphasizing different aspects of maternal behavior in their definitions of sensitivity. For example, whereas some studies define the central tenants of sensitivity as "promptness in response to infant signals of distress (i.e. crying)", others postulate that mothers must be able to not only accurately read the signals of their infants, but also show flexibility in responding to signals. Timing and pacing of behavior that is well suited to the individual baby at each developmental stage and state of arousal appears an important aspect of sensitivity (Hinde, 1982; Seifer & Schiller, 1995). Coding schemes used to classify sensitivity, however, often do not provide systematic definitions of what types of maternal behaviors are "suited" or "sensitive" to certain types of infant behaviors, especially in cases of extreme or difficult infant behavior. In particular, the question whether definitions of maternal sensitivity that were derived from and found appropriate for healthy full-term infants are appropriate and suitable for caregivers of at–risk infants has often been theoretically discussed but not empirically or methodologically resolved.

Preterm Infants

Interactions of larger preterm infants and their caregivers have frequently been described as less synchronous (Crawford, 1982; Murray & Hornbaker, 1997). Observational studies have revealed that mothers of preterm infants frequently show one of two different behavior patterns in interaction. Either they are found to be more passive, withdrawn from interaction and less socially engaging (Barnard, et al., 1984; Holditch, Davis & Thoman, 1988) and therefore appear less responsive to their infant's signals or they have been rated as more overstimulating, intrusive and overprotective (Bakeman & Brown, 1980; Brachfeld, et al., 1980; Beckwith & Cohen, 1989) than caregivers of full-term infants. Both patterns have been considered to indicate reduced sensitivity in these studies. It has been observed that preterm infants are often less readily engaged in social play, show less positive affect and are more difficult to console, mothers of very preterm infants stimulate their infants more and are more active in initiating and maintaining interaction than mothers of full-terms (Greenberg & Crnic, 1988). There is some debate whether this greater maternal activity is counterproductive or beneficial for the development of these fragile infants (Wolke, 1991). As mothers repeatedly try to elicit responses from their less active premature infants, they often display more gaze aversion and withdrawal than full-term infants, suggesting that greater maternal stimulation can represent overstimulation for these infants (Minde, et al., 1989). Similar patterns of overstimulating care giving and non-synchronous interactions have been observed in full-term dyads that were later classified as insecurely attached (Isabella & Belsky, 1991). It is therefore surprising that the interaction and care giving patterns of these lower risk preterm infants and their caregivers have not lead to a higher rate of insecure attachment in this group.

Few studies have investigated both maternal behavior and sensitivity in the first months of life, as well as attachment classifications at 12–18 months in preterm infants. Those studies that did have generally found a lack of association between maternal sensitivity during interaction and infant attachment classification (Brown & Bakeman, 1980; Wille, et al., 1991; in contrast: Goldberg, et al., 1986).

Several reasons for the lack of association between sensitivity and attachment classification in preterm infants have been offered. Some have questioned whether the definition of sensitivity used for caregivers of full-term infants is applicable to rate parental behavior towards very preterm infants: parental behavior that is perceived contingent to the needs of full-terms may not necessarily be the most appropriate and sensitive in response to preterm infants.

An alternative explanation would suggest that these past cohorts of larger preterm infants have been shown to "catch-up" in social behavior with full-term infants (Greenberg & Conic, 1988). It may therefore be speculated that parents of larger preterms are gradually able to respond more appropriately to their infants' difficult and non-responsive behavior over the first year, and thereby provide the foundation for secure attachment relationships. There is now ample evidence showing that larger preterm infants show catch-up in cognitive abilities and behavior by the second year of life. In contrast, higher risk very preterm infants are less likely to show this "catch-up" with full-term infants (Wolke & Meyer, 1999). In fact, they are more likely to display extreme behavior problems (i.e. irritability, excessive crying) early on (Wolke & Meyer, 1994), which may tax the care giving system to a degree that mothers are less able to respond sensitively to their infants. According to attachment findings in full-term infants, this would lead to a higher propensity for insecure attachment.

Maternal Attachment Representations

Sensitivity evaluates the mother's behavior toward her child. Many studies have focused on the impact of mothers' mental representations of attachment, which in turn are believed to influence their behavior and thus the formation of a secure attachment relationship with their infants.

A mother's account of her childhood attachment and separation experiences, together with her evaluation of these experiences has been shown to predict her child's attachment behaviors in the Strange Situation (Fonagy, et al., 1991; Steele, et al., 1995). Evidence for "the intergenerational transmission effect" has been provided by a number of studies showing the link between parental accounts in the Adult Attachment Interview (AAI: George, et al., 1985) and the infant's attachment classifications in the Strange Situation. Although internal working models are believed to be fairly stable, traumatic events have been shown to result in a shift towards insecurity in the adult's working model of attachment. Unfortunately studies on maternal representations of attachment and infant–mother attachment security have focused exclusively on caregivers of full-term infants (Van Ijzendoorn, 1995). No study to date has examined a) whether very premature birth has a detrimental impact on parents' internal working models of attachment, b) whether mothers' attachment representations in combination with a traumatic event such as premature birth can impact the formation of a secure attachment.

One study investigated childhood events and satisfaction with the current marital relationship in mothers of high-risk very preterm infants and found no relation to infants' attachment classifications (Minde, et al., 1983). This suggests that mothers' previous relationship and interpersonal experiences, which usually relate to later interactive behavior, were overshadowed by the experience of having a very preterm infant.

We can conclude that further research is needed to determine whether maternal sensitivity, early dyadic interaction patterns and maternal attachment representations are able to predict infant attachment classifications in preterm infants as well as in full-term infants. The findings that interactions of preterm infants and their caregivers were rated as less sensitive and synchronous, yet their attachment relationships were not classified as more insecure suggest that maternal sensitivity and interaction quality alone in these high-risk dyads cannot fully explain individual differences in attachment security. We speculate that the underlying mechanisms in the formation of attachment in preterm infants are more complex and different than in full-terms.

If other factors associated with premature birth are found to explain attachment security equally, or even better than maternal sensitivity, this could potentially challenge assumptions of traditional attachment theory with regard to high-risk infants. Very preterm birth is associated with medical complications, separation and severe psychological distress for parents (Singer, et al., 1999). How do many very preterm infants and their parents still manage to establish a secure attachment relationship?

It is necessary to take a closer look at the impact of medical risk and other infant characteristics associated with very premature birth on the formation of attachment relationships.

MEDICAL RISK AND SECURITY OF ATTACHMENT IN PRETERM INFANTS

Previous studies of attachment patterns among preterm infants predominately focused on preterm cohorts at low medical and developmental risk (as shown in Table 1). Those studies that specifically selected high-risk preterm infants reported discrepant findings on the influence of medical complications, length of hospitalization and intensity of care on maternal care giving, as well as on infant attachment patterns.

Minde, et al. (1983) initially proposed that the mother–infant attachment relationship is to a large extent determined by the mother's associated thoughts, fears or concerns regarding her infant's medical condition. During their initial visits to the neonatal intensive care unit mothers interacted less with their infants during severe medical complications, but resumed their initial interactive behavior once the baby's condition improved. However, with infants who remained ill for more than a month, mothers after 6 months still behaved as if these children were gravely ill. Likewise, it has been shown that children with specific chronic medical conditions (i.e. cystic fibrosis or congenital heart disease) were less often secure as infants than control children (Goldberg, et al., 1995), regardless of whether they were cured of their disease or not. Contrary to predictions, Minde, et al. (1984) did not find a higher incidence of insecure attachment in high-risk ill preterm infants compared to full-term infants in their follow-up study.

Two studies found a link between increased medical risk and insecure (specifically anxious–resistant) attachment. Plunkett et al. (1986) showed that their group of high-risk preterm infants, with respiratory illness and hospitalizations of more than 1 month from birth displayed a significantly higher proportion of anxious resistant attachment patterns (C: 36%) than healthy preterm infants. These findings are consistent with Mangelsdorf, et al. (1996), who also reported a higher proportion (C: 27%) of anxious-resistant attachment in their very preterm high-risk sample.

It is unclear, however, to what extent this pattern of increased medical risk and higher proportions of anxious–resistant attachment in preterm infants can be explained by differences in caregiver behavior, or by infant characteristics associated with medical risk. Long separations due to hospitalization and infant illness can create anxiety in the caregiver: anxious–resistant attachment relationships in high-risk infants may reflect the caregiver's prolonged difficulty in overcoming an initial need to disengage emotionally from an infant who may not survive (Minde, 1999), which may result in less sensitive care taking. According to transactional models of relationships, Plunkett, et al. (1986) suggest that high parental anxiety about having an infant who is at great medical risk, coupled with more difficult infant behavior associated with increased medical risk may lead to the higher incidence of insecure attachment.

Only one study which stratified preterm infants by risk status found a higher proportion of securely attached infants in their high-risk preterm group (mean hospitalization: 60 days) and, surprisingly, severity of illness was associated with greater security of attachment (Goldberg, et al., 1986).

It is important to point out that with fragile and acutely ill preterm infants, providing less stimulation and "sitting back" may be adaptive for the infant to recover, rather than indicating parental detachment (Als, et al., 1994; Wolke, 1987). There may be phases in the recovery from initial medical complications and transitions, for example to oral feeding that require very gentle and low key interactions that would be considered understimulating or insensitive for fullterms. When the preterm infant has recovered, however, appropriately stimulating and challenging interaction is indicated. Thus, there may be more phases in interactional adaptation that are challenging to parents of very preterm infants.

Clearly given the contradictory nature of these findings, further research is necessary to understand the effects of medical risk on the attachment relationships in very preterm infants. In addition, large samples are required that provide sufficient power to investigate the interplay between indicators of medical risk (i.e. degree of intensity of care, perinatal and postnatal complications, etc.) and later attachment outcome.

THE IMPACT OF INFANT NEGATIVE EMOTIONALITY ON ATTACHMENT

Full-Term Infants

There has been a longstanding heated debate over the relative contributions of caregiver behaviors (i.e. sensitivity) and infant characteristics (i.e. temperament) to the development of secure and insecure attachment (see: Lamb, et al., 1985; Sroufe, 1985, Seifer, et al., 1996, for reviews). Generally two opposing theories have been supported. Attachment researchers (i.e. Sroufe, 1985) have argued that infant temperament variations make no relevant contribution to the quality of attachment. They postulate that temperament differences will only influence the degree of distress the infant displays during separation, but not attachment behavior during reunion (Mangelsdorf & Frosch, 1999). Similarly, Belsky and Rovine (1997) found that temperament, although not related to secure vs. insecure attachment differences, did influence type of insecurity (avoidant or resistant) of attachment. Conversely, temperament theorists have argued either that infant temperament plays as important (or even greater) a role in attachment formation as maternal sensitivity (Goldsmith & Alansky, 1987; Seifer, et al., 1996) or that assessments of attachment are confounded by assessments of temperament (Kagan, 1982).

Although discrepant findings have been reported on the influence of normal variations in infant temperament on attachment classifications, studies have suggested that more extreme infant characteristics (i.e. reflecting high negative emotionality) are associated with insecure attachment. Van den Boom (1988; 1994) showed that infants identified as highly irritable in the newborn period on the Brazelton Neonatal Behavioral Assessment Scale (NBAS; Brazelton & Nugent, 1995) were twice as likely to be insecurely attached at one year in the Strange Situation then non-irritable infants. This is in accordance with other studies that have highlighted the link between infant proneness to distress and insecure attachment (especially the resistant attachment classification "C") (Bates, et al., 1985; Goldberg & Alansky, 1987; Seifer, et al., 1996). A third theory from a transactional perspective suggests that temperament mediates the impact of sensitivity on attachment security. Difficult temperament and poor self-regulatory behaviors per se therefore do not lead to more insecure attachment, rather these behaviors stretch the coping abilities of many parents, influence sensitive care taking and subsequently influence infant attachment patterns. However studies that have investigated whether high levels of infant difficult temperament or irritability lead to lower maternal sensitivity in the infant's first year of life have reported inconsistent results: some studies found a negative relationship between irritability and sensitivity (Crockenberg, 1986; van den Boom, 1988) whereas other did not find a significant association (Hubbard & Ijzendoorn, 1991).

Preterm Infants

Heightened levels of irritability in the first half year of life have been observed in very preterm infants (Medoff-Cooper, 1986; Washington, et al., 1986; Wolke, et al., 1994), but not in low-risk premature infants (Oberklaid, et al., 1986). It has been suggested that medical risk, neurological immaturity and disorganization may impede regulatory behavior (Wolke, et al., 1998; Wolke, et al., 1994). Neonatal examinations (i.e. Brazelton NBAS) revealed that twice as many very preterm infants were classified as highly irritable compared to full-term control studies (Gutbrod, et al., 2000). Stiefel, et al. (1987) compared emotional arousal and regulation in high-risk and low-risk preterm infants in the procedure of the Strange Situation in the second year of life and found that high-risk infants showed a greater proneness to distress and less ability to modulate arousal once distressed. According to the transactional theory of attachment, this pattern of infants being less effective at using their environment to regulate their arousal, in conjunction with mothers being less sensitive and inconsistent in their care giving, suggests that high-risk very preterm infants and their caregivers may be at risk for later attachment difficulties.

Although no study to date has investigated whether heightened irritability in very preterm infants leads to later attachment insecurity, recent studies have suggested that irritable infants display emotion regulation deficits in early interaction that may lead to later attachment insecurity. Gutbrod, et al. (2000) found that very premature infants classified as highly irritable in the Brazelton Neonatal Behavioural Assessment Scale at term displayed less successful emotion regulation after the still-face episode at 3 months and dyadic behaviors were rated as less synchronous during the reunion than non-irritable very preterm infants. This pattern of infant withdrawal and negative response after the still-face has been linked with insecure attachment at 12 months in full-term samples (Cohn, et al., 1991). As very preterm infants have been reported to be more irritable than full-term infants these findings suggest that their early neonatal deficits in arousal regulation may influence the formation of attachment, thus placing very preterm infants at risk for insecure attachment.

CONCLUSION

The question of whether prematurity has an adverse effect on the formation of infant-mother attachment has been the focus of this review. Firstly, larger, lower risk premature infants do not show a higher propensity for insecure attachment, although their mothers are often rated as less sensitive and their interactions are less synchronous. Methodological limitations (i.e. small sample sizes) of these studies were discussed. However, from a transactional perspective, this suggests that larger preterm infants and their caregivers are able to overcome the initial emotional stress related to premature birth by the end of the first year. At the same time, larger preterm infants do not seem to display sufficiently difficult behavior to jeopardize their caregivers' sensitive parenting and thus the formation of a secure attachment relationship.

Secondly, the very few studies that have focused on attachment relationships of high-risk preterm infants have suggested that they may be at higher risk for insecure attachment. This new generation of higher risk VLBW infants have been found to be more difficult and therefore present a greater challenge for their caregivers. According to a transactional perspective, we may speculate that infant difficult temperament, in combination with caregiver anxiety and stress related to premature birth can have a negative effect on sensitive parenting, which in turn can lead to insecure or even disorganized attachment.

If these high-risk infants are indeed at increased risk for insecure attachment, this will have both theoretical as well as practical implications. From a theoretical perspective, it would suggest that in certain situations (e.g. very premature birth) infant characteristics can either affect maternal sensitivity adversely, leading to insecure attachment, or that despite high maternal sensitivity infant behavior cannot be sufficiently modulated to deal with stress (e.g. separation). In addition, this would imply that mechanisms related to the formation of a secure attachment relationship in full-term infants may not suffice to predict secure vs. insecure attachment classifications in very preterm infants. The experiences and consequences of a high-risk premature birth are complex: various factors influence how a mother copes with premature birth, how sensitively she behaves toward her child, as well as how challenging her child's behavior can be. In addition, there is a large heterogeneity in high-risk preterm populations. The experience of a very preterm baby being born to a middle-class family as a result of IVF birth is very different to a high-risk baby born into a low-income, uneducated single parent household. Prediction models of attachment relevant to very preterm infants may need to incorporate other factors associated with high-risk birth, e.g. the role of stress and support, as well as medical risk and infant irritability in determining attachment outcome. Empirical studies are needed to shed light on the mechanisms involved.

The issue of attachment formation in very preterm infants also provides important practical implications. If the mechanisms leading to insecure attachment in very preterm infants are different from full-term infants, then specific interventions can be designed to improve parent and caregiver relationships, and prevent negative sequelae related to poor infant-parent relationships. Previous studies that have adopted intervention methods developed for full-term infants and their parents have been found to be unsuccessful in alleviating cognitive or behavioral outcomes in very preterm children (McCarton, et al., 1995; Wolke & Schulz, 1999).

For many years parents and health professionals caring for very preterm infants have wondered and worried about how this different start to life may affect the emotional well-being of these children. We owe it to these parents, health professionals and very preterm infants to provide the answers with sufficiently powerful empirical studies. Such studies are currently under way.

Table 1: Overview of Studies on Attachment in Premature Infants (1980–2000)

Year	Authors	N	Prematurity Criteria: Gestation / Birthweight / Hospitalization (mean weeks) (mean grams) (mean days)			Full-term control group?	Age (months)	A	B	C	D+	Group Differences (χ^2)
1980	Brown and Bakeman[1]	26	32.4	1627	26.6	Yes	12 pd	7 (27%)	13 (50%)	6 (23%)		None reported= "no difference"
1981	Field et al.	46	32	1600	32	Yes	12 pt	not reported	not reported	not reported		None reported= "no difference"
1981	Rode et al.	24	33.6	1851.5	26.7	No	15 pb	3 (12%)	17 (71%)	4 (17%)		None reported= "no difference"
1983	Frodi	20	34	1990	24	Yes	12 pt	3 (15%)	15 (75%)	2 (10%)		$\chi^2(2)=0.40$(ns) "no difference"
1986	Goldberg et al.	56	29.0	1087.9	60.4	No	12 pt	10 (18%)	41 (75%)	4 (7%)		$\chi^2(2)=0.80$(ns) (**) "no difference"
1986	Plunkett et al.[2]	23 (lo-risk) 33 (hi-risk)	33.9 30.7	2138.6 1419.5	10.2 60.5	No	12-18 pd	7 (30%) 3 (9%)	14 (61%) 18 (55%)	2 (9%) 12 (36%)		$\chi^2(2)=8.28$* (hi vs lo-risk) $\chi^2(2)=10.69$** (**)
1989	Easterbrookes[4]	30	<32	<1500	not reported	Yes	13 pt 20 pt	2 (7%) 5 (16%)	19 (63%) 21 (71%)	6 (21%) 3 (10%)	3 (9%) 1 (3%)	reported z scores "no difference"
1991	Wille[1]	18 (healthy) 18 (ill)	35 33	2039 1820	11 32	Yes	12 pt	5 (28%) 5 (28%)	8 (44%) 8 (44%)	5 (28%) 5 (28%)		$\chi^2(2)=7.57$* (preterm vs full-term)
1996	Mangelsdorff et al.	34	27.9	955.1	86.2	Yes	14 pt 19 pt	7 (21%) 9 (27%)	19 (55%) 16 (47%)	5 (15%) 9 (27%)	3 (8%)	$\chi^2(2)=2.58$ (ns) $\chi^2(2)=6.34$*

*p<.05; **p<.01; ***p<.001

Note: All studies listed in Table 1 have used the standard Ainsworth Strange Situation. Studies using other attachment assessments were not included, due to difficulty of comparison.

[1]Note: Brown & Bakeman (1980) and Wille, et al. (1991) compared samples of predominately low SES black preterm and full-term infants.

[2]Note: Plunkett, et al. (1989) compared high-risk infants with moderate to severe lung disease with low-risk infants free of respiratory illness.

[3]Note: Wille (1991) distinguished between healthy preterm infants (<48 hrs oxygen, no major medical problems) and ill preterm infants (>48 hrs oxygen or IVH).

[4]Note: Easterbrooks (1989) did not indicate mean birthweight, gestation or duration of hospitalization of their healthy preterm sample. They did not find group differences in mental development up to two years, therefore it is assumed that their preterm sample is quite low risk.

[+]Note: D classification regardless of secondary classification also includes A/C classifications

[++]Note: Compared to Ainsworth's original sample of 105 healthy infants (Ainsworth, et al., 1978)

pt=post term; pd=post hospital discharge; pb=post birth

Chapter 4

ON THE MEANING OF PRENATAL AUDITORY PERCEPTION AND MEMORY FOR THE DEVELOPMENT OF THE MIND: A PSYCHOANALYTIC PERSPECTIVE

Suzanne Maiello

IMPLICATIONS FOR NEONATAL INTENSIVE CARE

The newborn infant is a social being with a high degree of interactive competence. Through his behavior, he is capable of communicating precise clues about his needs and emotional state to the caregiver. Infant observation has shown that infants are not only an age group, but that every baby is born as an individual. The meeting between a unique mother and a unique infant gives rise to a unique relationship.

When does this relationship begin? In thinking about its origins, Balconi writes: "Is there an ancestral memory or the reminiscence of past experiences? How can we not imply the existence of a proprioceptive and heteroceptive sensory memory, since the newborn is able to react to the maternal heartbeat and recognizes the maternal voice and the sound of a piece of music which he heard in utero?" (1994).

Freud asserts that the ego is first and foremost a body ego and writes: "There is much more continuity between intrauterine life and earliest infancy than the impressive caesura of the act of birth would have us believe" (1926).

Only in recent years has psychoanalytic investigation started to explore proto–mental activity and prenatal psychic life. With great caution, and well aware of the risk of "projecting backwards in time" abilities which are acquired at later stages, an observational and psychoanalytic longitudinal study of children from the earliest stages of intrauterine life to the first years of postnatal life gives evidence of the extraordinary continuity of the children's characteristics before and after birth (Piontelli, 1992). The echographic and direct observations made by the author not only support the hypothesis of the prenatal origins of the intertwining of nature and nurture, but also confirm Freud's intuition of a surprising behavioral consistency between the fetus, the infant and the child.

This means that the fetus will not only *become* the individual who he will be, but that he *is* the individual who he is. Neurobiological research on prenatal life mostly refers to the fetus as an "it." His "it-ness" does not seem primarily to be meant to overcome the duplicity of gender identity, but rather to reflect the researchers' idea that it is too early to consider him as a human individual in his own right. By referring to the fetus as a "he," I underline his dignity as a person and at the same time differentiate him from the "she-ness" of his mother. The view on the fetus as an individual is particularly relevant when we think about the experience of prematurely born infants in intensive neonatal care.

In previous papers, I explored the area of fetal auditory perception and memory, as it can be inferred from infant observation and psychoanalytic psychotherapy (Maiello, 1995; 1997a; 1997b; 1999; 2000; 2001a; 2001b). The newborn infant shows through his preference of the maternal voice that traces of his prenatal auditory experience are stored in his memory. I suggest that prenatal proto-introjective processes connected with auditory experience may lead to the formation of what I described as the *sound-object,* which results from prenatal proto-mental activity and can be seen as a precursor of the child's later maternal internal object which will be nourished not only by her voice, but by the infant's global experience of the relationship with his mother. My hypothesis is that protoforms of an experience of relatedness may develop between the fetus and his mother not only at the tactile, but also at the auditory level.

PRENATAL SOUND ENVIRONMENT AND FETAL AUDITORY PERCEPTION[*]

During the first nine months of his existence, the child is immersed in the sonic intrauterine environment and lives in a state which Oremland (1987) describes as "primordial bi–unity." It is a state of fusion and suspension in an indistinct conglomerate of tactile and auditory sensations made of liquidity and movement, rhythmical and non-rhythmical noises and vocal sounds.

From the point of view of the fetus' perception of sounds, neurophysiological research has shown that the hearing capacity of the human fetus is fully developed at the age of four months (Tomatis, 1981; Prechtl, 1989). By that time, the fetus perceives the medium and high sound frequency range corresponding to the mother's voice. The low frequency range corresponding to the sounds produced by the maternal organism (heartbeat, breathing and digestive noises), is perceived at an even earlier stage, i.e. from

* An earlier version of parts of this chapter was published in:
Suzanne Maiello: The sound object: A hypothesis about prenatal auditory experience and memory. *Journal of Child Psychotherapy*, 21, 1, 1995.

the age of three months. Low frequency sounds have a soothing effect on the fetus and slow down his motor activity, whereas sounds of the medium and high frequency range corresponding to the maternal voice are enlivening and stimulate his mobility and heartbeat.

Not only are sounds perceived and listened to by the fetus, but research has shown that both the rhythmical sounds produced by the mother's organism and her voice leave traces in his memory.

Rhythmical Body Sounds

Recordings from the intrauterine environment show that "there is a very loud noise going on all the time in the uterus. It is a *rhythmical whooshing sound*, punctuated by the abdominal rumbles of air passing through the mother's stomach. The pulsating noise keeps exact time with her heart and is due to the blood flowing through her body" (Macfarlane, 1977).

Infants seem to retain a reminiscence of the rhythmical elements of their prenatal life. In fact, recordings of intrauterine sounds have a marked calming effect on newborn babies. Research has shown that the periodical exposure of newborns to the sound of an adult heartbeat leads to a marked decrease of crying and a higher weight increase as compared to control groups (Salk, 1973).

These earliest rhythmical experiences, which are rooted in prenatal life, seem to be fundamental, as we shall see, for the child's later emotional and mental development and for the quality of his interpersonal relationships.

The Maternal Voice

The auditory perception and memory of the maternal voice constitutes on the one hand the sound-code from which the child's future language, i.e. his "mother tongue," will develop in terms of the "deep language structures" described by Chomsky (1972). On the other hand, the specificity of the voice of each individual mother with its personal inflections and modulations puts the fetus in touch not only with the uniqueness of her personality, but also with the general state of her mind as well as the fluctuations of her emotions.

Since we know that the fetus actively listens to the mother's voice and reacts to it (De Casper & Spence,1986; Masakowski & Fifer, 1994; Moon & Fifer, 1990; Spence & De Casper, 1987), it is probable that he receives clues about her emotional states not only through biochemical fluctuations in her organism, but also at the vocal level. A depressed mother's voice has a flatter melodious line, a slower rhythm, a weaker tone and a lower pitch than the voice of a non-depressed mother. In this connection, Tustin's finding that the mothers of all her autistic child patients had been clinically depressed in the prenatal and/or perinatal period of their children's life is relevant (1986).

If in normal circumstances the maternal voice has an enlivening effect on the fetus, it may represent an essential factor for the onset of proto–mental activity (Maiello, 1995). And if the child is capable, from inside his intrauterine sound-universe, of distinguishing the mother's voice from other sounds and is stimulated by its presence, we may hypothesize that some form of proto-relationship begins already at this early stage.

The fetus is usually thought of as lacking the key-experience of separation which will allow the infant, from the moment of birth, to *meet* his environment, to gradually differentiate himself from it and thereby create the prerequisite for psychic growth. The question is whether birth is really the moment which inaugurates this level of mental activity, or whether we can hypothesize that the child has proto-experiences of separateness already in utero? If so, these could set in motion the development of primary nuclei of the later sense of self which are existent at birth (Klein, 1952).

Piontelli writes about the fetal stage: "The fact that characteristic behavior patterns are established so early and evolve developmentally but without losing their characteristic form suggests to me that they may well involve some very rudimentary form of 'me/not-me' differentiation" (1992). It seems legitimate to extend backwards in time into fetal life the far end of the *"developmental lines"* traced by A. Freud (1965) from birth through to adolescence.

In thinking about the fetus' auditory perceptions, the rhythmical sounds produced by the mother's body will be discussed separately from the sound of her voice. Although the fetus' actual experience is likely to be a cluster of auditory sensations, the two elements may have specific functions and meanings for prenatal proto-mental development.

CONSIDERATIONS ON RHYTHMICITY[*]

The *rhythmical qualities* of the sound-object may be rooted in the fetus' perception of the maternal heartbeat, the pulsations of her blood-flow and the rhythm of her breathing. In developmental terms, I would place the *rhythmical aspects* of the prenatal sound environment at the primordial end of auditory, and in part vibratory, experiences. Intertwined with kinaesthetic and tactile levels of experience, they may bring about the fetus', and later the infant's, primary awareness of pulsating life, and therefore be at the core of *basic trust* (Erikson, 1950).

These might be the levels of experience from which the child derives what Emde describes as *procedural knowledge* (1991). These proto-memories are not accessible to consciousness, but seem to include *relational knowing,* i.e.

---

* An earlier version of parts of this chapter was published in:
Suzanne Maiello: On temporal shapes – The relation between primary rhythmical experience and the quality of mental links. In: *Edwards, J. (ed.): Being alive – Building on the work of Anne Alvarez*. London: Brunner-Routledge, 2001.

"knowing how to do things with intimate others" (Lyons-Ruth, 1998).

I suggest that the dynamic temporal and rhythmical qualities of internalized patterns belong to these deep levels of proto-mental experience and have a bridging function in the transition from states of pre-mental psycho-physical at-one-ness towards mental activity and symbolic thinking.

Rhythm is an ever-present element in all that is living. The embryo begins his existence as a pulsating entity, and the end of life coincides with the last breath and heartbeat.

In prenatal life, sensori-motor materno-fetal interaction is characterized by *constancy* and *rhythmicity*. "Primary mental activity might consist of a process of "reading" or "decodifying" the rhythmical and constant stimuli that reach the fetus coming from the maternal container. Furthermore, by virtue of its rhythmicity and constancy, the fetus' object world might constitute the ground plan of a *primitive biological clock* that will permeate the prenatal psychic nucleus" (Mancia, 1981).

Ogden describes the normal infant's primary sensuous experiences with what he defines as the "autistic-contiguous" mode. In the author's view, their character of rhythmicity lays the base for the individual's sense of continuity of being (1989).

M. Papoušek underlines the constant rhythmic–dynamic stimulation during prenatal life coming from the maternal heartbeat, breathing and walking, and from the rhythms of maternal speech. She explores the synchronization of vocal and kinetic patterns in postnatal maternal behavior with the infant, as well as the infant's sensitivity to rhythmical patterns of behavior. Her analysis of euphonic cooing sounds produced by a two–month–old infant showed a frequency and rhythmical structure which corresponds to the rhythm of the heartbeat of an adult (1996).

Stern explored the postnatal structure and timing of mother–infant interaction and found that moments of engagement alternate with moments of rest and silence "at a surprisingly regular rate." Not only is there a "temporal patterning of human social behavior" as a result of experience, but "the infant seems to be equipped...to deal with the temporal world of his social interactions" (1977). Stern's later concept of *shared attunement* takes the importance of rhythmical aspects of experience even further (1985).

Trevarthen observed how mothers and infants adjust the timing, emotional form and energy of their expression to obtain intersynchronicity, harmonious transitions and complementarity of feelings between them in an emotional partnership of "confluence" (1993). Nursery rhymes seem to have similar characteristics in all cultures and languages. "They have predictable features of beat, rhythm, melody and rhyme that suggest innate foundations in brain activity for what turns out to be universals in the timing and prosody of music and poetry" (1996).

In my view, rhythmicity is of paramount importance at the earliest stages of introjective processes. Rhythm in fact combines presence and absence in a temporal dimension. A beat and a pause alternate at regular intervals. I suggest that at the earliest stages of awareness, the continuity and regularity of a sequence of beat and pause may be the prerequisite for the internalization of reliable *temporal shapes* (Alvarez, 1998).

The experience of rhythmical aspects of reality may lead from the primary state of unstructured fusional unity through the experience of reliable shapes in time towards the first dawning awareness of difference and the capacity to bear *variations*. However, a sufficient experience of rhythmical *continuity* seems to be indispensable for a safe exploration of *discontinuity*.

After birth, meeting the maternal breast is the infant's first experience of active rhythmical interplay with the external world. "A sucking movement involves pulling and slackening...there is huge activity, but hidden in the pulling and drawing is the letting go—the fundamental rhythm of life" (Alvarez, 1992). The "hidden letting go" is there, as the element that heralds in the possibility of absence, within the gratifying experience of presence, containment and nourishment.

I suggest that both aspects of rhythmical experiences have specific functions for psychic growth. Constancy and reliability are the indispensable ingredients for the establishment of basic trust, whereas variations and imperfections create the space for interpersonal and intrapsychic links to acquire flexibility and for mental activity to develop. At the earliest stages of life, rhythmical inconstancy and discontinuity are likely to be bearable only after a congruous experience of constancy and continuity, which begins during prenatal life, has been internalized.

On this basis, later rhythmical imperfections offer not only minimal spaces for frustration thanks to which attention is reoriented and thinking sets in train, but variations and discrepancies in the mothers' talk, singing or play can become pleasurable experiences (Papoušek, 1996; Tronick, 1989).

If we connect these considerations on the one hand with the fact that the fetus' auditory perceptive capacity reaches back to the fourth month of prenatal life, and on the other hand with the evidence given by newborns that proto-forms of rhythmical experience are stored in their memory, we can intuit the traumatic breach represented by premature birth in the area of primary experiences of rhythmicity.

A HYPOTHESIS OF THE FETUS' AUDITORY EXPERIENCE
OF THE MATERNAL VOICE[*]

If prenatal experiences of rhythmicity are stored at primordial levels of "procedural knowledge" and find expression in the individual's ways of existing in space and time, the maternal voice represents, in my view, the primary nourishment needed by the fetus for setting in train the most primitive forms of proto-mental activity.

From the psychoanalytic point of view, one prerequisite for the development of the mind and of symbolic thinking is the experience of the absence of the primary object and, consequently, the awareness of separateness. In other terms, the primary unit of "container/contained" (Bion, 1962) must be divided and one-ness must become two-ness. For thoughts to be thought by the mind, they must find an empty space to receive them. This space results from the abandonment of the primary fantasy of fusional at–one–ness. Without absence there is no thought, and without thought there is no language. Language, however, reaches the child already during intrauterine life through the maternal voice. A *sound language*, which is perceived by a being who, we are inclined to believe, lacks as yet the prerequisite of separateness necessary for mental activity to develop.

At first sight in fact, the intrauterine environment does not seem to offer the conditions for experiencing absence in any form. The environment of the fetus is a continuum. There is stability and constancy of place, medium and temperature, and there is continuity of nutritional supply and of low frequency background sounds, punctuated only by the rhythm of the mother's breathing and heartbeat. Rascovsky (1977) considers the umbilical flux, which includes an uninterrupted supply of oxygen, nutrition and heat, as the fetus' original object and asserts that the absence of the need for reality keeps the fetal ego in a state of total independence of external objects. According to the author, the relationship between the ego and the external objects is established only after birth, whilst during intrauterine life, the fetus is in contact with nothing but his innate internal objects. On the other hand, the author recognizes that sound, and therefore spoken language, necessarily exist in a temporal dimension.

The maternal voice does introduce an element of discontinuity in an environment which is otherwise characterized by continuity. At times the voice speaks, and at times it is silent. It *is* an external object, as unpredictable and uncontrollable as the breast will be after birth. Both the voice and the breast alternate moments of presence and moments of absence. The rhythm of

---

* An earlier version of parts of this chapter was published in:
Suzanne Maiello: The sound object: A hypothesis about prenatal auditory experience and memory. *Journal of Child Psychotherapy*, 21, 1, 1995.

alternation is not always regular, and is not necessarily in harmony with the fetus' needs. It can therefore be a source of both well-being and frustration.

In my view, the interactive competence of the infant from the moment of birth could be seen not only in terms of an innate primary inter-subjectivity, but, especially in its individual variations, also as the result of every single child's prenatal history and experience. I share the statement that "it is, in fact, only if the fetus has been able to elaborate external stimuli making internal representations of these, that we can explain the newborn's preparation for meeting reality; first of all the maternal breast" (Mancia, 1981).

Since the fetus not only hears the mother's voice, but actively listens to it, is it not likely, even in a situation of substantial indifferentiation between container and contained, that the disappearance of the enlivening and stimulating voice might give the child a proto-experience of absence and loss? Missing an object generates desire. And desire cannot exist without some, even though fleeting, awareness of an "elsewhere" and a "not-me." If so, the child's listening ear would no longer be completely fused in the primary sonic one-ness. There might already be some distance and differentiation between the voice and the ear, the germ of distinction between a listening "me" and a speaking "not-me," and hence of the experience of encounter and relationship. In other terms, the fetus' proto-mental nucleus capable of transforming sensory information coming from external objects (Mancia, 1981), could use the mother's voice for the creation of an internal proto-object with sound qualities, which in turn could become the ground on which rests the pre-conception of the breast (Bion, 1963). The absence of the voice on the other hand might give the child a proto-experience of emptiness, of the emptied space in which later thinking and language will develop and become the instruments for re-evoking, i.e. "giving voice again" to the lost object by naming it.

We know that the fetus is able, from the fifth month of intrauterine life, to put his thumb in his mouth and suck it. This ability appears at the time when the hearing capacity is fully developed and the fetus is ready to receive the sound-frequencies corresponding to the mother's voice. Is it too daring to think that there might be a link between the perception of emptiness following the silence of the maternal voice and the attempt to fill the gap by putting the thumb in his mouth? The loss of the voice might be felt as an emptiness in the mouth. The fetus is not yet capable of protecting himself from auditory frustration by producing vocal fullness to fill the silence of the mother's voice, but he is able to fill the tactile emptiness which he perceives in his oral cavity. This would imply that the fetus is capable from the middle of his intrauterine life, of *transmodal perception,* i.e. of "translating" a sensation from one sensory mode to another (Stern 1985).

The hypothesis of prenatal vocal and auditory interaction and communication between mother and child and the existence of a proto-experience of absence implies that the child may also begin before birth to lay the ground for some of his future patterns of defense and develop the precursors of his later response to the further and more diversified frustrations to which he will be exposed after birth. The experience of the present and absent breast might have a prenatal precursor in the present and absent voice. The cluster of pleasant sensations of "the mouth that sucks the nipple that gives nourishing milk" might correspond in utero to "the ear that listens to the sound of the enlivening voice." According to Mancia, the containing function of the skin as described by Bick (1968) might well have its onset during prenatal life (1981). Along these lines, the fetus' early hearing capacity may have an analogous containing function. The infant's *sound-envelope* described by Anzieu (1985) may well be rooted in prenatal life and correspond, at a time when inside and outside are not clearly distinguished, to the fetus' sound-object.

AUDITORY AND VOCAL EXPERIENCE AND PREMATURE BIRTH

The preceding considerations on the function of rhythmical sounds and the maternal voice during prenatal life show that premature birth represents a traumatic interruption of vital proto-mental processes connected with ongoing auditory experience.

From the point of view of the *rhythmical aspects* of fetal experience, the continuity and regularity of the background sounds of the maternal heartbeat and breathing disappear abruptly. I suggest that a sufficient experience of constancy and regularity may be the prerequisite for the individual to tolerate the awareness of discontinuity and gradually accept the absence of the object, and that the internalization of its rhythmical permanence may lay the ground for *basic trust* and for an existential *rhythm of safety* (Tustin, 1990) to develop and to acquire some degree of reliability.

What is to be said about the premature loss of the auditory experience of the *maternal voice* in prematurely born infants? In terms of its function and meaning for the developing fetus, we saw the maternal voice as the nourishment which may, once the neurophysiological prerequisites exist, stimulate the onset of mental development. It is important to note that auditory experiences are immaterial, as opposed to the concreteness of tactile and kinetic experiences. Furthermore, tactile perceptions can be reproduced by the fetus at will, whereas the maternal voice is not under the child's control and may therefore challenge the primary sensation of fusional at–one–ness and stimulate, as we saw, proto-forms of introjective mental processes.

In reuniting the two levels of prenatal auditory experience, i.e. its rhythmical and its vocal component, the continuity of the mother's heartbeat and breathing may bridge the spells during which the mother's nourishing voice is silent, and represent a reassuring background during the periods of the fetus' sleep, as well as during the periods of the mother's silence, rest and sleep.

If a child is born prematurely, the sheltered uterine space in which auditory proto-experiences of separateness and proto-introjective processes were safely contained, is lost. Neither physically nor emotionally the infant is ready to meet the external world. In terms of the sound-object, we could say that the interruption of his auditory experience and emotional interaction with the mother's voice leaves him insufficiently prepared to meet the breast in his postnatal life.

Preterm infants are exposed to a twofold trauma. Not only is the prenatal environment prematurely lost, but the incubator, the premature infant's first postnatal environment, is dramatically different from a mother's arms–eyes–voice–breast and loving attention, which in normal circumstances welcome the full-term infant at the moment of birth. The whooshing of the mother's blood circulation, her heartbeat and breathing, have disappeared together with her voice and are replaced by the mechanical sounds of machines and electronic signals.

AUDITORY AND VOCAL ELEMENTS IN FOLLOW-UP STUDIES AND IN PSYCHOTHERAPY WITH PREMATURELY BORN PATIENTS

We have seen that the fetus not only hears sounds and listens to them, but also maintains a memory of his auditory experience. The premature infant is not less sensitive to his sound environment in the incubator. Therefore, traces of his exposure are bound to have an impact on the quality of the developing sound-object in his internal world.

Research findings and psychotherapeutic experience with premature children give us clues about what their auditory experiences may have been during the first period of their postnatal existence after the untimely expulsion from their natural environment.

A follow-up study of twenty-two children born at a gestational age of less than 32 weeks and a birth weight of less than 1500 grams assessed the impact of premature birth on the structuring of the child's personality and the quality of his relationships. The age-range of the children was of 24–30 months (Latmiral & Lombardo, 2001).

The results of the study show that the development of premature children at this age is still significantly delayed and seems to follow developmental lines which are different from those of full-term children of the same age group.

In the area of speech, there was a slight delay in all the assessed children. One finding seems particularly relevant in relation to the breach of continuity of the prenatal auditory experience at the moment of birth. All the observed children made a peculiar repetitive and idiosyncratic use of their voice with low communicative value. They tended to accompany their activities with continuous vocalizations or words, significantly more than full-term children. The children who showed a more serious developmental delay tended to produce an almost voiceless mumble which could be heard only if the environment was perfectly silent.

The children who presented a higher verbal capacity tended to be less spontaneous in their interpersonal interactions than full-term children of the same age. Their talk had a mechanical and non-fluid quality and an artificial pitch.

All children seemed to show a peculiar lack of harmony both in their movements in space and in their vocal modulations.

The ongoing repetition of vocal sounds and the continuous babbling or talking of these children during play could be seen as a defensive clinging to a self-produced vocal presence as a substitute for the premature loss of the maternal voice. The apparent self-sufficiency of their non-communicative talk might say something about these children's loss of hope in an ongoing dialogue with a reliable other and about the tendency of parts of their personality to remain isolated from social interaction.

The artificial pitch of the more verbal children might be another attempt to try to come to terms with the same feeling of insecure internal and external auditory links. We could say that the socially interacting part of their personality tended to be disconnected from their deeper emotions in terms of a *false self* (Winnicott, 1971).

The lack of harmony in the vocal modulations of preterm children is another interesting finding which may well be related to both the interruption of the prenatal auditory experience of the modulations of the maternal voice and its sudden disappearance after the infant's premature birth. A full-term infant loses the water-borne version of the mother's voice, but meets and recognizes its airborne version at the reunion with her after birth. The no-man's land of the incubator represents a dramatic caesura of the normal transition from intrauterine to extra-uterine life also from the auditory point of view.

At the vocal level, another difference between severely preterm and full-term infants must be considered. The younger premature children are too weak to cry. A normal newborn is able to communicate his distress to his environment and call for relief. A preterm infant is unable to "voice" his forlornness and despair. May the early trauma of voicelessness be expressed in the toneless whispering of the preterm children who had more serious developmental delay?

When working in psychotherapeutic practice with both children and adults who were born prematurely, at some point invariably elements emerge from a kind of autistic-like encapsulation, which contain the nameless traumatic experience of the beginning of their postnatal lives. The clinical material has aspects of hardness and coldness, it conveys metallic or glassy sensations and contains violently intrusive elements.

In adolescents or adult patients, these inaccessible memories may take the form of hallucination-like fantasies, as in an anorexic adolescent girl who gave an obsessively detailed description of a building on an island where people were put in quarantine. The place had characteristics of coldness, hardness, sterility and isolation in a near-death atmosphere. The constantly impending life-threatening invasions were announced by an alarm-system. The disharmony of the sounds was in proportion with the degree of the impending danger. The patient felt that the function of the danger-announcing alarm in her fantasy was that of provoking a frozen panic-stricken state in the inhabitants who had to undergo threatening procedures (Kaës, 2000).

The patient seemed to know without knowing that she knew. To her listening analyst, she described what she experienced as a hallucinated fantasy, but it reached him as a chillingly precise description of her life in the incubator and a message of the nameless split-off anxieties of annihilation which she had endured. The acoustic alarm-system played an important role in the life-threatening place of her fantasy.

Prematurely born children are often referred to psychotherapy with symptoms of either developmental delay and social isolation or violently destructive behavior (Maiello, 2000). At the vocal level, my experience corresponds to the findings of the mentioned follow-up study. All prematurely born child patients had a disharmonic relationship with their own voice. They seem to have difficulties in using its pitch, loudness, rhythm and intonation to convey unconscious clues of their emotional state as naturally as other children and adults do. Many of these children have high-pitched piercing unmodulated voices of a brittle "glassy" quality. When they learn about their vocal power, they may use it to scream endlessly at an almost intolerable pitch for any human ear.

A screaming child may try to escape his nameless sensations of helplessness by inverting the power relationship with the therapist who is forced to hear and listen to his piercing vocal emissions. But through his screams, the child also desperately tries to expel and rid himself of the cutting and stinging intrusive quality of his early nameless experiences. His screams may contain both his rage and his despair at not having been heard and listened to at a moment when his need was inversely proportional to his ability to communicate it.

THE AUDITORY AND VOCAL AREA OF EXPERIENCE IN NEONATAL INTENSIVE CARE

When premature infants were initially being cared for, physical survival was the first priority. Today, progress in neonatology and modern technology has resulted in the survival of more and younger preterm children, and more attention is given to the quality of the infant's environment and to his emotional and relational needs. Neonatal intensive care units have been "humanized," first and foremost by giving the baby's parents free access to their child and offering them guidelines to facilitate establishing this primary relationship (Klaus & Kennell, 1971). Unfortunately, the importance of the parents' presence and participation is still far from being fully recognized in many European countries.

More systematic psychological investigations of both short-term and long-term effects of the relational deprivation of preterm infants in intensive care still need to be undertaken, with the aim of offering the traumatized infant not only a substitute container which has as much as possible in common with his lost intrauterine universe, but takes into account the fact that the baby needs to be in-relation and that he can be an active partner in its making. Today, a premature child is often still too much of a "survivor," with his later personality traits of fragility, lack of basic trust and the tendency to isolate and split off emotions.

The importance of touch in normal early development has been widely recognized (Klaus, 1995; Tronick, 1995), and the introduction of the kangaroo care method extends these insights to the premature infant's need for tactile contact with his mother (Anderson, 1995). In the incubator, infants are laid on water mattresses and surrounded by rolls, in order to offer them an environment which reproduces as closely as possible the lost uterine containment.

At the level of the preterm infant's auditory needs, however, much remains to be thought over and done. It has been recognized that the noises produced by the mechanical life-saving equipment of the incubator are very disturbing, but the intrusiveness of alarms is an aspect which needs to be given more attention. To alleviate the monotony of machine noises, "sound-therapy" has been introduced (Peltzam, et al., 1970; Negri, 1994). It can include the reproduction of the beat of an adult heart, which has a soothing effect on preterm infants, as well as the diffusion of soft music.

The particularly problematic area of the premature infant's auditory deprivation is the absence of the mother's voice, which is unique for every single baby, and with which, as we saw, he enters in relation during prenatal life. It was a unique presence then, and it is a unique loss now in his untimely postnatal existence. If every fetus is an individual, every preterm infant's personal needs must be taken seriously, not only in terms of diminishing the auditory intrusions of the equipment, and not only by finding the optimal balance between filling the gap of his auditory deprivation and protecting him from over stimulation. This can primarily be offered by listening to his need to retrieve the lost familiar sounds, first and foremost his mother's voice, as soon as possible after the rupture of his traumatic birth.

A difficulty in this connection may arise when the infant's mother is not immediately physically available. Also, her own traumatic experience must be taken into account. Her anxieties around the survival of the baby, her depression and guilt feelings may make it difficult for her to create the emotional link, which her baby is waiting for. Mothers often need support themselves to become able to look at their child, to touch him and talk to him in a way that conveys to the baby feelings of hope and trust more than of failure and anxiety.

INFANT OBSERVATION IN NEONATAL INTENSIVE CARE: THE MOTHER'S VOICE

The infant observation method (Bick, 1964) has been used in neonatal intensive care units and offers precious insights in the early experiences of preterm infants. The uniqueness of the observed baby with or without his mother and father is at the center of the observer's attention. The infant has a chance to be seen in the multifold expressions of his "mind-mapping" struggle, and the observer's emotionally open mind allows her to discover the infinite means by which the preterm human infant is able to signal his internal state (Cohen, 1995; Lazar, Röpke, & Ermann, 1998; Mendelsohn, 1999; Szur, 1981). As Mendelsohn puts it: "Hitherto the emphasis had been laid on parent–infant interaction, which implied that it was the mother who was the prime instigator of the bonding process...". However, "...as maternal behavior in relation to her baby was being observed and studied, so too was the baby in relation to his mother, and the baby in relation to the nursing staff, the doctors and the incubator environment" (1999). Infant–parent interaction is observed as much as parent-infant interaction. In this way, the preterm infant is not only the passive recipient of scientifically determined "optimal care," but he becomes a precious source of information himself. He is in fact capable of signaling his needs and can be an active partner in the relationship with his caregivers.

In the area of vocal expression, infant observation gives evidence of these children's first attempts to cry, at a time when "the voice is still too weak, and his experience of response to it still too slight for it to be recognized as 'crying–for–somebody'" (Lazar, et al., 1998). Yet, research has shown that preterm infants do feel pain and distress when submitted to invasive therapeutic procedures (Negri, 1994; Sumner, 1993).

A little boy born at thirty weeks of gestational age was observed in the incubator from birth. He clearly showed his distress, caused by the intrusive procedures he had to undergo. On the second day, Leo was visibly disturbed by the tube in the corner of his mouth. He grimaced and moved his little hand towards his cheek. On the 14th day, he found out that if he slipped his hand between the tube and his cheek and pulled firmly, he could partially liberate himself of the foreign body in his throat. Every time, the alarm went off and the nurse pushed the tube back into Leo's throat. As he insisted in pulling it out, the tube was strapped more firmly to his cheek to prevent him from displacing it (Maiello, 1999). Obviously, the tube was necessary for his survival, but Leo had been able not only to signal his distress, but also to find a way to give himself relief. Not all painful procedures can be eliminated, but knowing emotionally about the infant's suffering may help the caregivers to be more understanding when submitting the baby to inevitable intrusions.

In the area of preterm babies' auditory experience of the mother's voice, an infant observation in a neonatal intensive care unit assessed the response of infants to the mother's singing voice. The babies were not yet mature enough to be taken in kangaroo-care, and the mothers were asked to stroke their children lightly and sing nursery songs to them through the openings of the incubator. All the observed infants listened eagerly to their mother's singing as they do to her speaking voice. One mother commented: "It feels as if he is drinking the stroking and the song with his whole body." The infants not only listened, but also communicated their preferences with their facial expressions and movements, in particular by relaxing or contracting their muscles. Thanks to the babies' clues, the mothers could adapt the loudness and rhythm of their voices to the infant's needs. The babies' signals were even more sophisticated. All the observed infants showed a preference for slow songs with a falling melodious line and small tone intervals, as they are universally found in lullabies, and tended to withdraw from brighter rising melodies with larger tone intervals. It seemed that the primary need of the infants at that point in time was on the side of soothing more than of excitement (Maiello, 1999).

These observations, as other research findings have clearly confirmed (Nöcker-Ribaupierre, 1994) not only give an indication of these children's need to be nourished with the sound of their mothers' voices, but give evidence of the ability of even very premature babies to perceive and express the specific quality of their auditory needs and to communicate them in preverbal and prevocal, but unequivocal ways to their caregivers.

It is not easy to observe and to "listen" to what a premature baby is able to communicate. The painfulness of these observations is often at the limit of bearability and has something to say about the infant's experience and state of mind. His mute suffering stirs emotions, which are difficult to tolerate. This may be one of the reasons why so much remains to be done in working towards understanding more about the depth of the psychic side of the preterm infant's trauma, of which the auditory aspect is an essential part.

Only if the emotional aspects of the preterm infant's experience are further explored, neonatal care can offer him, after the catastrophic caesura of premature birth, a harbor which has in common as many aspects as possible with his intrauterine experience. In other terms, only if we are ready to be emotionally receptive to the depth of these children's trauma can we listen to and hear their desperate need for relatedness.

Chapter 5

COMING TOGETHER—RESONANCE AND SYNCHRONIZATION AS A REGULATING FACTOR IN RELATIONSHIPS

Gisela M. Lenz and Dorothee von Moreau

AN UNSUCCESSFUL ENCOUNTER

GEORG - *Georg was 10 weeks old at the onset of therapy and was an excessively crying infant. During one of our first therapy sessions he began to scream. His mother tried to breastfeed him. He was so upset that he couldn't nurse and kept screaming. Ms. N. looked at me[1] - helplessly. I took a rattle and began to try and match Georg's intensity of screaming. I managed to get his attention and he looked directly at me. I modulated the rhythm, was able to quiet him down and began to speak to him. Georg relaxed, burped and smiled. A moment later, he began to scream again. His mother said to him, "You can't be hungry, we've just tried to take care of that." But his reaction was clear. He stuck his fist in his mouth and began to suck it and then screamed. I cautiously intervened by diverting her attention to his behavior. She asked, "He really seems to be hungry. Should I try to feed him again?" Ms. N. was surprised how readily Georg drank this time, but remained anxious about what would happen next.*

MICHAEL - *Michael and his mother had a difficult beginning. Michael was also an excessively crying baby and almost drove his mother over the brink. This was extremely painful for her, as she had wanted a baby very much. His father pushed her to breastfeed him, whenever the infant was restless. Although Ms. S. often had the feeling that he wasn't hungry at all, she gave in to her husband. Thus, Michael often experienced being misunderstood by his mother and lost any motivation to try and communicate with her.*
Such a series of misunderstandings can prevent a mother and infant from developing true intimacy. Both are in an agitated state, which usually escalates with neither finding a way out. Some mothers describe the situation as being locked in a vicious circle. When these unfortunate interactions repeat

---

[1] All case studies refer to the first author, Gisela M. Lenz.

themselves, they can have fatal consequences. The infant never really has a chance to calm down. The agitation increases with each incident and becomes a habit. The mother is constantly under pressure: When is he going to start screaming again? How long will it last? This fear of failure can develop into a continuous cycle, making it almost impossible to have any intimacy with her infant and suffocating any joy they may have in one another. Both try to reach each other and can't. In this situation, the infant usually pulls back from his mother and begins to rely on himself. However, with some intervention and support, it may be possible for the mother and child to find a solution and begin bonding.

COMING TOGETHER

When Michael began music therapy he was already 22 months old with a diagnosis of delayed speech development. He had been an excessively crying baby, and now almost two years old, had a vocabulary of five words. His mother reported that when something did not suit him, he began to "scream like an animal" and she had to guess what the matter was. He gave no sign of what he wanted.

In our first session, Michael appeared insecure and unable to recognize boundaries. He propelled himself aimlessly around the room and showed no reaction when spoken to. I began to interfere with his wandering by using different instruments to interpret the dynamics of his movements. The rattles especially fascinated him and he stopped to grab two of them, one after the other. He began to play with great concentration, graduating in intensity, threw his arms up with complete enthusiasm, and opened his mouth, without uttering a sound. It was possible to observe that affective movement and verbal expression do not always go hand in hand.

In such moments, I usually try to intervene. I took two rattles, played, imitated, accompanied and commented on his playing as well as my own until we came together, free and joyful. At the end of the session, Michael's reactions and sounds were matched for the first time.

In the next session, he discovered the fun in vocal games (babbling, echoing) although they were not age appropriate. After interacting with me, he ran to his mother and got her to join in. She was initially very inhibited and embarrassed to play along. Michael continued to try and get her involved through his enthusiasm. I encouraged him from my seat and she gradually joined in. Michael appeared to be the happiest child in the world.

This was a turning point in their relationship. From then on, he addressed her as "Mama" and showed her what he wanted. His speech developed rapidly and was age appropriate within a few months. The change in his social behavior was impressive, as was the way others reacted to him. Later on, his mother had even forgotten that his delayed speech had been the initial reason for beginning music therapy. She remembered a feeling of hopelessness about their relationship. "We couldn't find a common ground. It was tortuous, so unsatisfactory—a feeling of growing aggression on both sides— I was afraid that I would eventually start hitting him."

TURNING POINT—A SPECIAL MOMENT

Michael was initially unreachable, even through the sounds of the rattles, which he had chosen. Through my intervention, he was able to experience the sound himself, how it feels when affect, movement and expression come together—a short moment of self-encounter, supported by interaction with another.

Of course, I first had to find a way of establishing contact with Michael and sustain it. Thus, I began to imitate his playing, commented on his actions and accompanied his movement. Gradually, the game took on its own form and I was able to forget therapy as such. Our intensity increased and our playing developed into a free and satisfying experience for both of us. It became a moment in the here and now, when two people are able to be together in the moment. They share the same emotional intensity in their contact with each other, feel *the same feeling shape,* according to Stern (1985) and are so emotionally close to each other, that one can say they are resonating with one other.

Although these moments are experienced as very satisfying, they do not always easily occur. They demand a readiness and courage to go with whatever may happen; an acceptance of the unknown or that which can not be controlled (the basic quality of improvisation). Michael's mother was able to cautiously take part in her son's childish play, while Georg's mother was not yet able to let go of her fears. In both cases, the potential to change was there. The difference being that one mother had an easier time interacting than the other. A hungry infant is quieted when it is fed, but it reacts differently when the mother is anxious while nursing. Real intimacy and closeness are missing.

When Ms. N. saw how positively Georg reacted to the sound of the xylophone, she began to play the xylophone with him at home, especially when he was agitated. Georg relaxed and became attentive and the mother's own blood pressure returned to normal. The autonomic response was the same in both of them: relaxation and normal physiological functions—a wonderful example of mutuality and being in the moment.

Through sharing an experienced affect, mother and child are able to share a deep bonding and the relationship can take on another phase of intimacy. I assume that Michael and his mother experienced an emotional closeness for the first time in the above anecdote. This appeared to be a newly won basis for opening a locked door, leading to self-encounter. Such moments of meeting are key moments in an infant's development, which will become apparent in the following theory.

In my music therapy work with excessively crying babies, I continually experience special moments when the medium of sound and music creates the groundwork, where mother and child are able to reach each other—to meet each other. The tones quiet both of them, allowing new experiences—a longer attention span, letting go of a held breath, eye contact, smiles, amazement, and encounter. All of this brings them together. In these moments, they both experience being connected with one another. The mother–child relationship takes on new qualities in spontaneity, mutual pleasure in each other, and allows a lightheartedness to shine through. This builds a foundation for them, as both of them learn they can trust one another and will start to move away from the difficult and confusing situations. The excessive screaming begins to diminish and other problems with sleeping or eating slowly correct themselves (Lenz, 2000).

In order to better understand these processes, we are presenting the following theoretical principles to clarify how and why music therapy may be used with the newborn.

DEVELOPING SELF-REGULATION

Research richly documents that infants are born with a wide range of abilities (Dornes, 1993; 1999). In spite of the newborn's helplessness with motor skills, he can experience diverse areas of his environment through his sensory organs (Papoušek, 2001). Before his birth, he can recognize the different emotional states and arousal, which he is experiencing. After birth, physically and hormonally separated from his mother, he has to learn to begin relying on himself.

According to Stern (1990) the newborn perceives objects and events predominately emotionally which awaken in him. Everything that a child experiences has its own special feeling tone—for example, as a lit room filled with sound, an onslaught or a wave. He is interwoven within his environment and experiences a dynamic flow, colored by his feeling states. These affectual states differ in their sense of time, intensity, tension and release.

In experiencing the world around him, the newborn develops a diverse pallet of inner states. Basch (1994) describes these states as precursors of feelings. They show similar qualities such as *vitality affects* (Stern, 1985) and *background-feelings* (Damasio, 1999). These may be described as quickly changing states of tension, which are dramatically experienced or are hardly recognizable in their delicacy, like a dancing filigree of light. It is significant that these states are regulated. The infant is born with many possibilities—eye contact or turning away, screaming, sucking or kicking. This behavior allows him to communicate but he is dependent on others to correctly understand and react to him. Otherwise his messages go unrecognized. His instinctive behavior loses its meaning, cannot be used for a self-regulating process and is results in a vicious circle of pre–occupation with himself.

Yet the newborn is dependent on others in regulating his sensitivity. Basch (1994) emphasized that newborns learn to regulate their feelings in their first six months by interacting with others. Thus, the infant learns to adapt to the world through experiencing a consistency and repetition in his daily life. This interaction allows his life to take on structure and clarity. An inner give and take grows into a feeling of confidence and security.

This mutual regulation is a pleasant experience for both sides: for the moment, the world is in order. The infant is open to reacting to what is happening. Through this openness towards his environment, he learns to experience "being in the world" and flexibility. The more people who react to him in this way, enable him to grow and become more encompassing in his ability to fit into his environment. The interaction with the important people in his life will establish his social sensibilities, interaction and flexibility in the psychological system of childhood.

But what happens if the newborn is not regulated? If he is highly agitated and unable to calm down? If the smallest irritation ends in disaster? If each encounter is blanketed in a shadow of tension and continues to build a chain of misunderstandings? What experiences of "being in the world," what implicit knowledge of the world will he learn? Which patterns of agitation will be established and how large is his foundation that allows him to flexibly react? In order to survive the complex world of emotions, a basic quality of first interactions is decisive. His future life will be built on these experiences and he will either find life a struggle or be able to master it with relative ease.

There is no doubt, that the infant's temperament or general tendency to be irritated also plays a role (Kohnstamm, et al., 1989; Spangler & Scheubeck, 1993). However, these processes are also influenced by the sensitivity and flexibility of the mother.

THE DEVELOPMENT OF SOCIAL INTERACTION

Different chapters of this book show that inborn behavior helps the child and his mother be intimate with one another and build a relationship, beginning with the onset of pregnancy. During the first weeks of his life, the infant strongly supports this process through his interest in human faces (Morton & Johnson, 1991), in the human voice (Papoušek, 1994) and his preference for processing movement, dynamics (de Schonen & Deruelle, 1994) as well as his pronounced ability to imitate (Meltzoff & Moore, 1992) while learning social interaction. We have observed an astonishing readiness on the part of adults to effectively react with the newborn, to interpret his behavior as social and to develop thoughtfulness and deep emotional bonding (see also: Klaus & Kenell, 1987). In addition, children, adults, and older adults all possess an intuitive behavior in dealing with newborns in appropriate ways (Papoušek, 2001).

These instincts are the prerequisites for the actual development of the bonding process and the development of highly complex world of affective interaction. However, the newborn's instincts must also be allowed to further develop. This is dependent on the child's age and diverse skills.

From Unison…

The interaction between an infant and his mother is not a dialogue from the beginning. The earliest form of interaction can most easily be described as being together. The newborn experiences his environment of sounds, colors and spaces with all of his sensory organs; registers the atmosphere and mood of those around him; and reacts to fine movement and the differences in tension and dynamics (Stern, 1990). The relationship to his caregiver during this phase of forming an emergent self (Stern, 1985) is based on simultaneous and reciprocal sharing of states and affects. The first interaction and communication is therefore regulative. This is a process of being in a part of each other and mutuality. It continues again and again in synchronization and certainly in unison (Beebe, et al., 1992). While appropriate reacting and regulating are most important in this initial stage, this begins to shift to reciprocal attunement during the stage of inter–subjective relatedness.

… to Interplay…

The newborn gradually begins to leave this *unison* phase between 3–5 months. His development is moving forward. His attention span is increasing. Visual acuity and the ability to see forms and distances are developing (Atkinson & Braddick, 1989), resulting in direct eye contact and sustained eye contact through better eye control (Bremmer, 1989), initial cognitive aptitude and the ability to handle longer periods of excitement through more appropriate and self reliant behavior (Basch, 1994).

The infant now begins to exhibit real interest in the faces of those around him (Papousek, 1984). In order to pursue this new interest, he begins to distance himself from his mother's body by putting more space between them. He spends more time intensely observing the faces of those around him, thus reaching into their worlds. While emotionally experiencing others, he also experiences himself in their reactions, as if looking into a mirror. While advancing through this exploring type of contact, he not only experiences the dynamics of states and feelings but he begins to understand how others see him and react to him. Thus, he is learning to better get a feeling of himself through his social contacts (Beebe & Lachmann, 2002).

In addition to the changes in physical closeness, his interaction with others also changes in its form and structure. During his intense observation of others, the infant is amazingly attentive and then reacts with kicking, strong arm and leg movement, lip movement and vocalization in order to express what he is experiencing (Papousek, 2001). This interplay develops through observing, listening, kicking, vocalizing and reacting. A give and take will be repeated in all its forms, playfully, varied and differentiated. It is the first form of play, long before the infant is interested in objects and can play with them. This is the time for the first nursery rhymes and songs, which can be repeated with simple variations in dynamics and tempo.

Of course, the quality of simultaneous and mutual sharing is not lost in this developmental stage. Rather, as the infant begins to separate himself from his mother, the interaction takes on a more mutual, playful and diverse quality. He is learning to identify himself as a separate entity and becoming sensitive to the mutual structure of a relationship.

… and Dialogue

After the infant has mastered the above developmental phases of affective attunement, experiencing resonance, mutuality, the sense of emergent self and the quality and structure of relatedness, it is just a small step to actual dialogue. The sense of a subjective self (Stern, 1985) is normally reached at about 9 months. The infant now perceives another person not only as separate from himself, but as a complete person with his own inner world, experiences, opinions and feelings.

The maturing process includes different developmental steps. At about 6 months, the infant develops "joint attention" (Adolph, et al., 1993) — the ability to orientate his attention to the direction of where someone else is looking, He begins by alternating his attention between his surroundings and the person opposite him. An exchange with the world is now possible and is important in acknowledging the other person may have a different viewpoint. The commencement of crawling strengthens the infant's experience that another person may have a different idea about what is pleasing, allowed or forbidden.

Thus, the first inter–subjective dialogue begins between both sides and the initial experiences of fighting for their own way.

CONNECTING

Experiences of mutuality, contact, resonance and relatedness become the basis for further development. While interacting with others, the infant begins to further stretch his skills in dealing with affects. By experiencing relatedness he builds a sense of security for existing in the world and develops into a sense of self, which Stern calls the *sense of a core self* (Stern, 1985). The infant must be validated in his own sense of self by others, so that he is able to build his own structure and further develop himself.

However, the *sense of a core self* does not tend to build a stable inner balance, but rather a more dynamic one—a balance that is constantly endangered and must continuously be regulated and rebuilt. While appropriate reacting and regulating are especially relevant for the newborn, the emphasis in this phase on inter–subjective relatedness is mutual attunement between mother and child.

Yet, when contact can't be established and an appropriate quality of coming together does not happen, the infant continues searching for an answer. As he does not yet have his own structure to fall back on, nor an appropriate reaction from his mother, he begins to take over the mother's mental world and makes it his own (Stern, 1999). At the same time, he also begins to assume the mother's image of himself. This results in difficulties in setting boundaries and developing the feeling of personal identity—"I am me." The enfolding of his own structure is inhibited through a lack of resonance. His sense of self is disturbed. The shaping of his *core self* is not happening or the *core self* cannot be formed. This directly affects his development, his sense of being a part of the world, his implicit understanding about himself and his world. "I am lost without response."

IMPLICIT KNOWING—KNOWING ABOUT THE WORLD

Implicit knowing is the sum of our entire sensory and social experiences. It is the essence of our impressions, our feelings about the world and ourselves. This knowledge is not symbolically nor verbally represented, but rather purely sensory coded. "Implicit knowing is procedural, non-verbal, non-symbolic, pre-conscious or unconscious (but able to be experienced in relationships), hard to sum up in words, but dynamically conscious" (Stern, 1999). Stern describes it also this way: "You have always known it, but never thought about it."[2] We can't call it up on command or simply change it with a cognitive strategy. Structural changes in *implicit knowing* are only possible through new multi–sensory and/or social experiences, or as Roth (2001) says when we are emotionally deeply moved.

With his new existence as a separate being at birth, the infant begins a life long process of growing into the world of social relationships. This *implicit knowing* which has been gleaned from his prenatal experiences will develop at

---

[2] The term "procedural" describes the automatic, but not the dynamic and emotional process of learning. Therefore other authors prefer "moody memory" or "state-dependent learning" (LeDoux, 1999, 2001). Roth (2001) refers to an unconscious emotional representation or experience dependent memory.

this early postnatal stage into *implicit relational knowing* (Stern, 1998). This *implicit rational knowing* builds a basis and background on which the infant enters new experiences, is aware of them, gives them meaning and integrates them. How the new experience is processed depends on this background—if the infant is open or prejudiced and experiences the new encounter as interesting, boring, strenuous or even dangerous.

Based on the structure of *implicit knowing*, changes in *implicit relational knowing* are possible only through new, immediate experiences in relationships. This has important implications for our therapeutic work with babies and their mothers: the most important task is to make new experiences in relationships possible.

PAINFUL BEGINNINGS

We can only begin to imagine what happens to a newborn or infant's development when there are medical problems, involving long hospital stays or other causes that hinder sensitive contact, which normally help him to regulate himself in order not to be overwhelmed by his own reactions. A mother's sensitivity and motherly instincts may be blocked by her daily stress; the emotional distress of the mother brought on by her confusion in her role as mother; conflicts between partners; insufficient support combined with feelings of being overwhelmed or trying to do everything correctly. This, of course, causes a multitude of difficulties in her relationship with her infant.

Without the mother's help in learning to regulate himself, without answers and resonance, the child is left to his own devices. He has no help in working through his affects and if the situation is repeated, he will react irritated, fearfully and/or tense to anything stressful—such as hunger, outside stimulation or his mother's attempts at interaction. A vicious circle results in tension, fear, misunderstanding and a lack of resonance and synchronization between infant and mother, where the baby seems to be constantly irritated (Van den Boom & Hoeksma, 1994). This leads to chronic crying and to eating and sleeping problems as discussed in the beginning of this chapter.

The infant has difficulties in adjusting to his environment and he is no longer able to trust his instincts. This has emotional consequences and also affects the development of the neuron structure in the brain, making the infant's life even more difficult (Huether, 2001). In our opinion, early professional intervention is necessary.

THERAPEUTIC HELP—BUT HOW?

When I began working with excessively crying babies, I often asked myself what I could do to break the vicious circle in interaction that was tormenting the mother and child. During therapy, I was almost always able to stop the child's screaming and to quiet it down. However, it is not enough to show the mother small steps to help her better understand her child's reactions and learn how to act more effectively. It is more important that she learns to trust her own motherly instincts again. Relaxation exercises can help her to calm down and often to be more able to recognize and react to her infant's signals. Verbal therapy and conflict centered music therapy can help her to eventually work through serious conflicts in her own life or those with her partner. But how can I dissolve the misunderstandings or established patterns of interaction between the mother and her infant? How can I change implicit structures and establish new and better patterns of interaction?

We all know those "magic moments" in relationships, those special feelings of coming together, of being connected, understood and accepted, which touch us so deeply. These moments which we called "turning points" in the aforementioned cases occur when effective attunement is happening. Therefore we may also describe them as a phenomenon of affective resonance.

In my therapeutic work with excessively crying babies, I am concerned with presenting a space where such moments of change may happen. The main goals of these music therapy interventions are not to initially train certain skills or make up for developmental deficits. It has much more to do with the natural enfolding of a shift in the established interaction to allow mother and infant to come together and have another chance. Thus, the implicit patterns in the structure of their interaction can be brought into play and changed.

NOW MOMENTS—A LOOK BACKSTAGE AT A FASCINATING PHENOMENON

Why do humans so strongly long to feel emotionally related and experience a sense of inter–subjectivity? Why does the dissolution of this emotional relatedness have such disastrous results on the emotional development of a child?

Tronick, member of the *Process of Change Study Group in Boston* (Tronick, Stern, Brushweiler-Stern, Lyons-Ruth, Morgan, Nahum, & Sunder) developed the "Dyadic Expansion of Consciousness Hypothesis" (Tronick, 1998). This hypothesis describes a micro–regulative, social–emotional process of communication, which creates the dyadic, inter–subjective conditions of a divided consciousness. Each individual—mother and child—presents a self-organized system, producing its own consciousness (neuronal organization). Combined with other self-organizing systems, this can expand into complex and coherent states of consciousness. We also find the meaning of sharing with each other for the creation of dyadic states of consciousness in the root of the word consciousness: con–scire, meaning to know together.

The Boston Group refers to this coming together of two self-organized systems as *now moments*. Walter J. Freeman (1994) first used this term describing changes in the brain as it reacts to new stimuli. His study of electric patterns in rabbits demonstrated that the olfactory system not only registered a new pattern in reaction as a new smell, but also organized an already existing pattern into a new whole. Sound, as well as all the phenomena of sensory awareness, follows the same principles as that of the Freeman experiment. For example, when we hear a note of a flute and then another note is added, we do not just hear one note separately after another. Both tones begin to sound together and mix with the overtones, changing the way we hear the sound. We no longer hear two single tones, but rather a new sound, something more, the relationship (harmony or dissonance) between them.

We take for granted that different aspects of nature combine and create a new "whole." This is not quite as simple in interpersonal relationships. Stress, irritation and prejudice can block our readiness and openness for a *now moment* and ultimately the possibility of change.

The Boston Group has used these principles to demonstrate how deep change can happen during psychotherapy. In the following quotation, Stern (1998) describes how this *now moment* comes about, what criteria are necessary for it to happen and what follows.

The process starts with *moving along*, a certain atmosphere similar to the *staying in the present* in psychoanalysis. Stern later replaced *moving along* by *relational move* in order to point out the aspect of relatedness.

The relational move is in its character similar to "the parent–infant–interacting-process consisting of matches–mismatches, ruptures and repairs. This is especially evident in situations such as free–play, in which there is not even a specific goal except to amuse one another. This process is almost pure improvisation. These repetitions become extremely familiar canons of what moments–of–life with a specific other person are expected to be like while *moving along*. In this form, present moments become represented as 'schemes of ways of being–with–another.' The schemes are in the domain of implicit relational knowing" (Stern, 1998).

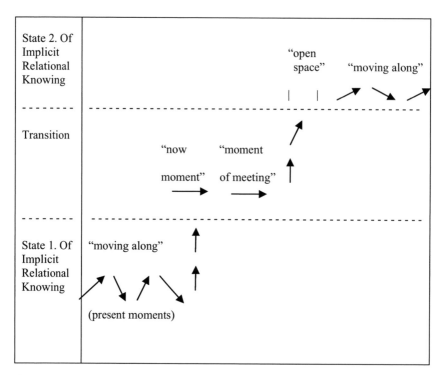

Figure 4: The process of therapeutic change involving implicit knowledge: Some implications of developmental observations for adult psychotherapy. Infant Mental Health Journal 19: 300-308; from Stern (1998).

During this *moving along* all of a sudden a qualitatively different and unpredicted moment arises. It is a "now moment." "This is a 'hot' present moment, a sort of 'moment of truth' which is affectively charged. It is of potential importance for the immediate or long-term future. It is a moment called *kairos* in ancient Greek, the moment that must be seized if one is going to change their destiny. It is also a moment that pulls the two participants fully into the present. The *now moment*, as an emergent property, disequilibrates the normal, canonical way of doing business together. In infancy pre-programmed developmental shifts, as well as the intrinsic mutual regulatory working of the system, create emergent properties within the dyadic system" (Stern, 1998, p.303f).

Thus, a *now moment* is just an opportunity to change. This moment must be used so that a *moment of meeting* may take place, with both individuals participating. Stern describes this emotional reaction as catching affects, the basis for inter–subjective intimacy. Beebe (1994) refers to such experiences of closeness and mutuality as key moments of interacting—when something comes together so that a true, deep interaction is possible. (How a negative emotional spiral can be broken in an interaction during a *now moment* and *a moment of meeting* is seen in Michael's case at the beginning.)

RESONANCE AND SYNCHRONIZATION

As we have seen, a special quality of relatedness occurs in a *now moment*. As in the early processes of interaction and regulation between mother and child, it occurs through synchronization and resonance.

According to Cramer (1998) resonance is nature's way of bringing together different elements or individuals without any loss of energy. This process does not need any energy. It creates even more energy. Cramer proposes that all cycles of nature are connected to each other in this way and strive for a harmonious development.

In human relationships, the process is more complex, as indicated in the model of the *now moments* of the Boston Group. The conditions that enable such moments to take place are the previously established *moving along* or *relational move*. The *now moment* appears, but it also may fail. The real change will happen, when it becomes a *moment of meeting*. "For instance, when the social smile emerges along with sustained mutual gaze and vocalization, the parent and baby amuse one another with facial and vocal exchanges. They are moving along. Then, something unpredictable happens (e.g., a funny expression or an unexpected vocal and facial synchronization), and all of a sudden they are laughing together. The interaction has been kicked up to a new and higher level of activation and joy that the baby may never before have achieved and which has never before been shared between them as an intersubjective context" (Stern, 1998, p. 305).

The *moment of meeting* is the moment which lifts us to another plane. We experience everything as feeling different. Feelings of happiness, being alive, lightheartedness, being affected may arise—and this even in situations of grief, when the grief is shared.

The role of the synchronization process in establishing deep emotional relatedness was mentioned above. It aids in developing bonding. It is found both in children and in the animal world. Establishing synchronization appears to be a basic need, which we also often observe in our work.

At the age of 7 months, Georg (whom we introduced at the beginning) tried to copy his mother's rhythm on the xylophone. He couldn't do it. Frustrated, he turned to me and began a vocal game and I played along. He became agitated and eventually completely taken with it, but did not forget his original goal. He picked up his rattle again, turned to his mother and accompanied her in rhythm. She turned towards him and both of them looked at each other. He had "reached" her. He was completely satisfied afterwards and played peacefully by himself and then returned to play happily with his rattle.

We are convinced that such moments of synchronization contribute to a secure attachment pattern. Daniel Stern believes that human relationships serve reciprocal regulation. The level on which the reciprocal regulation plays itself out depends on the quality of the relationship. Especially at the beginning of life, the quality of *being–with–another* and the level of regulation achieved are decisive. Music plays an important role among primitive tribes in establishing synchronization and bonding but one also doesn't have to travel far in the Western world to observe this process.

A village in Tuscany. The older people are sitting together on a bench. The owners of the grocery store and the butcher join them when there aren't any customers. They gossip and listen. Younger people pass by and stay for a moment. Children play in the street. There is seldom a car. A woman walks by, carrying her 6–months–old daughter. The children in the group quickly encircle her. The older people remain seated. A lively discussion ensues over the daily events. The infant begins to whine. The entire group turns towards the child and begins to imitate the child in a chorus. A give and take starts—the group modulates the child's "melody" and the infant quiets down.

It is especially fascinating because the group as a whole establishes contact. Through pitch rhythm and phrasing, they perfectly match the infant, as if a conductor had given a downbeat. They have come together in an astonishing unison at the "right moment," demonstrating the ability of a group to regulate tension.

WHY DO WE NEED MUSIC THERAPY?

When the interaction of the mother and her infant constantly goes amiss, develops into rigid behavior, or occurs in an atmosphere of fearful tension, both need help. Their unsuccessful attempts with and around one another have failed. Both need a new space in which fresh contact can be made—a space for being together in a relaxed, playful and lighthearted way without any goals.

Any therapy should always offer such a space. Music therapy is especially well suited for infants and children. In discovering simple instruments such as rattles, xylophones and bells, mother and child are presented with a neutral way to be with one another level—a new, playful one. This level is usually new to both of them and offers an opening—a space where they can move forward. Developing their play, they may first play side by side and all of a sudden meet more by chance than on purpose. They may come together and separate again. Their play will be in harmony or not. With music, both mother and child are involved in what has been described above as *moving along* or a *relational move*. The music bonds both of them in an increasing dynamic *being–with–one–another*, offering them an opportunity to meet in a fun and free way. They may find a common space where they learn to enjoy being together. Affects may unfold. Affective experience is contagious. Both share the same affects and experiences, coming together in mutuality.

Something else may happen. Something begins to swell and sound—a wave, an unusual sound, a spontaneous coming together where mother and child can both laugh and perhaps experience for the first time how it feels to be on "the same wavelength"—when one is understood and experiences resonance, when mother and child are connected in a common experience. It is a special moment, a turning point or *now moment* which gives the relationship another quality, or as Stern says, "The interaction has been kicked up to a new and higher level of activation and joy" (Stern 1998, p.305).

With small children and infants this type of direct interaction happens through vocal and facial contact. In a therapeutic setting, it is an interaction with three partners. In the process of *moving along* the therapist helps them to come together, to share affective ways *of being–with–another*, to synchronize and resonate in a lively manner.

We believe that music is the most effective medium for this kind of contact, as the earliest forms of interaction use primarily musical parameters: pitch level, sound, volume, melody, intensity and dynamics. Music is the most closely related to what Stern refers to as the *vitality affects* of newborns. This refers to all of the dynamic qualities in regard to the flow of play, tempo, volume and intensity—qualities that the mother and infant need in order to experience the "tuning" process and guarantee emotional regulation. In addition, music offers both players a natural way to find synchronization and resonance, as music lives from these phenomena. Musical improvisation, either with voice or instruments, leads to the process of *moving along* or a *relational move* and offers a common space where change is possible. Music offers special moments when we find ourselves--now moments, we happily engage in. Music offers the possibility of what the mother and infant are looking for and need so desperately: pleasure, happiness and joy.

This may be the most important aspect of music therapy with infants and their mothers. The parent will be encouraged to trust the power and dynamics of their improvisation, and replace fearful tension, over-concern and control with joy and fun. Only in this way can a rigid pattern of interaction be exchanged for one more flexible, allowing each of them to enjoy the pleasure of each other's company.

We have seen that shared happiness has the capacity to dissolve a negative emotional spiral. *Implicit knowing* stands out for a certain slower pace in learning and constancy. It is like knowing how to ride a bicycle—you cannot forget it. In order for implicit patterns to change, you must have experienced moments of meeting with another person. By these moments you are deeply affected. Music therapy has a direct access to these deeper levels: Thus, old patterns and structure begin to resonate and enable a gradual transformation and new beginning.

PART 2

RESEARCH AND CLINICAL PRACTICE

Chapter 6

MEDICAL MUSIC THERAPY FOR THE PREMATURE BABY—RESEARCH REVIEW[1]

Fred J. Schwartz

The effects of stress play a dominant role in most disease states. This is particularly true during physiologic processes where there is less reserve such as pregnancy. Since the process of pregnancy, childbirth and prematurity are a continuum it is useful to look at some of the mechanisms of stress throughout. During pregnancy blood flow to the fetus is regulated by a complex interplay of hormonal and neural influences. An exaggerated stress response during pregnancy can cause decreased placental blood flow to the fetus, which can cause intrauterine growth retardation as well as varying degrees of fetal distress. Intense anxiety has been associated with fetal death in the 3rd trimester (Myers & Myers, 1979). During childbirth, elevated levels of stress hormones cause decreased effectiveness of uterine contractions (Simkin, 1986). Some of these patients end up needing Cesarean sections because of this. An exaggerated stress response can also lead to premature birth. Increased levels of stress during pregnancy are also associated with the development of pregnancy induced hypertension (PIH), cardiac disease, and stroke in the mother.

Music, guided imagery, and hypnosis have all been utilized in the treatment of the pregnant patient. While exaggerated maternal stress response can lead to the initiation of preterm labor, hypnosis has been used to prolong the pregnancy during threatened premature labor (Cheek, 1995; Omer, Friedlander & Palti, 1986). Besides the documented clinical use of hypnosis in the treatment of preterm labor, both the use of hypnosis and meditation have been documented to decrease stress hormone levels in various clinical situations (Sudsuang, Chentanez & Veluvan, 1991). Music alone has been shown to diminish surgery-induced increases in stress hormones (Spintge & Droh, 1987). It has also been shown that music combined with guided imagery decreases stress hormone levels (McKinney, Tims, Kumar & Kumar, 1997), as well as the Bonny method of Guided Imagery and Music (GIM) (McKinney, et al., 1997). The psychological aspects of maternal stress during pregnancy in adolescents have been shown to decrease with music therapy (Liebman & MacLaren, 1991). Music's ability to slow respiratory rates and decrease the stress response is beneficial during labor. It has been shown to have the ability to shorten labor

---

[1]This chapter draws heavily on two previous writings. See references and copyright permissions at end of chapter.

(Winokur, 1984). Even when the course of labor does not speed up when music is utilized, the perceived length of labor decreases (Clark, McCorkle & Williams, 1981). Other studies have shown that when music is played, pain is decreased (McKinney, 1990; Hanser, Larson & O'Connell, 1983).

Increased levels of stress in the mother are associated with initiation of preterm labor. Thousands of years ago, Hippocrates believed that the fetus decides when the birth process begins. There is now good evidence to show that the fetus does initiate labor (Nathanielsz, 1995). Evidence points to fetal initiation of labor about 2–3 weeks before birth. In the fetal brain, the hypothalamus increases secretion of CRH (corticotrophin releasing hormone) and this stimulates the pituitary to release ACTH (adrenocorticotrophin). The fetal adrenal cortex responds by increasing its secretion of cortisol. The placenta then produces more estrogen and less progesterone and this eventually sets off the contractions of labor.

Besides the communication of stress, there is a constant interplay of communication between mother and fetus which is transferred by hormones as well as sound. The expression of love, nurturing and acceptance are expressed by the mother to the fetus by her voice; through the wide gamut of tonality, rhythm and inflection produced by her talking and singing. The fetus also responds to the rhythm of her mother's placental blood flow and picks up emotional content in this way. It is also likely that other learning takes place via informational content in the rhythmic variability of these womb sounds. It is intuitive that there is a profound interplay of information and emotion involved here and this dialogue is sacred and precious.

For the premature baby, the adverse effects of stress in the NICU are reflected by increasing oxygen consumption and decreased blood oxygen levels, marked blood pressure and heart rate fluctuations, and increased levels of agitation. The NICU infant cannot always communicate the feeling of pain, yet when pain is sensed this sets off a stress reaction, which includes an increase in stress hormone levels (Arnand & Hickey, 1987). The consequences of an exaggerated stress response for the premature baby is that there is a great deal of energy expended which does not get used for growth and development.

Since the intrauterine acoustical environment is a dominant part of fetal life, it is useful to explore this in order to gain insight into ways to positively shape the sound environment of the premature baby. Ultrasound studies have shown that at 16 weeks gestation the fetus can respond to outside sound (Hepper, 1994; Shahidullah & Hepper, 1992). Hearing is the first sense to develop and the last to deteriorate in the life cycle. Babies learn to adapt to their mother's breathing, her movements, and her voice as she speaks or sings. The sounds of the blood flow through the placenta are the predominant sounds in the uterus. The fetus hears the mother's heartbeat about 26 million times. This rhythm protects us, and throughout our lives it will attract us as one of the most important components of music, because it symbolizes primary security and dependable return (Decker-Voigt, 1997).

The womb acts as a high pass filter, with a 40–50dB attenuation of the higher frequencies above 500Hz by the time sound energy reaches the inner ear of the fetus (Gerhardt & Abrams, 1996). The frequencies below 500Hz are attenuated by 10–20dB, so that in this frequency range mean sound levels are between 70 and 80dB. The adult male voice has an average fundamental frequency of 125Hz, and for the female this is 250Hz. The noise floor of the uterus is produced by blood flow, respiration, digestion and maternal movements and is between 40 and 50dB for the frequencies below 500Hz. Speech becomes unintelligible when the noise floor sound level exceeds the level of the speech by about 10dB. What actually is discernable by the fetus is determined by how much attenuation of sound levels there is at different frequencies, which depends on transmission through mother's abdominal wall and tissues, uterus and amniotic fluid, transmission via fluid to the inner ear of the fetus, and the noise floor in the uterus. As a result, the fetus can hear speech and music in the frequency range below 500 Hz only when the airborne sound levels exceed 60dB (Gerhardt & Abrams, 1996).

It would be natural to suppose that the sounds and rhythm of the placental blood would have an effect on the newborn. Some studies by Dr. Lee Salk (1973) stemmed from an observation that most new mothers exhibited a natural preference for holding their infants on the left side of their chest near the heart. Salk analyzed a number of then popular books containing a large number of photographs and artistic representations of infants and adults. Almost 80% of these showed mothers holding their infants on the left side of their chests. This preference extended across all cultures. Balancing groups for left and right-sided dominance, Salk then replicated this left-sided preference in a large group of new mothers and babies (and used these heart sounds to calm newborns in the hospital nursery). He reasoned that there is an imprinting of the placental sound in utero so that similar sounds after birth have a functional connection with the original experience. This would explain some of the rhythmic similarities of modern music to intrauterine rhythms.

Others have connected the similarities between womb sounds and the "nonsense sounds" that mothers use in talking to their babies. Some of these calming sounds are "hush," "shush," "shah" (Yiddish), "ushuru" (Ethiopian), and "enshallah" (Egyptian). Perhaps the similarities to womb sounds also explain the spiritual use of similar sounds in different religions, i.e. Om (Buddhism), Shalom (Hebrew), Tibetan overtone chanting, and Gregorian chants.

Despite the filtering out of the higher frequencies of speech and music, a great deal of learning takes place in the womb. The newborn can recognize voices, distinguish words, and show preference for stories read during pregnancy (Fifer & Moon, 1994; DeCasper & Spence, 1986). The newborn can also discern songs and musical sequences (Hepper, 1989). The mother's internally generated sounds and rhythms in the womb may contain information important to the development of the fetal brain (Devlin, Daniels & Roeder,

1997; Shetler, 1989). The newborn can differentiate a recording of his own mother's prenatal womb sounds from a recording of another mother (Righetti, 1996). The newborn can also differentiate emotional content in the recording of his prenatal womb sounds and respond with changes in movement and heart rate (Righetti, 1996). The emotional content that can be sensed via maternal heart rhythms by the fetus and the newborn include love, acceptance, anger, and fear.

The synaptic network in the fetal brain as well as the infant brain undergoes learning dependant reorganization. This process involves synaptic pruning, the regression of neural circuits as well as the synaptic sprouting of the developing brain. There is a substantial reduction in neurons and synaptic connections that occurs during the last trimester as well as a more modest reduction during childhood. This is consistent with the observation of psychologists that infants and children may have enhanced behavioral abilities that diminish later in life (Johnston, 1995). It also gives significance to the enduring effects of fetal life.

There is a vast amount of potential information available to the fetus that can be given in the playing of just one musical note or in singing or talking a single syllable. The content of this sound is full of informational and emotional content (Schwartz, 1997). The fetus and newborn have an innate capacity to perceive this information at a very deep, profound level. To label an interaction with a newborn as infantile is to ignore the genuine receptivity of the newborn, who is already prewired for the reception of love, nurturing and emotional wisdom. These communicative processes which take place before and after birth contribute to the promotion of the child's physical development, behavioral characteristics and level of intelligence (Lipton, 1998).

The intrauterine environment plays an essential role in the growth and development of the fetus. The whole "nature vs. nurture" controversy has ignored the influence of the womb on intelligence and personality. Most previous studies have looked at identical twins in examining genetic and environmental effects on intelligence. The assumption in these studies was that identical twins that are separated in infancy share only genetic effects on their intelligence. This approach ignored the shared environment these twins shared in the womb. A meta-analysis of 212 studies spanning the last 70 years showed that the womb accounts for 20% of the shared IQ component of these identical twins separated at birth. (Devlin, Daniels & Roeder, 1997). This explains the striking correlation between the IQs of twins, especially those of adult twins raised apart. The intrauterine environment undoubtedly contributes much to effect human behavior and the relationship with the world throughout life. Since fetal hearing is probably the major component of this learning dependent synaptic pruning and sprouting, the fetus is participating in a 2nd and 3rd trimester auditory amphitheater that is perhaps more important than any other classroom.

THE PROBLEM OF PREMATURITY

Over the last 25 years there has been a marked increase in the population of low and very low birth weight infants, whose care requires large resources in technology and personnel. The economic cost of care in the United States for Neonatal Intensive Care Unit (NICU) and Intermediate ICU averages between $1,000 and $2,000 per day or over 10 billion dollars a year. The added costs of special education and continued cost of medical care for these children are larger than the initial costs for their NICU care (Lewit, et.al., 1995). Many of these babies suffer hearing and visual disabilities, mental retardation, cerebral palsy or learning disabilities.

These infants are deprived of their normal intrauterine environment and they are susceptible to the effects of stress in the NICU. While it is felt that sensory stimulation is necessary for optimal neurological development, the sights and sounds of the modern NICU provide an inappropriate sensory environment for the premature infant (Collins, 1996). An infant in the NICU is exposed to average ambient noise levels ranging from 50–88dB, with peak levels of over 100dB from sources such as ventilators, monitor alarms, incubator fans and motors, conversations, radios, telephones, water faucets, and cabinet doors (Lynam, 1995). The act of closing an incubator porthole can reach over 110dB, or the equivalent of a riveting machine. Loud noise and abrupt peaks in sound levels can be highly arousing for the medically fragile premature baby. Subsequently, conditions such as hypoxemia, blood pressure instability, increased apnea and bradycardia, altered cerebral blood flow, and a predisposition for intraventricular hemorrhage can occur (Lynam, 1995). Besides causing distress, these sounds can inhibit sleep–wake cycles and prevent descent into REM sleep states necessary for maturation and weight gain.

Since the 1980s, a number of studies have looked at the institution of developmental care, in the NICU (Als, et.al., 1994; Petryshen, et.al., 1997). This approach recognizes the importance of the environment and the appropriate level of stimulation necessary to foster brain growth and to integrate physiological and behavioral processes. Developmental care incorporates light and noise management, positioning/bundling, use of pacifiers, kangaroo care consisting of skin contact with mother or caregiver, and "clustering" of stimulative procedures, allowing for delineation of awake and restful state cycles. Some of the very significant benefits of developmental care are improved clinical outcomes as well as faster weight gain, earlier discharge from the hospital, and significant decreases in the cost of hospitalization. The inclusion of playing music and other sounds is a natural extension to the practice of developmental care.

The use of music in the NICU can consist of programmed music that is appropriate to the gestational age of the neonate. This type of setup will be one of the least costly ways to provide psychological and physiological benefits. It should be noted that including a music therapist and using live music in the NICU has more potential to communicate beauty and love, and this human contact can transcend any of the individual elements in a recording (Abrams, et al., 2000). The physical connection between mother and infant as she sings, the complex biologic rhythms between mother's body as she sings to a child nestled in her arms, these cannot be duplicated by recorded music (Bolton, 2000).

If sound is used therapeutically in the NICU the sound volume must be considered. There has been minimal research on what the most effective music sound levels are. There have been recommendations on "permissible noise criteria for occupied, newly constructed or renovated hospital nurseries" (Philbin, et al., 1999). These recommendations were based on previous studies looking at decibel levels and patterns of noise and their effect on infant sleep. The recommendations stated that nursery design and patient care should be utilized so that there is no noise above 70dBA for periods of one second or greater, and that sound levels should not exceed 55dBA for greater than 6 minutes per hour. An maximum hourly Leq of 50dBA was also advised. This would ensure an "equivalent sound level" where the amount of sound energy per hour would not exceed the sound energy of a constant 50dBA per hour.

These recommendations were based on previous studies on the effect of noise on the sleep state of the preterm infant. In contrast, most of the studies on music and music therapy in the NICU have used sound levels between 65 and 80dB, and music played at these sound levels have been found to promote sleep. These sound levels are clearly above the recommended levels for noise. However, music is different than noise. It is organized, contains less dynamic changes in sound amplitude, communicates information, and frequently decreases stress levels in the NICU population. Many of the previous studies on music intervention used sound levels of between 65 and 80dB, and the result was soothing behavioral changes, higher oxygen saturations, as well as more rapid weight gain (Cassidy & Ditty, 1998). These results are clearly different and mostly opposite the effects of noise within these dB ranges.

Another consideration is the potential for high sound levels and ototoxic drugs to cause loss of hearing acuity in preterm infants. The few studies that have addressed this have been inconclusive. There have been no recommended criteria based on human studies that address the potential relationship between nursery noise and hearing loss. There also have been no studies looking at the most effective sound levels of music intervention in the nursery. Until there is further knowledge, it would be conservative to keep mean sound levels of music intervention at no more that 65dBA. At these music sound levels the background noise level in the NICU should not exceed 50dBA, since premature babies would have a difficult time discriminating between the similar frequencies of the music and the background NICU noise (Werner & Marean, 1996).

STUDIES ON NICU MUSIC

Some of the hindrances to growth and earlier discharge from the NICU are decreased blood oxygen availability and increased oxygen consumption from stress. The increased stress response also consumes precious calories. The use of music in the NICU has been shown to decrease the stress response and increase oxygen levels. Womb sound music has been shown to soothe the pain-elicited distress from heel sticks (Bo & Callaghan, 2000). Similar music has also been shown to be helpful in the care of mechanically ventilated, agitated premature babies with low oxygen levels. Significant increases in oxygen saturation as well as decreased levels of agitation were found with the use of womb sound music (Collins & Kuck, 1991). Another study showed that when lullaby music was played in the neonatal intensive care unit (NICU) there were less episodes of oxygen desaturation (Caine, 1991).

There is no doubt that some of the high decibel sounds from alarms and equipment in the NICU are harmful to the neonate. In one study a group of premature babies were insulated from their audio environment with earmuffs (Zahr & Traversay, 1995). They had higher oxygen saturations and more time in the sleep state compared to a control group.

Several studies using music with premature babies in the NICU have shown a 3–5 day earlier discharge from the NICU. In a study at Tallahassee Memorial Regional Medical Center, Janel Caine studied 52 premature infants with an average birth weight of 1.6kg. Beginning on the fourth day after birth, half of these infants were exposed to recorded lullabies and children's music for 30 minutes three times daily. The babies in the music group had significantly increased daily weight gain, decreased stress behaviors, and decreased length of stay in the hospital (see figure 5).

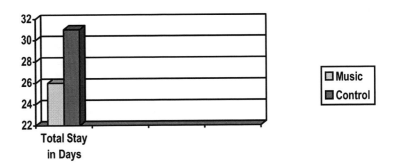

Figure 5: Vocal lullabies decrease length of hospital stay in NICU patients (modified from: Caine, 1991).

Coleman, Pratt, and Abel studied 66 premature infants between 25.5 and 34.5 weeks gestational age at Brigham Young Hospital. Half of these infants were exposed to 70 minutes each day of taped and spoken lullabies for a period of 4 days. The infants exposed to the music showed doubled weight gain as well as an average decrease of stay in the NICU (see figure 6).

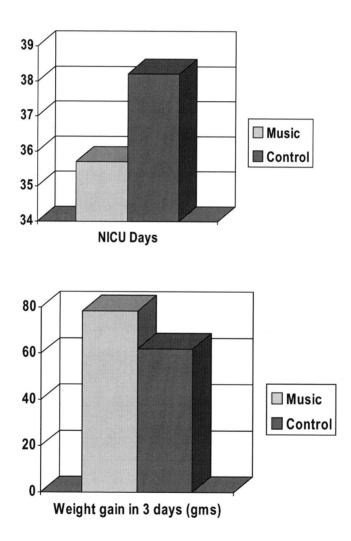

Figure 6: Vocal lullaby music increases weight gain and average 3 day earlier discharge from NICU (modified from Coleman, Pratt, et al., 1998).

Jayne Standley studied 40 premature infants at Tallahassee Memorial Regional Medical Center with an average gestational age of 30 weeks. Half of these infants received multimodal stimulation consisting of live nonvocal humming of Brahms' Lullaby, as well as rocking and tactile stimulation for 15–30 minutes, one or two times per week. The multimodal stimulation group were

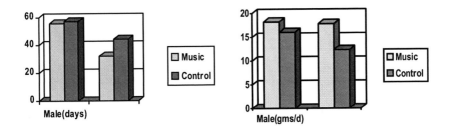

discharged from the hospital earlier and gained significantly more weight per day.

Figure 7: Music and multimodal stimulation decreases hospital stay and increases weight gain (modified from: Standley, 1998).

A gender difference as far as music benefits has been observed in most studies, with the benefits of music predominantly benefiting the female babies (Standley, 1998). This can probably be explained by the fact that newborn girls have more sensitive hearing than boys at birth (Cassidy. & Ditty, 1998).

"After music was introduced in our NICU at Piedmont Hospital, Atlanta, Georgia in early 1998, we noticed a trend for faster growth of head circumference (HC) in our premature babies exposed to music" (Schwartz, 1998). In a post hoc analysis this effect of music on HC growth was found to be significant in Standley's study on effect of music and multimodal stimulation in the NICU (Standley, 1998).

It seems logical that the early loss of the intrauterine sound environment would affect brain maturation in the premature baby. Previous work on prenatal intrauterine sound stimulation has shown increases in newborn head circumference and developmental abilities (Logan, 1991). Head circumference is a reliable indicator of brain size in the first 2 years of life (Sheth, 1995; Bray, 1969). We know that malnutrition during infancy leads to reduced head circumferences and IQs later in life (Winick, 1969). There is a definite negative effect on cognitive abilities in the very low birth weight baby (<1.5kg) with subnormal head growth in whom catch-up growth does not occur. Decreased head circumference at age 8 months is a strong predictor of decreased intellectual capacity at eight years of age (Hack, 1991). Low birth weight babies who do not catch up in their HC growth have decreased cognitive abilities later on.

Since it appears that we can foster increased brain growth along with increased synaptic connections in premature babies with music stimulation, the implications are that we can use music to decrease the developmental delays that are common in premature babies. It has been shown that by exposing premature babies to a recording of the baby's own mother's voice in the hospital, the results at age 5 months showed a significant enhancement in verbal and motor development (Nöcker-Ribaupierre, 1995; 1999). At age 20 months there remained a trend for these infants to maintain these leads in verbal and motor development despite a small sample size (24 patients control, 24 patients audio stimulation). At age 6 there was still a trend for better verbal skills in the stimulated group. It becomes clear that there is indeed an effect of music and sound on brain development which extends as far back as the fetal period. This is a natural extension of some of the studies with preschool children, which showed that music training can enhance language development, spatial and mathematical abilities (Rauscher, et al., 1997).

The newborn baby, and especially the premature baby have a distinct framework of experience with sounds and music. We know that newborns prefer female voices to male voices, and prefer their own mother's voice to other women's voices. Some of the most commonly used audio stimulation in the NICU have been lullabies, classical and womb sound music, as well as mother's spoken voice and singing. Previous studies on the use of music with premature and term babies have mostly looked at the benefits of lullabies, classical and womb sound music (Cassidy & Ditty, 1998). Musical selections for fragile premature babies must be carefully considered. The emphasis must be given to simplicity, as well as gentle rhythms, flowing and lyrical melodies, simple harmonies, and a soft tone color. Transient changes in amplitude must be avoided, as well as abrupt tempo changes. Complexity of sound timbre and color should be avoided as well as complex combinations of different instruments. However, the premature baby responds to quality and precision of musical expression, and has the capability of responding to a beautiful recording which expresses love and wisdom.

Lullabies may be particularly effective because in general they combine the benefits of the female voice in a simply orchestrated format. All lullabies have the same characteristics: they are slow (about 60–82 beats per minute—about like a normal resting adult heartbeat). They are regular and monotonous, and repetitive; there are no exciting disruptions in rhythm or melody; and they are most effective when sung in a low voice. Research has shown that high pitches tend to create tension, or excitement, while lower pitches tend to promote relaxation. All these characteristics contribute to a baby's sense of security, safety and strength.

CONCLUSION

Music can decrease the stress response during pregnancy, labor and delivery, and for the newborn. The premature baby in the NICU is particularly susceptible to the effects of stress and can benefit dramatically from music in the NICU environment. Numerous studies show the benefits of utilizing an NICU music program including either a music therapist or a neonatal nurse. Despite this evidence, most NICUs do not have organized music programs. A recent study surveyed attitudes of nurses and physicians in a university hospital setting where music is not routinely played in the NICU (Kemper, et al., 2004). A majority agreed that music can reduce stress and crying, and improve sleep and cognitive development in the premature baby in the NICU. The physicians were likely to have less favorable attitudes about using music in the NICU.

Despite some ambiguity in the medical literature distinguishing between "NICU music" and "NICU noise," it is clear that using NICU music in a clinically sensitive manner has distinct benefits. Not only are there medical and economic advantages but also immediate benefits which enhance survival, as well as long-term developmental benefits which will allow our little patients to approach their full potential as human beings.

NOTE

This chapter draws heavily on the following writings, and has been reprinted by Barcelona Publishers with kind permission from the American Music Therapy Association and Satchnote-Armstrong Press.

- Schwartz, F., & Ritchie, R. (1999). Music listening in neonatal intensive care units. In C. Dileo (Ed.), *Music Therapy and Medicine: Theoretical and Clinical Applications* (pp. 13-22). Silver Spring, MD: American Music Therapy Association.
- Schwartz, F. (2000). Music and sound effects on perinatal brain development and the premature baby. In J. Loewy (Ed.), *Music Therapy in the NICU* (pp.9-20). New York: Satchnote-Armstrong Press.

Chapter 7

THE MOTHER'S VOICE—A BRIDGE BETWEEN TWO WORLDS:

SHORT- AND LONG-TERM EFFECTS OF AUDITIVE STIMULATION ON PREMATURE INFANTS AND THEIR MOTHERS

Monika Nöcker-Ribaupierre

Following the improvements of intensive medical care within the last decade, more and continuously younger and younger very low birth weight infants are able to survive. At the same time, survival is no longer the only goal. There is more interest in the infant's quality of life in the NICU and later and developmental and social issues. Therefore, more and more attempts to maintain some of the "natural" environment of the womb are being added to the NICU's very high tech environment. This includes music and its recognized beneficial impact on human emotions and physiology. Music can be a serious intervention for premature babies in order "to create a peaceful environment in which the premature infant can relax and achieve the levels of development that would normally have taken place had the pregnancy gone to full-term, and appropriate stimuli that affect such measures as development of physiological functions" (Pratt, 1999). Besides the benefits through selected music programs, the musical elements of the human voice allow the mother to establish emotional contact with her infant.

My work with Auditive Stimulation reaches beyond the documented supportive impact of music. It is based on the effect of the mother's voice as a basic fundamental during the process and development of bonding and establishing a relationship with her infant.

The fetus lives within an acoustic intrauterine environment characterized by biological sounds—the heartbeat and visceral sounds. Under these many acoustic influences, the mother's heartbeat can be seen as the continuous acoustic experience and starting point for the relationship between rhythm and the human, and insofar has a psychological impact on character formation.

This rhythm of the mother's heartbeat protects the baby because it symbolizes security and reliable return. Rhythm is also the most important component of music.

The mother's voice is the basis for a more distinct impact in the relationship between the mother and the fetus. It is created not so much by the discursive but the presentative content of the voice and its emotional message is decisive. Sound, melody and the rhythm of the voice have an essential and formative psychological impact.

After premature delivery, especially very low birth weight infants (VLBWI) are exposed for several weeks or months to a noisy technical environment characterized by chaos and unexpected extremes of over- and under-stimulation. They are not ill but physically and emotionally vulnerable and therefore need more care and attention than time born babies. Their mothers are also in an extremely difficult and sometimes desperate situation, often suffering from fear, depression, guilt, and feelings of inadequacy. Therefore, they need more care and attention than mothers of normal weight babies. Both the deprivation of the VLBWI from normal sensory experiences from within the womb and the emotional problems of their mothers may contribute to the long-term sequelae of VLBWI.

During my many years working as a music therapist in a Newborn Intensive Care Unit (NICU), I developed a program for providing these babies with acoustic impressions different from the noise of the machines surrounding them.

We first decided to mask the technical noise level and stimulate vital functions by exposing infants to the music of Mozart and the mother's voice, based on the theories of Tomatis (1981; and my personal experience). However, I soon discovered that most of these mothers found it very strange to play music for their babies, often music they did not even like. However, they were all very willing and happy to make a spoken cassette for their baby.

Two issues became very apparent: 1) that, especially at the beginning of this extreme situation, mothers found it very difficult to establish a relationship with their baby, and 2) that this opportunity of being active offered the mothers a possibility to re–enter into a relationship with her baby.

I suppose that the mother's voice is able to create a bridge on several levels:
   1) for the infant from the intrauterine life to the extra–uterine life,
   2) for the infant from the intrauterine life through the technical life in the NICU to life at home,
   3) for the mother from the experience of being pregnant to suddenly not being pregnant anymore, and
   4) for the emotional connection, the bonding process of both.

Theories and methods from related disciplines such as medicine, developmental psychology, psychoanalytical and bonding theories and infant research are necessary to better understand the situation of a premature birth and thus the importance of developing a program including the infant *and* the mother.

LITERATURE REVIEW

Follow-up studies such as the *Vermont Intervention Study* (Achenbach, Howell, Aoki, & Rauh, 1993) have shown that intensive early and subsequent support of mothers/parents leads to a significantly better development of VLBWI. These findings are in line with documentation in infant research and observation, psychotherapy, and bonding research, which postulate that the mother and her premature infant should be regarded and treated as a unit (Winnicott, 1965; Klaus & Kenell, 1976; Brazelton, 1985; Miethge, 1978; Stork, 1986). Als includes these ideas in her NIDCAP concept (Als, 1998).

Humans develop the ability to hear at a very early stage of life. According to Rubel's research (1984), the auditive system is developed at 18 weeks. Unborn infants react to sound after 24 weeks of gestation (Birnholtz & Benacerraf, 1983), sometimes after 19 weeks (Hepper & Shahidullah, 1994). This means that this ability exists before birth, and, subsequently, during the time when the premature baby has to remain in an incubator in order to survive. For this reason many multi-modal and purely acoustic stimulation programs have been carried out: isolated music stimulation such as Brahms' lullaby, a mother's voice, lullaby-type singing, female vocal sounds or music based on womb sounds and heartbeat. These have shown to be particularly effective and have offered significant results, such as reducing observed stress behavior and pacification (Busnel, 1986; Caine, 1991), significant increase of oxygen saturation levels (Caine, 1991), significant increase of oxygen saturation levels and decreased levels of agitation (Collins & Kuck, 1991; Cassidy & Standley, 1995; Standley & Moore, 1995), increased weight gain (Chapmann, 1979; Caine, 1991), stronger positive effects on female infants than on male infants in increasing weight gain (Coleman, Pratt, Stoddart, Gerstmann & Abel, 1998), length of hospitalization (Caine, 1991) and significant earlier discharge (3–5 days) from the hospital (Coleman, et al., 1998).

In summarizing these studies, Schwartz and Ritchie (1999) have evaluated and described the benefits of different acoustic stimulation programs for the physical well being and the development of infants as well as the influence on their clinical stay.

The infant's ability to store and remember the maternal voice during the prenatal period is essential to this study. This has been observed in other studies with newborn babies, especially in the United States, regarding such questions as whether newborns can remember vocal sounds they had heard before birth, and if they have preferences for certain voices. Measurements were made using different parameters, such as behavior and oxygen content in arteries. These studies documented that newborn infants can distinguish the words they had repeatedly heard during their prenatal life from unfamiliar words (DeCasper & Fifer, 1980). They prefer female voices to male voices and the mother's voice to other women's voices (DeCasper & Fifer, 1980; Standley & Madsen, 1990) and they can distinguish an ascending intonation from a descending one if both scales are sung by the same voice on the same vowel (Fernald, 1982). One very early study on the maternal voice (Katz, 1971) suggested that compared to infants in a control group, auditory stimulation of VLBWI by the maternal voice (presented intermittently through a tape recorder) resulted in enhanced maturation and better function of motor, tactile, auditory, and visual responses.

As a whole the above studies verify that the ability to perceive acoustically is determined genetically. That means it already exists before birth and also when the premature infant's survival requires that he remain in an incubator.

PSYCHOLOGICAL BACKGROUND

In order to offer substantial support, it was necessary to understand the psychological state of both, infant and mother from the perspective of developmental psychology (Bowlby, 1969; Klaus & Kennell, 1976), psychoanalytic theories (Winnicott, 1965; Eagle, 1984), and infant research (Stern, 1985).

In terms of the mother–infant bonding process, premature birth causes an infant and mother to be separated from each other at the most inopportune time. When this psychophysical continuum is broken, they both lose the experience of being together during this essential period of life, but with a different impact on each of them, as described below.

Impact on the Infant

In the psychoanalytic treatment of adult patients, messages and dreams often emerge which are interpreted as memories of our earliest life experiences. Since the 1940s this has led a number of psychoanalysts (Graber, 1974; Hau & Schindler, 1982; Schindler & Zimprich, 1983; Fedor-Freyberg, 1987) and representatives of prenatal psychology (Graber, 1974; Ammon, 1982; Janus, 1990) to assume the existence of prenatal experience. They concluded from this that various psychological disturbances could be traced to this prenatal period.

But trying to understand the psychodynamics of prenatal life or to reconstruct the experience of premature infants on this basis is, I believe, subject to the danger of adultomorphism. I, therefore, searched for any theories that attempted to explain the understanding of the emergence of traces of memory within the self of the child.

When these early traces of memories are painful and disruptive, they may cause physical and emotional development to possibly assume pathological forms. It is therefore possible that premature birth requires archaic psychological forms of defense to enable psychological survival, such as they have led to the conclusions of the above mentioned authors.

It thus became necessary for me to understand the psychodynamics of prenatal life, and more specifically to try to reconstruct the experience of premature infants. Daniel Stern (1985) proposes a theory for understanding the emergence of traces of memory within the self of the child. Based on observational data in infant research, Stern concludes that the infant does have a subjective experience. He describes the emergence of self-esteem as a primary, organizing, and structural principle, which already controls the earliest developmental stage. *Supplementing* psychoanalytic theory, he offers the hypothesis of a holistic development principle, including the caregiver from the beginning. Stern postulates that the psychological regulation of life *occurs with help of the exchange* of social behavior, that is, the interaction between the child and his mother or caregiver. In this context, the different ways of feeling, which accompany all elementary events of life, play a decisive role. Stern (1985) is referring to *"vitality-affects."* He explains them as follows:

> *"Abstract dance and music are examples par excellence of the expressiveness of vitality affects. Dance reveals to the viewer-listener multiple vitality affects and their variations, without resorting to plot or categorical affect signals from which the vitality affects can be derived. The choreographer is most often trying to express a way of feeling, not a specific content of feeling."* (p.56)

And later:
> *"Like dance for the adult, the social world experience by the infant is primarily one of vitality-affects before it is a world of formal acts."* (p.57)

From the onset of life, the infant demonstrates many genetically determined abilities that allow it to connect with different social and cognitive experiences. These abilities either exist at birth or can develop later, providing the developmental–neurological conditions and the environment are adequate.

The infant's ability to react to acoustic influences proved to be essential for this study. Very small premature infants react visibly and measurably from birth to the numerous, unpredictable mechanical noises in the unit. Reactions include psycho-physiological disturbances such as restlessness and crying, reduction of oxygen saturation, and acceleration of heartbeat and breathing (Wolke, 1991). After a period of about two weeks, these babies no longer react to such disturbances because they have become desensitized. There is, however, no desensitization to the mother's voice, even after playing the same tape for a period of several weeks. These infants react to their mother's voice with full attention, except when they are ill, sedated and/or are asleep.

The observations of Morris Eagle (1984) explain this phenomenon. Eagle addresses the different theories of the development of object relationship. He states:

> *"All results suggest that the interest in objects as well as the development of feelings of attention are not.... the result of having other needs satisfied, but that they are a decisive independent aspect, which is the expression of a congenital desire to establish cognitive and affective ties to objects in the world."* (p.18)

From the very beginning, tactile and kinaesthetic stimulation is the decisive dimension to which the infant reacts. In this context, an infant's selective preferences for certain stimulative figurations are autonomous congenital abilities that can already be observed at or immediately after birth.

Impact on the Mother

I exclude mothers of multiple births here, because they are prepared to end their pregnancy often many weeks ahead of time. In my clinical practice I have seen them physically weakened, of course, but mentally more stable and active. However, for every mother of a single baby, its premature birth is a traumatic event. Assessment measures (Caplan, Manson, & Kaplan, 1965; Cramer, 1976) indicate that every mother has to overcome severe emotional, psychological stress consisting of guilt, fear for the infant's survival and development, and loss of self-esteem compounded by the separation from the infant. Therefore the following postnatal maternal depression could be seen as a result from the interruption of the mother–infant relationship due to this unexpected, often traumatically overwhelming too-early delivery.

In addition, the mother is physically weakened and finds herself psychologically isolated. Sometimes a mother has just begun to really accept her pregnancy and emotionally relate to the new life growing within her. So very often, she is emotionally unable to understand the situation. She does not see or feel her baby to be a separate person. In identifying with her baby, she regards herself as the cause of anxiety in this overwhelming technical environment.

Some approaches to addressing this situation include helping the mother to understand the problems that come with prematurity, and encouraging her to articulate her emotions and ask for information and help (Caplan, 1960). This necessitates support from her family and/or the clinical staff. An effective way to help a mother is to give her the opportunity to be active. The first opportunity to be active (e.g., kangaroo care, or simply talking to her baby) often causes this initial event for the mother to develop a new emotional strategy, producing a new set of tendencies, sensibilities, fantasies, fears, and wishes. Stern (1995) refers to this as the *"motherhood constellation"* which is the basis for the mother's ability to bond after birth.

When feeling helpless, the mother can thus be empowered by *actively* responding. One way is by helping the mother to give something of herself through physical contact. Often the opportunities for tactile stimulation, such as touching, holding, cuddling, kangaroo care, are very limited for many weeks.

Therefore it is only logical to suggest to the mother to reach out for her infant through another sensory channel, the acoustic one. She can talk to her baby, give him a name, tell him something of herself. She can imagine that her baby is able to listen to her and that they both share a common experience, like "*intermediary space*" (Winnicott, 1965), in which both listen to what she is conveying to him. The mother's voice is something alive through which her vitality is conveyed to the infant in this impersonal world of the incubator.

The mother's entire personality, the manner in which she moves and acts which is familiar to the fetus, is also reflected in her voice. During the prenatal period the mother's voice is an element of connection. Her voice is physically near, offering the whole range of verbal communication. In terms of development psychology, this type of communication takes place later.

The vocal expression and not the word or its meaning is of importance at this stage, along with its musical parameters, according to the early state of the infant's development. At the same time, this kind of vocal expression guarantees the continuity of pre- and postnatal life.

THE STUDY: AUDITIVE STIMULATION WITH THE MOTHER'S VOICE

The purpose of this study was to examine the effect of the mother's voice on the physical activity and transcutaneous oxygen pressure ($tcPO^2$) of VLBW oxygenated infants, during the first years of their development, and the effect of this approach on the mothers' behavior and stabilization.

The local ethics committee approved the study. Participants included infants being treated in the NICU of the Dr. von Hauner'sches Children's Hospital, Ludwig–Maximilians–University, Munich. The mother of each infant participating in the study was carefully informed on the purpose and the procedures of the study.

Infants

The short and long-term effects were studied in two different groups of very low birth weight infants (VLBWI).

For the short-term observation, 9 randomly selected infants, 26–30 weeks gestational age, with a birth weight of 780–1270g were their own control in a repeated measures design. All infants were patients in the NICU in this hospital.

For the long-term observation, 24 randomly selected infants in the experimental group were compared with 24 infants in the control group in an independent group design. The infants in the control group were carefully matched for gender, birth weight (w/i 100g), gestational age, and clinical stay in the Munich units in which the study took place. Infants in both groups were 24–

30 weeks gestational age, with a birth weight of 650–1270g. All infants were subjects in the *Munich Regional Prospective Long-term Follow-up Study* (Riegel, Ohrt & Wolke, 1995), which supplied the developmental data for this study. Children were excluded from the follow–up measures after 6 years, if there was evidence of neurological or cognitively impaired infants, because this later was a test for school age children.

Method

High fidelity cassette recorders were used. The transcutaneous oxygen tension (tcPO^2) was continuously monitored by means of a Kontron electrode (Eching, Germany) and monitor; the behavioral states of the infants were recorded by two independent observers throughout the observation periods with help of the Prechtl Behavioural State Scale (Prechtl & Beintema, 1974).

The assessment program of the follow-up used selected instruments of the *Bavarian-Finnish Development Study of Infants Born at Risk* (Riegel, Ohrt, Wolke, 1995): Griffiths Developmental Scales (GDS) were applied at 25 months of corrected post term age (Brandt, 1983); at 4.8 years, the IQ and achievement levels were tested by means of the Columbia Maturity Scales (Schuck, Eggert, Raatz, 1975), a Test of Active Vocabulary (Kiese & Kozielski, 1979), a Logopedic Test of Understanding (Wettstein, 1983); and, at 6.3 years, by means of the Heidelberg Test of Speech Development, subtest, understanding and construction of sentences (Grimm & Schöler, 1991). In addition, the intensity of neonatal morbidity was scored (Casaer & Eggermont, 1985): three clinical and three neurological items were assessed daily with a three digit score, and also the social classes of the families, to take eventual differences into account for the comparability.

All developmental tests were standardized with a regional representative normative sample (Wolke, Ratschinski, Ohrt, Riegel, 1994). For statistics variance analysis (Scheffé-Test), t-Test, X^2-test and ANOVA were used.

Protocol

The study with the mother's voice took place in two parts, after a pilot study with high and normal frequency ranges of acoustic stimuli, with music by Mozart and the mother's voice (following the Tomatis–Method), in order to rule out negative side effects, such as restlessness or cardio-respiratory events (bradycardias and apnoeas).

Short-Term Observation

This first part focused on the direct effect of the voice on the child. The mothers spoke, sometimes sung, onto tape in the second week of the infant's life or as soon as the baby was clinically stable. The mothers decided what they wanted or were able to do, singing and/or speaking.

Here I would like to comment on the stimulus: at the beginning of this study I assumed that a mother should sing, e.g. lullaby–type songs, and I suggested that they try it. But it became obvious that in such an extremely desolate situation, it is almost impossible for a mother to sing. Singing seems to bring up more emotions than a mother can handle in this situation. During all these years, I have only met 2 mothers out of more than 200 who were able to sing. Very often it was even impossible for them to speak easily. I then proposed that they read something personal written for their babies or from a book, e.g. "The Little Prince" by Antoine de Saint-Éxupéry. The recording lasted at least half an hour, as this long duration allowed the mother to calm down from possible anxiety and excitement, which could be reflected in the sound of her voice. She was then better able to really talk to her infant.

This 30–minute recording was played through a small loudspeaker, with 65–70dB and about 20cm from the infant's ear. The 9 infants were observed throughout the 6 weeks, alternating one day with the mother's voice stimulation, and the next day without stimulation, at the same time of day. Observation on the stimulation days began 15 minutes before stimulation, continued though the 30-minute stimulation, and ended 15 minutes after stimulation. Thus, we received a total observation period of 60 minutes. Observation on the non–stimulation days also took place over a 60–minute period at 10–second intervals.

Two independent observers recorded the behavior and alertness, following the Prechtl Behavioural State Scale, and the monitored $tcPO^2$. Variance analyses were used to compare the changes in the infants' alertness and $tcPO^2$: the mean values of both of these parameters within the four 15–minutes sequences of each observation hour, with and without stimulation.

Long-Term Observation

The aim of the long-term observation was the influence of Auditive Stimulation on the development of the children's and the mothers' behavior, seen as an indicator for her ability to bond with the infant.

The experimental group of infants received the 30–minute recording of the mother's voice, five times daily in the incubator, starting in the second week of life or as soon as the infant was clinically stabilized. The stimulation continued throughout each infant's stay in the NICU, the mean stimulation time being 9 weeks. Stimulation periods were set with a timer. Times of regular manipulation by nurses or physicians were avoided so that the infants were not disturbed and did not associate their mothers' voices with disturbing procedures.

At the ages of 5 and 20 months, 4.8 and 6.3 years, the motor and verbal/ cognitive development of the experimental group was compared with that of the control group as described above.

RESULTS

Short-Term Observation

First an example of two recordings in a preterm infant with 31 weeks postmenstrual age (PMA) during one hour: one hour without and one hour with stimulation of his mother's voice, on two following days at the same time. Both figures show activity and transcutaneous oxygen pressure (tcPO²) recorded every 10 seconds. The mean values of 15 minutes periods and the mean values of the whole hour (+- SD) are given. Significant deviations (p< 0.5) are marked (*).

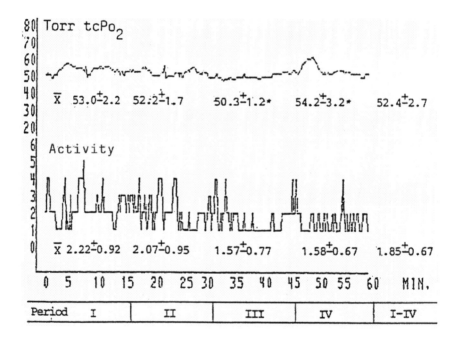

Figure 8: Observation of (tcPO²) and activity during one hour without stimulation.

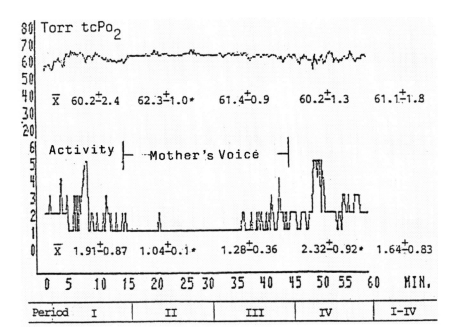

Figure 9: Observation with stimulation of the mother's voice in period II and III: tcPO² went up during period II from 60.2 to 62.3 Torr, the activity score decreased simultaneously from 1.9 to 1.0, and increased during period IV. Both reactive changes are significant.

The salient results of the 9 infants were:
1. Without stimulation, there was no difference in increase and decrease of activity and in transcutaneous oxygen pressure (tcPO²).
2. During the stimulation period, infants showed significantly decreased activity (p<0.001) and increased tcPO² of mean 5 Torr (p<0.02) (Nöcker, Güntner & Riegel, 1987).

As a whole the results showed that
    a)   infants reacted visibly and measurably after the age of 26 weeks PMA to the mother's voice without the interference of stronger stimuli or drugs,
    b)   the maternal voice had a soothing effect on the preterm infant, and
    c)   the effects of the stimulation on activity and tcPO² seemed to increase with increasing postmenstrual age.

Long-Term Observation

Data analysis found that, at the corrected age of 5 months, the children in the experimental group showed significantly advanced motor and verbal development (*Griffiths Scales*, p<0.05). This trend was still present at the corrected age of 20 months and 4.8 years, but not significant in the tested areas of cognition, language, and visual–motor integration.

At the age of 6.3 years, 18 children exposed to the intervention and 18 children from the control group were reassessed. The post-test *Heidelberg Language Developmental Test* (HSET) documented a significant lead in speech understanding from the children in the experimental group. Because of the small number of cases one can regard this only as a tendency. But this tendency provides important indications for the significance of early auditory stimulation, and the emotional stability of the mothers that accompanies it.

Mothers' Behavior

a)   The mothers of the infants in the experimental group breastfed with significantly greater frequency (50% vs. 12.5%) and for longer periods than mothers in the control group.

b)   Using independent observers for group comparison at the 5-month assessment, the mothers in the experimental group were less emotionally burdened and physically more stable.

c)   Five months after discharge all mothers were asked to give a written statement on their impression of the treatment. All these mothers reported the "recording" to be very supportive for the development of their infant and for their own stabilization (Nöcker-Ribaupierre, 1995).

According to findings of developmental psychologists (Bowlby, 1969; Klaus & Kennell, 1976) all these behaviors support the developing bonding process.

At this point I would like to add a psychoanalytic interpretation. As mentioned before, a premature birth, in addition to being an anxiety crisis, can also devastate self-esteem and produce feelings of guilt, a severe narcissistic indignity. This situation makes it difficult for the mother to reach her baby in a way which is going to be very different from what she had anticipated.

During my clinical experience, I observed a mother's behavior changing immediately when she had the opportunity to do something for her baby, to think about what she could tell him. While speaking, her voice allowed her to be a separate entity and she did not have to create a "We." The infant was, vis-à-vis, an individual separate from the damage of her narcissistic feeling. Later, when a nurse described her infant's reactions as calming down, becoming attentive, sometimes smiling or falling asleep while hearing her voice, or she could observe it herself, she saw that her baby was getting to know her in spite of the separation and that it was responding to her offer of a relationship. As a result she visited her baby more frequently and stayed longer. She had discovered her own potential. The mother's activity and infant's response are of primary importance for resuming the interrupted bonding process.

I would also like to mention that I share Graven's opinion about sound and the developing infant in the NICU (2000), "Recorded sound cannot replace interactive experience with another human, preferably a parent." It has been my experience that the mother's "recorded voice" is able to build a bridge from the interrupted pregnancy to the reality in the NICU. This interactive experience nurtures the mother's new confidence.

This program was developed at a time when parents were not allowed to enter the unit at all (unfortunately a practice still found today in many units) and also for parents who are not able to visit their baby daily, whatever the reason may be. A mother, who could only visit her baby once a week, put it most eloquently:

"I put down the schedule for the time when the tape is played on a piece of paper and took it home with me. Now I know when my baby is listening to my voice... then I feel that I am with him."

CONCLUSION

On the whole, the observed differences in the developmental tests between the index and the control group cannot be explained by differences in perinatal and neonatal risk factors or by differences in social demographics. Therefore it is unlikely that the monitored increases in the $tcPO^2$ during Auditive Stimulation contributed to improved development.

I assume the following:
1) similar to the individualized care as documented in the NIDCAP (Newborn Individualized Developmental Care and Assessment Program—a brain based framework for NICU environment and care; Als, 1998), Auditive Stimulation may also support the development of the neurobehavioral functioning of the central nervous system, and
2) mothers of infants with Auditive Stimulation appeared more emotionally stable then those in the control group. This has a positive impact on breastfeeding (the mothers breast-fed more often and longer) and because of the related impact on the relationship, on the development of the VLBWI (Achenbach, et al., 1993).

DISCUSSION

There is ample biological and psychological evidence that the auditive system already plays a major role in infant development in early pregnancy (see Maiello, chapter 4).

The present study has shown that Auditive Stimulation with the mother's voice is beneficial for both the mother and the very low birth weight infant, for the support and the stabilization of the mother, the infant's development and the bonding process.

Regarding these benefits, the results of this study are in line with early intervention programs and their follow-up results (Achenbach, Howell, Aoki, & Rauh, 1993; Wolke, Ratschinski, Ohrt, & Riegel, 1994; Als, 1998) and attachment research (see Gutbrod/Wolke, chapter 3).

As a whole, my approach of Auditive Stimulation combines two different approaches: a therapeutic–functional approach of retaining or replacing something lost and a psychotherapeutical approach, addressing the developing subjective experience within the relationship between mother and child. Besides the significant physiological and developmental support for the infant, an essential approach of this study is the psychological and emotional impact of the voice.

From the psychological point of view, the mother's voice during prenatal time is a connecting element. Through the sound of her voice the baby experiences the mother's physical closeness. Her voice contains the whole concept of relationship through verbal communication, which, in terms of developmental psychology, takes place at a later stage.

Regarding Eagle's theory (1984) on the development of object relationship, one can expand his description of tactile and kinaesthetic stimulation to apply to auditory stimulation as well. Since the infant's auditive system is developed after 18 weeks of gestation (Rubel, 1984), it is obvious that, next to the neurologic-developmental significance of acoustic stimulation, the mother's voice during pregnancy plays an important role in the development of intra-psychological elements at the beginning of bonding and the beginning relationship. Therefore, during the period of intensive medical care after premature birth, it is possible with the help of the mother's voice to open a psychological and emotional space for the child, a space where development can occur.

Full-term infants, immediately after birth, demonstrate the ability *"to recognize an object with the help of one sense, with which they have become acquainted through another sense"* (Eagle, 1984). This developmental step has possibly already taken place several weeks prior to regular term birth, since, from about the 36th week onward, the premature infant can no longer be pacified by the recorded maternal voice, but only through a combination of acoustic and tactile stimulation.

These results indicate that it is supportive to continue the prenatal acoustic environment in respect to the mother's voice. Due to its ability to help form relationships, it is a continuum, building bridges from the intrauterine world through the technical world in the NICU on into life at home. Thus, Auditive Stimulation enables an independent intra–psychological activity towards a renewed relationship between mother and infant. This is a decisive basis for the bonding process, interaction and development.

Chapter 8

PREMATURE BABIES HAVE
PREMATURE MOTHERS:

PRACTICAL EXPERIENCES WITH PREMATURE
INFANTS AND THEIR MOTHERS
USING AUDITIVE STIMULATION
WITH THE MOTHER'S VOICE

Marie-Luise Zimmer

According to Nöcker-Ribaupierre (1995), Auditive Stimulation of very premature babies is a music therapy method, solely using the mother's voice. This treatment technique focuses on both the mother and the premature infant. For the baby, it is a form of music therapy, whereas for the mother it is a crisis intervention. The objective is to support and promote the bonding process between mother and child, which has been seriously threatened by a much too early birth.

The fetus is exposed to a multitude of acoustic stimuli in the intrauterine environment, such as heart beat, intestinal sounds, breathing sounds, and, in particular, the mother's voice. The voice represents the mother. It does not only sound like the mother, it is the mother. The mother's voice conveys security, intimacy and warmth. It represents an emotional "home" and is distinctive for the infant, unique in tone, melody and emotional substance (Stern, 1995).

According to Rubel (1984), from the 18th week of pregnancy the unborn baby is able to perceive acoustic signals, process them, discriminate between them, and recognize them postnatally. Therefore, the mother's voice can play an extremely important role in the treatment of very premature infants. "Under the aspect of its relationship-forming qualities for mother and child, I believe that the voice makes possible a connection, builds a bridge from prenatal life across the time of intensive care to the point of coming home, and that it allows a new liaison after the abrupt and too early separation" (Nöcker-Ribaupierre, 2001).

In the last 2 to 3 decades, the chances for survival for these infants (less than 32 weeks gestational age and less than 1500 grams) have improved drastically, thanks to advances in intensive medicine. Despite the immaturity of all organ systems and the connected risk of secondary illnesses, an increasing number of children are surviving. Therefore, we have even more responsibility to help such children achieve the best possible quality of life (Albrecht & Zimmer, 2000).

The importance of a stable mother–child–relationship for the child's quality of life is underlined by longitudinal studies of premature infants, indicating that developmental parameters correlate even more with socio-economic family factors than with the severity of prenatal and postnatal risk factors (Achenbach, Howell, Aoki, & Rauh, 1993; Riegel, Orth, Wolke & Österlund, 1995).

Furthermore, there is abundant evidence (Klaus & Kennell, 1976; Brazelton, 1981) demonstrating that the mental state of the mother plays an important role in the child's prenatal as well as postnatal development.

Before addressing issues of relationship and attachment theories and describing my practical work and experiences, I would first like to present an actual case study.

Case Study: "So that it will not hurt so much when he leaves me."

The ward doctor of the neonatal intensive care unit asked me to contact Ms. R.[1] She had had a Caesarean section due to an imminent HELLP syndrome. Her son weighed 650 grams. Although the child was experiencing the typical medical difficulties of premature infants, no serious complications had arisen. The doctor was concerned about the mother's behavior. She stood next to the incubator without moving, had not taken up any contact with her baby, and remained strangely unaffected when nurses and doctors talked to her.

Our first contact took place next to the incubator, where I said hello to both of them, mother and child. I told her about the possibility of recording her voice on a disc for her son, which could be played for him in her absence, and offered her my psychotherapeutic support. Ms R. listened without any visible reaction. She appeared to be numb, almost as if she were paralyzed, or as if she were behind a glass wall, staring out of the window, past the incubator, during the entire conversation. Her face remained blank. "No," she didn't want to talk about it, didn't need any help. The other thing: "That with the voice... well, I just can't imagine that... but maybe." She said, it is okay if I wanted to come again. It was all the same to her.

I took her "but maybe" and her hesitant "OK" as a weak sign of some willingness to enter into a relationship. In the evening I dropped by Ms. R. again—she was standing at the incubator in the same way I left her. I thought, "She couldn't have been standing there all day." The nurses told me that she had gone back to her room in between, but had again been standing next to the incubator for a long time without moving, staring out of the window. I approached Ms. R., stood next to her without saying much and was more physically present, looking at her baby in the incubator. All of a sudden Ms. R

---

[1] All names have been changed in the following case descriptions.

turned her head, looked at me first, then down at the floor. Her eyes quickly darted to the incubator, then through the room, and back again to me, as if she did not know where to look. In answer to my question if she would like to come to my office, she gave a relieved nod. We sat there for a long time. Ms. R. held her head in her hands, staring down at the table. Once more, I described my function on the ward and told her that I had been asked to offer her and her son therapeutic support during this very difficult time. Suddenly I saw her tears dropping on the table. She began to talk quickly, softly, and without any inflection. One morning she had been working in her office. Everything was normal and by evening the baby had been born. And she had not even been "really" pregnant. Hardly anybody had noticed anything and she was looking forward so much to getting a big belly. "I feel as if I were in a dense fog, everything is so unreal. This is supposed to be my son.... I don't want him to get close to me so that it will not hurt so much when he leaves me." He was a planned child. She had waited years and years to get pregnant—and now this! She was very frightened, everything in the hospital scared her, and she felt as if she had failed. It was impossible to look at her child. It nauseated her to see all those tubes and needles, it was just awful. "And what's going to happen now?" Ms. R. continued weeping softly. I could only tell that she was crying from the tears on the table. Her crying, too, was silent and motionless.

I asked her if she could imagine writing down everything that was going through her head—what scared her, what she found revolting, like writing in a diary. Ms. R. nodded again in response. I suggested that she write a letter to her son. That would enable her to tell him what had happened, describe the home waiting for him, who would be waiting for him there, or simply tell him what came to her mind. Ms. R. shrugged her shoulders: "I don't know." I noticed how exhausted she was. Before parting, we made an appointment for three days later. I wanted to give Ms. R. enough time to consider my suggestion. The next day I received a call from one of the nurses, who told me that Ms. R. wanted to see me as soon as possible. We met that day.

Ms. R. was again standing by the incubator, looking out of the window. In response to my hello, she regarded me with the hint of a smile, which immediately faded as she stared back out the window. Then she took a little book from her pocket: "My husband brought me this today. I wrote something in it." She asked me if we could go to my office. "It should be easier for me, here I feel as if I were on exhibit." She wanted to read something to me from the book, and asked me to tell her if she had done "everything right."

"To my son," that was the surprising beginning. Ms. R. cried, this time accompanied by a flood of words, as if she wanted to unburden herself and get all her troubles off her chest. Oh, she had wanted the child so much. It was her last opportunity. She had given up all hope. Her husband had not spared reproaches either, telling her there must be something wrong with her if she never became pregnant. That's why she decided to undergo hormone treatment. Not long after, she became pregnant. "I was sick and tired of the permanent

discussions about whose fault it was, mine or my husband's. It turned out that he was right, it was mine." That's why her disappointment was all the greater that *"something like this had to happen. It's my fault again."* Ms. R. spoke quietly in a monotone voice about the disappointments in her marriage, her shame and anger about her supposed inability to conceive, and the humiliations she suffered. She described her pride and joy when she finally became pregnant and at last felt that she was a *"complete woman."* That is why she was in such great despair about this *"disgrace."* She couldn't give one thought to the condition of her son, otherwise she would *"go crazy."* After a short pause she said: *"Something is changing a little bit, but I don't know why."*

We made arrangements to meet the next week. In the meantime, I encouraged her to keep on writing the letter to her son. She could tell him hopes for him, how she imagined their life together in perhaps 5 years from now, what they would all like to experience together. During our next appointment we would make the recording. Maybe she would like to record the letter to her son then. Ms. R. agreed and took her book, leaving without looking at me again.

During the next few days the nurses told me about some small positive changes in Ms. R.'s behavior. She was still very quiet, but she had some contact with another mother. Once in a while she would risk a glance in the incubator. In general she did not appear to be as numb as before. She would often sit and write in her book, or she would observe what was going on in the baby unit. Right now one of the nurses was showing her how to change her son's diapers in the incubator.

A week later we met to make the recording. She asked me to leave the room, as she otherwise would not be able to read out loud, not knowing that I usually leave the room to respect the mother's privacy. After the recording was finished, we took it to her son, where I had installed a small loudspeaker at the head of the incubator in the meantime. Both of us were curious and a little nervous. What is going to happen? Will we be able to observe anything at all? I appropriately adjusted the volume. We were *"all ears,"* listening at the open door of the incubator. Then we shut the door and waited. Ms. R.'s whole body was shaking. I put my arm around her, and we waited some more. Her son's eyes were shut. Suddenly, he tried to open them. First he pulled up one eyebrow, then the other. But he was not able to get them open. Again and again, he furrowed his brows in the attempt to open his eyes. And then, very very slowly, after a long time and numerous attempts, his eyes opened up to tiny slits. His head rolled back a little, as if he was trying to look at the loudspeaker, and a smile appeared on his little face. Ms. R., standing next to me, cried and laughed at the same time. Her whole body was trembling. She then gave me a big hug: *"That's impossible—I just didn't believe it."*

RELATIONSHIP AND ATTACHMENT THEORY

Pregnancy is not only accompanied by physical changes in the expectant mother. Psychological changes are of particular significance. Daniel Stern (1995) categorizes the socio–cultural factors in the following four points in his concept of *"the motherhood constellation."* The mother's success in dealing with these themes plays a significant role in successful mother–child–bonding.

- Is the mother capable of keeping the baby alive?
- Is the mother successful in developing an emotional relationship to her child, in other words, can the mother love her baby, can she feel that the baby loves her; can she recognize and believe that it really is her baby?—"Primary relatedness."
- Can the mother create a reliable and protective environment and also accept it so that she can fulfil the first two tasks?—"Supportive matrix."
- Is the mother able to develop and maintain a new self-image of herself as a mother, in other words, a new identity?

In connection with the concept of sensitivity, Mary Ainsworth (1977) also stresses the importance of the child's reactions for evaluating the quality of attachment between mother and child.

In reference to *motherhood constellation,* it is not difficult to imagine how different the "starting conditions" for a successful mother–child relationship are in a premature baby, and (as illustrated in the aforementioned case) how deeply hurt and insecure the mother of a prematurely born baby can be. For whatever reason, the mother was not able to carry her child to the full-term. And she is not able to sustain the child's life. She is "replaced" by doctors, nurses, and intensive medicine, and is confronted with feelings of her own inadequacy, incompetence, and failure. Thus, through her role as the mother of a premature infant, she does not experience an increase in esteem from her social environment—what normally happens with full–term babies—but instead is often confronted with the opposite.

Because of the very early birth and the isolation of the baby in the incubator, the mother is unable to communicate spontaneously with her child, and it is very difficult for her to develop an emotional relationship. How can she show her child that she loves him? How can she recognize that her baby loves her? The mother is not able to build and organize the supportive matrix herself. The institution "hospital" must take on this role to give the mother the security, support, and assistance she needs, as well as the respect and esteem she deserves. The mother is forced to accept the circumstances and adapt to them. Because of the premature and abrupt termination of pregnancy, the mother has not had the normal nine months to grow into her new identity as a mother.

Even under normal circumstances, motherhood is considered the greatest stress factor in the life of a woman (Barnett & Baruch, 1985). How much more is demanded of a mother who experiences the bio–psycho-social stress of a much too early delivery.

For the child a very premature birth always means an early trauma both physically and mentally. This is the conviction of psychotherapist Ludwig Janus, (1997) who states that: "Because of his or her prematurity, the human being is born not only in a physically, but in particular in a mentally immature state." At the same time, premature birth always presents a threat to the mother–child relationship, endangering later ability to form attachments. In order for the mother to develop a relationship with her child, she needs intensive support. For this reason crisis intervention plays a significant role in my practical work.

THE PSYCHODYNAMICS OF THE MOURNING PROCESS

Through the premature end of a pregnancy the mother is usually confronted by a new situation in which she has to say goodbye to the desires and goals she had in connection with a full-term baby. New plans for the future are not yet viable, because everything, which is connected with the baby's future, is still uncertain.

In the course of my work I have found parallels between the psychological coping processes of these mothers and the clients in my practice who are mourning the death of a close person.

In other words, when I speak of the mourning processes of mothers, I explicitly mean all mothers of premature infants who have to cope with this situation, not just the mother whose baby has died due to premature birth and the resulting complications. Of course, these cases also exist, but they make other psychological demands on the mother. Furthermore, I have repeatedly observed that the experience of a premature birth can re-activate earlier traumatic events or earlier losses, which have not been adequately resolved.

The Swiss psychotherapist, Verena Kast (1982), describes the following stages of the mourning process and explains how important it is to work through each phase in order to be able to renew one's confidence in life and develop new life perspectives: "What seems critical to me in working through mourning is the experience that we are not only able to bear the separation, but that through the grief it leads us to experience ourselves from a new side, also with new evaluations: As persons, who are not broken by separation."

These stages can also be found in the mourning processes of these mothers who are bereaving the premature end of their pregnancy and premature birth of their child.

Stage 1: Denial

The mother who has no time to mentally prepare herself for a preterm birth, who is initially in a state of emotional shock, often expressed by numbness.

It is important for the mother to know that this does not mean she has no feelings for her baby. She is allowed to be numb—to "cry no tears." It is also imperative that no one has any expectations of her or her behavior.

Stage 2: Emotional Outbreaks

Restlessness, fear, guilt, grief, rage, anger, and despair—a chaos of feelings usually follow emotional paralysis. The mother can be tormented by the question "why me?" The search for a cause or a person to blame begins, which does not exclude the mother herself.

Grief is accompanied by anger that the situation can't be changed, that there is nothing one can do about it. This feeling is at first very painful and almost unbearable. Also, a mother can very seldom admit her anger with the child as the "cause" of the situation. Her feelings of guilt would be overwhelming. So, the anger is usually vented on others. Kast refers to shifted anger. The mother feels anger toward the partner, anger toward the gynecologist, who may have noticed something too late. She may be angry with the ward, the nurses, the orderlies, and doctors, because not everything functioned the way she wanted it to function. She may be angry with me if I am not immediately available for a talk. But on the other hand, this is all connected with feelings of shame for feeling angry at all. Buried under all this anger, there is the great fear that her child may not even survive, or if it does, that he or she may be seriously handicapped.

The more the mother realizes that she does not have to be ashamed of these feelings, the greater is the support for the mother. When she understands that they are justified and a part of her struggle to come to terms with reality, she has a better basis for building a new and viable relationship with her child. The kindest approach is to listen, allow it, and not argue against it. Only after this emotional volcano has been expressed the mother is free to deal with reality and formulate new goals.

Stage 3: Introspection and Letting Go

At this point the mother often starts the inner search for what she can rescue from her former plans as a new mother and what she can integrate into her new life as mother of a premature baby. What is still feasible, what must be thought over again, and which solutions must be found? Despair and grief may still wash over her, because her life will never be the same as before and probably not quite how she had wished and hoped for. Nevertheless, the mother's greater confidence in coping with the situation allows her to assume an active role, by distancing herself from previous expectations.

Stage 4: The New Orientation Toward Self and Reality

The mother begins to accept her fate, to make the best of it. She starts thinking about how to improve outer conditions and where she can get more support. She begins establishing contact with other mothers and imagining her future at home with her baby. Many mothers start to make realistic plans, even though it may still take many weeks to actualize. She is able to take "time out" for a weekend and go home. She is confident that her baby will be well taken care of on the ward during her absence.

In order to make it at all possible for the mother to develop a new emotional relationship with her baby and the situation, she needs time, quiet, and a person to be with her as she works through her grief. She must be allowed to mourn, as Kübler-Ross (1975) calls it, without feeling guilty. This presents a chance for mother and child to develop a new identity out of this vulnerable period in their relationship, or—as Mechthild Papoušek states (oral paper in Lindau 2001)—*"a devil turning into an angel."*

GENERAL SETTING

This data on Auditive Stimulation is based on my work at the Clinic for Neonatology and Pediatric Intensive Medicine and the Children's Clinic of the Central Hospital, Bremen. Approximately 240 infants under 2500 grams birth weight are treated annually. I offer Auditive Stimulation with the mother's voice on two intensive care units and one newborn unit, where the babies are transferred immediately after birth. To date I have worked with 426 premature babies and their mothers.

METHODOLOGY

The technical equipment consists of mini disc recorders, a microphone, headphones, 1 cassette deck, 20 mini-disc walkmen, 20 active loudspeakers. I also have a small library of picture books and story books in different languages as many of our patients have other cultural backgrounds.

The doctors or nurses suggest those babies whom they consider appropriate for Auditive Stimulation. I then establish contact with the mother. Either I visit her in the maternity ward or we meet at the child's incubator. I introduce myself and the method, and we arrange an appointment in my therapy room to talk about everything in more detail.

This conversation revolves around three central themes:

The Mother's "Story:"

- What happened?
- How were the pregnancy and birth?
- Is it her first child?
- Were there any other prior negative factors, for example, premature births, miscarriages?
- How is the relationship with her partner, with her family?
- Does she get social support from them; is there an additional social network?
- Can the mother remember any previous crises which she coped with successfully? (resources)
- What has she experienced in the clinic?
- How is her relationship to the nurses and doctors?
- Does she have contact to other mothers?
- Does she feel that she and her baby are receiving competent hospital care?
- How is she feeling physically and mentally?

The Premature Infant and the Mother–Child Relationship:

- How is the baby's present condition according to doctors/nurses?
- How does the mother experience the baby's condition?
- Which feelings come up in her?
- Is the mother able to accept the baby as her child?
- Is the mother able to imagine establishing a relationship with her child or does she refuse to have any contact?
- Does the mother feel it makes any sense for her to be with her child or does she feel unneeded?

Explaining Auditive Stimulation

- Explanation of hearing development in the womb
- Why the mother's voice is more important than the father's
- How the baby recognizes the mother's voice
- What the mother's voice convey to the child
- Has the mother repeatedly read or sung to other persons, for example, to her other children, during the last weeks of pregnancy?
- The effects of the method on mother and child

- Practical application
- What the mother can talk about or sing on the recording
- How she can prepare herself for the recording
- How much time she has
- When it is important *not* to play the recording of the mother's voice

In the beginning, mothers are often anxious and uncertain, frequently appearing to still be under shock and incapable of taking in everything I tell them. For this reason, I especially emphasize the following and point out that there are a number of ways to make the recording:

- The mother can speak freely and talk about anything.
- She can write a letter to her child and then read it out loud.
- She can read out loud from a book.
- She can sing a song.

The recording should last about 30 minutes and can consist of all the described alternatives. I remind the mother that while her baby may not understand the meaning of her words, it is important that she feels comfortable with whatever she wishes to tell her child. Furthermore, I mention once more the significance of familiar material, perhaps something that she read or sang to another person during her pregnancy. The baby already knows this sound and is able to recognize it. After birth an infant is able to distinguish between a text that has often been heard prenatally from an unfamiliar text (DeCasper & Fifer, 1980). It is important for the mother to understand that only she is able to give this to her child. No one can replace her voice, no doctor, no nurse, no medicine, not even Mozart or Brahms. She is now playing a very important role in helping her child to make progress. This gives her a feeling of autonomy and competence in her role as a mother.

I explain that the CD should not be turned on when medical treatment is being conducted in order to prevent the infant from associating it with the medical intervention. The recording cannot replace her actual presence. It is merely a supportive measure for the time they are separated from one another.

I usually make the recording appointment a week later. I ask the mother to bring the photograph of her baby, which was taken on the ward after birth, to the recording session. I intentionally extend the time period before doing the recording for several reasons. I want to give her enough time to think about what she would like to give her child. This can lead to a change of perspective. Perhaps in this week, her child's survival is not in the foreground, but her role as mother—what she wishes for her child, what she would like to tell and give him or her, in other words, positive thoughts about a mutual future.

Recording Procedure

When we meet again, the mother shows me what she has prepared. She places the child's photo on the table, so that her baby is there with her. I explain how to operate the equipment, and we make a short sample recording. I ask the mother not to make any pauses during the recording session in order to avoid disturbing noise. Before leaving the room I show her once more how to turn the recorder on and off and tell her that I will return in about 30 minutes. I deliberately leave the mother alone because many mothers are too shy to speak in the presence of another person.

While the mother is recording, I install the walkman in her baby's incubator. When I return to the room, the mother often appears transformed: relieved, freer, quieter, but also very exhausted. We listen to the beginning of the recording to make sure everything functioned properly. This often leads to a talk. In the course of my work I have discovered that on the day of the recording it is better to first record the CD and then talk with the mother. The mother can often be so emotionally involved that she is no longer capable of making the recording.

After talking, we visit the incubator together, insert the CD, and watch how the baby reacts to it. This is a very decisive and moving moment for the mother, because she can see that her baby recognizes her voice and that she is not a stranger to her child. These are the first feedback signals (Ainsworth, 1977), which are important for the quality of attachment between mother and child. Then I remind the mother once more that she should not turn on the CD when her child is receiving treatment. I tell her that the nurses will play the CD 6–8 times a day and that she can turn on the CD when she leaves to go home so that a part of her remains with her child. This gives the mother the feeling that she has done everything possible so that her child does not feel left alone.

Coda

The infant's discharge is usually around the child's normal birth date, except in seriously ill babies. We then talk again. When possible, we go through what happened at the baby's birth through the discharge date and talk about any remaining problems, anxieties, or worries.

CLINICAL EXPERIENCES AND OBSERVATIONS

In working in a neonatal intensive care ward, one constantly encounters the limits of human existence. Everyday experience shows the fine line between birth and death.

Auditive Stimulation often works like a key—a door opener—to the mother's life-story and to conflict loaded topics from the past, which can further hinder the development of normal mother–child bonding.

I have repeatedly encountered the following problems:

- unconscious or conscious partner conflicts
- the child perceived as "rescuer" of the marriage or unwanted by one or both parents
- failed abortion
- previous premature births, miscarriages, or stillbirths in the past (multiple)
- the infant seen as a "substitute" for a dead child
- long-standing desire and difficulties to become pregnant with infertility treatment
- multiple births in which not all children survived
- special problems of immigrants, for example, communication, applying for political asylum, impending deportation, unemployment, appalling living conditions, isolation
- single mothers, very young mothers and first pregnancy for older women
- adverse childhood experiences of the mothers
- illness of a parent and fear of disease transmission
- anxiety, addictions and mental disorders, attempted suicides

With the following two case studies, I would like to illustrate psychological conflicts and how they affect the mother–child–relationship.

MELANIE - *In the 29th week of pregnancy Ms. P. gave birth to twins (1060g / 1200g): a boy, Michael, and a girl, Eva. Her oldest son was 17 years old. Ms P. appeared to handle the current situation in a very practical way and did not seem very anxious. However, what did stand out was that she completely devoted herself to her son, Michael, and usually let the nurses take care of her daughter. All attempts to reduce the distance between Eva and her mother seemed to fail. Ms. P. was open to the idea of Auditive Stimulation. She was happy to be able to do something for her children. However, she was not willing to make a separate recording for each child. Her position was "That's not necessary, one CD is enough for both. You can make a copy."*

During our talk I noticed that Ms. P. repeatedly calls her daughter Melanie instead of Eva, without being aware of her mistake. When I called her attention to the fact that we were talking about her daughter Eva and not Melanie, she came out with the suppressed truth. She had had another daughter Melanie, who would have been 10 years old now. At the age of three she suddenly died from an infection. Ms. P. said that she did not notice her slip and did not say anything about Melanie because she did not want to think about it any longer. But she was just not able to look at Eva because this immediately reminded her of her deceased daughter, automatically bringing up all the pain and fear from the past. She had absolutely no idea how to have a relationship with Eva. It had been her greatest wish to have twin sons.

The grief over the death of her older daughter, which had not been worked through adequately, was reactivated by the current stressful situation. For this reason, Ms. P. was not able to establish an emotional relationship with Eva. Only after this talk was Ms. P willing to make a separate recording for her daughter.

MANUELA -*The unresolved conflict of Ms. W., which hindered her in making contact with her daughters, was of a completely different nature.*

Ms. W. was an Aramean from a very religious family from Syria. She already had five children between 6 and 14 years and had given birth to twins (28th week of pregnancy, 800g / 865g), both girls, in our hospital. The family had been living in Germany for many years and gave the impression of being stable. Despite the premature delivery, everyone seemed overjoyed about the twins. Ms. W. started looking after both children very soon after delivery and agreed without reservations to begin Auditive Stimulation. At first there seemed to be no problems. However, after a while Ms. W. visited the babies' incubators less and less frequently. When I tried to talk to her in order to plan the recording session, she avoided me. She seemed to be more and more unhappy. One day, she suddenly asked me for an appointment, during which she broke down. She couldn't make the recording. She had wanted to name one of her daughters Manuela, which means "God be with you". But instead she bowed to her husband's wish to call her Daniela. Now she was reproaching herself for not having asserted herself. She believed there to be connection between this and the premature birth. God has punished her for this, and now she felt to blame for her children's state of health. She was not able to talk about this with anyone, not even with her husband and saw no way out. I was able to arrange a talk among the three of us, Ms. W., her husband, and myself. After Daniela — still in the incubator—had been renamed Manuela by a priest and he had given both girls his blessing, Ms. W. was able to renew the contact to her children and record a CD for each of them. With a beaming face she told me that in the recording she prayed for her children and told them that the priest had blessed them.

Of course, some of these mothers are referred to social workers and psychologists for continuing therapy and support.

ISSUES WHICH REQUIRE SPECIAL CONSIDERATIONS

LOWER INCOME, ILLITERATE AND MENTALLY RETARDED MOTHERS. For some of these mothers it is difficult to understand the basic principles of Auditive Stimulation. Still, they are willing to participate. If the mother is not able to sing, talk, or read, then I suggest that she describe pictures from popular children's books. For mentally retarded mothers, the emotional contact to the baby appears to be less disturbed. Perhaps such mothers are not always able to grasp the potential consequences of the risks involved in a premature birth.

MULTIPLE BIRTHS. When focusing on the relationship between a mother and her child, it is necessary when multiple births occur that the mother make a recording for each child. This implies that the mother builds a personal relationship with each of her children.

Unfortunately it often happens that not all of the infants survive. This is a tremendous strain for the mother, causing even more inner conflict. She is simultaneously mourning a dead infant and establishing a relationship with her remaining babies. The mother usually must first cope with the death of her baby and take leave of him or her, before she is emotionally able to attend to the surviving child or children.

LANGUAGE, RELIGIOUS, AND CULTURAL ASPECTS. In our multicultural society, mothers often have other native languages and cultural backgrounds. We often need an interpreter, in order to explain Auditive Stimulation. In such cases, other conversations are almost impossible. If the mother is bilingual, I suggest that she makes the recording in her mother tongue, if this is the language she has spoken most of her life.

In the course of my work I have become more and more aware of how important it is to have at least basic knowledge of the rituals of other religions and cultures, so that no additional problems are created by interventions, which may conflict with such traditions. For example, Moslems often give their child a name only after they are sure that it will survive. In this way the Moslem mother hopes to lessen the pain and grief connected with a possible death of her baby. Here the establishment of a relationship between mother and child is especially complicated, because until the baby is named, bonding may be avoided. It is helpful to point out to the mother that a relationship between herself and her baby has been established and developing during the intrauterine stage. Many Muslim mothers then like to read from the Koran for the recording and often place a small Koran in the child's incubator.

Some of these mothers are also silently suffering because they are beaten and mistreated by their husbands if they have not produced a son and have also brought disgrace upon their family because of the premature birth.

CHECKING THE RECORDINGS. Many mothers are afraid that they will cry during the recording. I try to lessen their fears by reminding them that they surely must have cried sometimes during their pregnancy. What we will be doing is nothing that the baby has not experienced in the intrauterine stage.

However, if the baby repeatedly cries when hearing the mother's recorded voice (Stern, 1986, affective attunement), then with the mother's permission, I examine the CD. If it turns out that the mother has cried for long periods during the recording, we make a new one.

On principle, I only listen to the beginning of the CD together with the mother to check the technical quality. What the mother tells her child on the rest of the recording is their private sphere.

MOTHER'S REJECTION OF AUDITIVE STIMULATION. A few mothers do reject Auditive Stimulation. This is evident when it becomes very difficult to make appointments, when other things seem more important to the mother, or when she repeatedly misses appointments. It is important to talk about this with the mother in order to uncover possible unconscious fears and conflicts, and support her to build relationship to her baby. Those mothers who continue to reject the offer, often show a rejecting and conflictive attitude toward their infant.

FATHERS. I initially explain to parents that in Auditive Stimulation the focus is on the relationship between mother and child: it is a method to at least partially compensate for what has been abruptly taken from the child. In this respect the mother's voice is of prime importance for the child's later ability to form close attachments. Parents often wish for the father to participate in the recording. Here, it must be pointed out that although the baby has already been born, we are actually still dealing with the time of pregnancy, the very close and symbiotic phase between mother and child which the baby needs for his or her physical and mental development.

It is then easier for the parents to accept this special role of the mother. I explain that they are actually looking inside the uterus when you look at your child in the incubator. I tell them that when the original birth date arrives, the father's voice then becomes very important for the baby.

WHEN THERE IS NO MOTHER'S VOICE. In this case study, the mother had died during the birth of her son, Moritz. My task was to give the father and the 5–year–old sister, Maria, emotional support.

Obviously it was not possible to apply the method of Auditive Stimulation in its original form. Nevertheless, I used the technique in order to establish a relationship between the remaining family members and the baby. On the one side, Maria mourned the loss of her mother, on the other hand she found herself in an ambivalent conflict between being happy about the birth of Moritz and at the same time blaming him for her mother's death. The father was completely overwhelmed—both physically and emotionally and was unable to handle the situation. By working together on the recordings for Moritz, they were no longer "victims." They were now able to develop and nurture their relationship to one another and to Moritz. The family also received psychotherapy for a number of years.

This is an example of how often we are suddenly confronted with situations which no longer fit the "rules" and which require individual solutions. Even where Auditive Stimulation with the mother's voice is not possible, it can still be used in other ways as an important aid for bonding.

CONCLUSION

My experiences with Auditive Stimulation substantiate the results of Nöcker-Ribaupierre, indicating that this method makes an important contribution to building or re-establishing the relationship and bonding between the mother and her prematurely born baby.

Doctors and nurses on our ward report that the mothers who have partaken in Auditive Stimulation seem to be more balanced, quieter, and more stabile and that this behavioral change has positive effects on their babies. If babies' level of oxygen saturation decreases, the nurses first turn on the recording with the mother's voice in the incubator before they resort to other technical measures. Only in very seldom cases does a child react negatively to the mother's voice, and in such cases it is necessary to first examine the recording to find out if there is an external cause. The nurses also report particularly positive effects of Auditive Stimulation for restless babies.

The operation of the technical equipment is the nurses' task because of the limited amount of hours I have to do this work. Of course, this is connected with problems. The nurses have decided against the use of timers which automatically play the mother's voice 6 times daily, in order to consider each baby individually. There is no doubt that this is an additional burden for the nurses. This problem has not yet been satisfactorily resolved. Is music therapy possible in an intensive care unit full of high-tech equipment? How can a form of therapy, which is also artistic, be integrated in such a setting? Must it necessarily be limited to technical apparatus and verbal interventions? Isn't there also the chance to make use of the potentials of music therapy in a better and more effective way?

I would also suggest receptive and trophotropic music for relaxation and relief as a supportive measure for these mothers who are undergoing extreme strain and pressure because of breast-feeding as well as for those who are anxious and depressed.

Finally I would like to add a personal suggestion: I often work with patients who are suffering from eating disorders or so-called early childhood disorders. Such clients quite often report particularly difficult early childhood experiences. Perhaps Auditive Stimulation could be an important intervention in the early prevention for infants born at risk or for those with early hospital experiences which lead to disorders connected with bonding and attachment problems. We are only able to truly live if we are able to form relationships with other human beings

Chapter 9

LIFE IN NEONATAL CARE—OR THE SITUATION OF THE PREMATURE BABY

Elisabeth Dardart

INTRODUCTION

The Neonatal Department of the hospital complex situated in Evry (Essonne), a southern suburb of Paris, was opened in 1982. Since its opening, premature babies were admitted who had undergone general observation, following a stay in the neonatal intensive care unit. In addition, newborn babies who were ill or slightly premature were also treated. Over the years intensive care beds were added for these premature babies, who are more fragile than other infants. They usually receive much more rigorous medical treatment and some have to be hospitalized for several months.

From the start, my role has been to improve the quality of the parent-infant relationship by means of music and massage. The parents of infants in intensive care units are concerned that their infants may become handicapped or even die. Thus, I have consequently begun offering more psychotherapeutic support for the parents.

THEORETICAL BACKGROUND

The ear is the organ used for hearing as well as for balance. The fetus' vestibular system is functional from the 14th week, his auditory system is developed by 18 weeks (Rubel, 1984), and his hearing is fully developed by the 8th month (Busnel, 1986).

Busnel has shown that the fetus is capable of auditory memory—recognizing its parents' voice, a melody or a poem regularly heard during pregnancy and even differentiating between certain words and syllables. After birth, these voices or music heard in the womb generally have a soothing effect on the newborn baby.

Touch is the first sense to develop. At 8 weeks, the fetus reacts to stimulation in the perioral region. By about 18 weeks it is sensitive to any exterior contact and through its movements begins to interactively communicate with its mother (Busnel, 1991).

Skin is not just an organ of touch. It supports a number of functions, such as the perception of pressure, temperature and perspiration. It forms the body's first protective membrane (Montagu, 1979). Anzleu (1988) defines the skin as the first receptor of emotions and refers to the "me–skin" as representing the difference between the inner and outer. It is where exchanges and communication occur, a "unifier."

The skin is also a resonance receptor, requiring coenaesthesia and weightlessness. The fetus is thus carried or cradled by this "bath of sound." Lecourt (1988) found this link between touch and hearing to be one of an infant's first experiences of its own "self limits." She develops the concept of a "sonorous cocoon," backed up by touch, sound and sight, contributing to some of the infant's basic psychological experiences.

THE EXPERIENCES OF PREMATURITY

Premature birth is always an overwhelming event for the newborn baby as well as its parents. The premature arrival of a baby is often experienced by its mother as a brutal interruption of her pregnancy, which she may experience as extremely traumatic.

The admission of a newborn baby to the Neonatology Department is an entrance into a surrealistic environment. This can include resuscitation, strong lights, loud voices, noises, alarm sounds, ventilators, drips, tests, fear of the environment and the lack of a mother's presence to reassure the infant (as she is at this point still in the obstetrical room). If the father is present during the birth, he will generally stay with his infant and it is with him that the infant will experience emotional contact. However, in these first few moments, both father and baby are extremely overwhelmed by medical procedures. It therefore seems imperative to offer this helpless family as humane a welcome as possible.

The first moments are dedicated to explaining the interventions which have just been carried out, and examining the infant. The functioning of the various machines—feeding and thermal tubes, cardio–respiratory monitoring, oxygen saturation, the use of drips or catheters and, if necessary, ventilation is demonstrated to the parents. Afterwards, the length of the baby's hospitalization is discussed along with possible complications arising from the prematurity, future treatments and development, which the newborn baby will go through. "When will he leave the hospital?," "What will he be like?" One of the difficulties of neonatal medicine is the inability to give parents a realistic prognosis, particularly in the first few days after the birth. How many times do parents hear, "Today he's well, but we can't yet tell you how he's going to be tomorrow." In addition the physiological state of premature babies can change rapidly, so that in one day, an infant who is well may have to undergo a cardio–respiratory decompensation, sometimes requiring resuscitation. A few hours later, the infant may stabilize. These neonatal uncertainties only add to the parents' existing concerns.

The parents are confronted with conflicting feelings. The mother experiences her pregnancy as unfinished. She is no longer pregnant, but does not yet feel like a mother. Her womb is empty, but so are her arms. She can not take the baby home. In addition, she is dreading returning to her home environment (family, neighbors and friends), often experiencing their reactions as hurtful. The mother may feel guilty. What did she do or fail to do that resulted in her baby being born so early? Her personal image as a mother may be damaged.

From a psychoanalytical perspective, at this point her relationship to her own mother resurfaces. While she is pregnant, she becomes like her mother, she is no longer her little girl, her status changes: from that of little girl to mother. Often a feeling of rivalry sets in, but this is tainted with a feeling of failure: "I wasn't able to succeed, while you were able to accomplish things." The relationship with her mother (or mother–in–law) may become more fragile and former conflicts may once again come to the fore. However, this relationship may also be strengthened and new bonds may be forged (Mathelin, 1998).

As for the infant, the change from an imaginary infant to a real–life baby and adapting to the birth of a premature baby is once again more difficult. During the pregnancy the fetus (whether wanted or unwanted) and partly glimpsed during the ultra-sound scans, has aroused the interest and desires of its mother and her family members. The image of the actual newborn, small, thin and fragile, and often requiring life support is completely different from how the mother imagined her baby would be. In the first few days of the baby's hospitalization, the mother and father may be incapable of adapting to this new situation. Some parents may even suffer from shock or be overcome by distress, repeatedly asking the same questions to the hospital staff without so much as registering the answers. Such reactions are even more frequent, when it is suspected or announced that the baby is handicapped or suffering from the after-effects of the pregnancy. Time and psychological support will help the parents accept this reality. The parents may behave in different ways: infantilism, resignation, "knowing better," rivalry with the staff, aggressiveness, distrust or over-confidence. In such moments, it is important to listen to what the parents are experiencing, allowing them to express their feelings, in particular those which are the strongest and most disturbing. It is the latter that foster feelings of guilt and other ensuing attitudes. For example, the parents may hope the infant dies—this infant which has turned out so differently from how they imagined and is causing them to undergo such agony.

While the infant's life or death prognosis can only be established by the doctors, the parents experience a sometimes almost insurmountable mental conflict:

- *"Are we going to like this baby who might die? The suffering might just be too hard to bear."*

- *"Wouldn't it be better for him to die now, than for us to go through this tortuous wait and perhaps end up with an infant which is handicapped or dead?"*
- *"I must be a monster for thinking such things while my baby is so ill."*
- *"I'm really a bad mother. My baby doesn't need me. The staff is taking care of him using medical treatment, which I'm incapable of carrying out."*
- *"The hospital has stolen my baby from me. He is experiencing his first relationships with the nurses. As for me, I'm just second best."*
- *"The department is doing all they can to treat our infant. Nevertheless we begrudge them for taking our place."*

These effects may overwhelm the parents during this perinatal period when we know that the subconscious can more easily resurface and that former conflicts may re-emerge, because suppressed emotions are more likely to come to the surface (Mathelin, 1998).

In this hospital context those mediating the parent-infant relationship can prove to be extremely helpful, as the direct contact between parents and infant is sometimes difficult (particularly during the first few days). We use music, massage and the "Kangaroo Baby" technique in order to help the parents in initially communicating with their baby.

MUSIC

Music has been used for 18 years at the Evry hospital. Its use has been modified over the years. In 1982, two different kinds of music were used, firstly, one for "relaxation" and secondly, one for "stimulation." We used these techniques at calculated times, which appeared to us to correspond with the moments when the premature baby woke up or cried. This very quickly led to us broaden our concept. Supported by Busnel's research on fatal hearing (1991) we used music selected by the parents.

The fetus is able to hear from the 5th month: both sounds as well as voices are detected, although these are filtered through the mother's abdominal wall. Music is organized sounds. It affects the body with its resounding vibrations and the emotions with its melodious, rhythmic and harmonious constructions. Music is also a blanket of sound, which surrounds the baby, serving to reassure him.

Using the parents' musical selections gives them a sense of recognition and of sharing in their baby's development. They feel valued in their parental role. Accepting the parents' music means accepting their emotional world, permitting communication between the parents, the baby and the nurses. For the department this denotes the discovery of an element introduced by the parents, which allows them to turn the situation around. In addition, premature babies show a clear preference for music listened to by the mother during her pregnancy.

Music also brings about a moment of social interaction and of exchange of comments on the babies' reactions. It's a "meeting place" where parents and caregivers are equals in one of the infant's non-medical moments.

Furthermore, for immigrant parents, often having a much harder time than native French parents, an acceptance of their music means accepting their cultural differences and their identity.

> *N'Day (2 days old), premature and suffering from hypotrophy, was the first boy in a family of five girls from Mali. When his father arrived in the department, he was very nervous and reserved. He asked if he could touch his son and talk to him. The baby was under observation in an incubator. N'Day had fallen asleep. He immediately reacted as soon as his father's hand covered his body. The father, still very nervous, asked if he could bless his son and explained to us that being a Muslim, tradition dictates that his baby is only considered whole once he has pronounced the words of the "invitation to life." N'Day's father took his son in both his hands, lifted him up and chanted a prayer with gravity and solemnity. N'Day opened his eyes and started to move in a harmonious fashion while looking wide-eyed at his father. After the blessing, N'Day's father, visibly happier, continued to talk to his son and thanked us warmly while explaining to us the importance that this ceremony held for him and his son's destiny.*

Besides favorite taped music and those rituals, parents often bring their own music in form of a music box. Thus, music boxes or musical toys, which can be placed in the infant's incubator or crib, are also very popular. They may boost an important emotional experience: the mother's music box from infanthood days, a musical stuffed toy, which is a present from the grandmother or older brother. One mother told us with emotion how, one evening on arriving home, she discovered her husband sitting on the floor in front of their infant's empty bed, listening to his music box and crying.

We also encourage the parents to sing or record their voices and those of brothers and sisters on cassette, but this does not happen so often.

> *Laura, a third infant, born after 33 weeks, was in a monitored incubator with a feeding tube and a drip. During her pregnancy her mother regularly sang and played the guitar. At home she recorded a cassette with children's songs. While recording this, Laura's brother and sister came into the room where the mother was playing and asked to sing for their little sister. The siblings very quickly started to argue as to the choice of songs and whether or not they would sing solo. The*

mother let the cassette continue recording and brought it, complete with her children quarrelling. While listening to this cassette, Laura liked her mother's singing voice very much. But she particularly reacted to her brother and sister's dispute by opening her eyes wide and listening more attentively, which made her mother laugh. When she listened to it again, Laura's reaction was always more marked and more positive when her brother and sister started to argue. Perhaps during her time in the womb Laura regularly heard the shouts of her brother and sister and these constituted a reference point of sound for her.

Premature babies are sensitive to music as well as to sounds. As previously stated, the "sound environment" in a neonatal department is usually extremely noisy. All of these sounds create an element of insecurity for the baby. Even when the staff takes care to minimize them, they still cause a certain stress. Music can thus soothe, envelope, reassure or help the newborn baby to become alert. However, it is necessary to avoid playing it all the time, as it can thus become an additional sound, an excessive negative stimulation for the infant. The premature baby has great need for rest and of sleep. Quiet and darkness are equally indispensable for its healthy development. But sometimes unexpected difficulties have to be taken into account and dealt with.

Not all parents want music played to their infant. Some don't even want members of the staff to play the department cassettes. Whatever the reasons, they should be respected without making the parents feel guilty. For example, one such mother didn't want music played to her son, as she "was afraid that he would feel too happy and not want to go home."

Music Can Have Unexpected Effects

Loïc's mother was a professional violinist. She regularly played Celtic music to her son. Loïc was in a crib. Another baby, Kevin, was in the same room. The staff and Loic's mother wondered if his "music" was disturbing Kevin. During this musical performance Kevin failed to react. His father came a short time later and we told him that his son had just been listening to some violin music. His father panicked and explained to us that if Kevin didn't react, it could mean that he was deaf like his brothers and sisters. The department thus became more attentive to Kevin's reactions to sound and a hearing examination was scheduled.

Music Can Also Reveal How a Couple Interacts with Their Infant

Adrien, 7 days old, was in an incubator. The parents visited regularly and were interested in the music used in the department. They told us about their musical tastes. The mother listened to a lot of light music during her pregnancy. The father considered himself a music lover and preferred listening to what he termed "good" music. The father made a cassette for his son, choosing the majority of works according to basically technical criteria and was what he classified as his "good music."

Of the six works on the cassette, his wife had chosen only one song. The father took over the musical selections for his son, considering himself to be more expert than his wife.

The first few times he listened to this music, Adrien particularly reacted to the song chosen by his mother, which resulted in her feeling more interested in the music. In spite of this, when she was alone with her son, she very rarely played music to him.

During a medical visit after Adrien had been released, the mother mentioned to the doctor that her arms were more effective than music for calming her son's tears.

In this case, music seemed to us to be a controlling device used by the father, which brought the existing parental rivalry into play.

From time to time music is used more collectively. The staff is often under a great deal of stress: it is impossible to find an infant's vein, a baby who is suffering from decompensation and has to be resuscitated or receive a blood transfusion, machines breaking down, staff shortages etc. In such cases, the nurses deal with the crises and put all their energy into solving the problems as best they can. They need to work with the utmost concentration. However, the anguish in such moments is something that affects all of them. In the aftermath of such crisis, music can help to soothe and help everyone to recover and find some inner peace.

The Neonatal Usage of Music Should be Understood in the Broadest Sense of the Term

Baby Mathieu was very premature—29 weeks. His mother came to see him every day. She was delighted that we were playing music to her son. Having neither cassettes nor compact discs at home, she chose 2 or 3 cassettes from our collection. One day she shyly asked us if she could bring along the children's books that her parents read to her when she was a little girl. The next day and every day after Mathieu's mother read him a story. She experienced these events with a great show of emotion and Mathieu always remained calm. This mother was sharing something from her own childhood with her son, more intimate and personal than the music offered by us—though much appreciated.

Newborn babies often suffer from irritated buttocks. We use a hairdryer to dry the skin, which is affected, and this always serves to relieve the pain. A little girl reacted in particular to the noise of the hairdryer, her ears picking up as soon as she heard this sound, even if it was another baby that was being treated. On reporting this to her mother, she started to smile. She told us that she was a hairdresser.

Another aspect of music for purposes of social interaction can take place during certain feeding sessions. The staff gathers together in a room, holding the babies in their arms, and together begin singing a children's song. Our experience leads us to believe that music can be a source of exchange, of vitality and of pleasure shared in a medical environment.

COMPLEMENTARY TREATMENTS

Kangaroo Care

From the opening of the department in 1982, we have also been using Kangaroo Care. The newborn baby is placed (dressed in just one layer of clothing) against its mother's naked stomach. This technique, originally from Colombia, enables the mother and baby to re-establish sensory contact. The premature baby rediscovers the noises of its mother's body (heartbeat, breathing, intestines, etc, her heat, her odor, the vibrations of her voice). We very frequently observe that when a baby is in the kangaroo position, heart and breathing rates as well as oxygen saturation become more regular, the alarms sound less frequently and that the babies practically never cry (except when experiencing physical pain). Mother and baby find themselves as close as possible to the state of pregnancy or the environment of the fetus. The mother feels less empty with her baby—she too can sense the heat, the smell of her infant's body, its sighs, and its noises. She gains a physical sensation from this, which she can retain for the rest of the evening. The baby finds itself "cocooned" by its mother's body and arms and is also able to retain the sensory memory of this moment of intimacy. In the same way, we place scarves, which have been worn by the babies' mothers, in their incubators.

We also suggest that the father use Kangaroo Care. Even if he is not feeling the inner emptiness which may be felt by his wife, he has just as much a need for a sensory relationship with his infant. In fact, one father didn't dare to pick up his son and as he was hesitating, a nurse placed his infant in his arms. At the beginning the father was motionless as if he had been paralyzed. He then began to breathe in the scent of his infant's head and said, "But he smells good, he smells like sweets." He gently relaxed as if he were holding a valuable treasure. The next day, the father arrived and proudly announced with a big smile, "I've come to see my sweetie." From that day on, this father took his infant in his arms without anyone helping him.

The body of a premature baby or of a newborn baby which is ill, is regularly "attacked" by his treatment: daily pediatric examinations, palpations of his abdomen in order to check his digestion and whether or not he is bloated, blood samples, electroencephalograms and other examinations. The problem of drips is more difficult to deal with as premature babies have fragile veins, which are often damaged by injected medication. Thus the newborn baby's "venous reserves" are rapidly exhausted. The solution offered by a central catheter may solve this problem. The positioning of the catheter is a surgical process, which only pediatricians are authorized to carry out. This catheter is sometimes also impossible to position, the infant reacting to the positioning by completely retracting its veins. This process can also be the cause of possible infections and the catheter may get clogged up.

Respiratory support is also a source of stress. The intubation of a newborn baby is an intrusive act and during the positioning and maintenance of a nasal tube or oxygen mask, there is a risk of injury to the infant's nostrils.

Touching and Massage

These few examples, which are by no means exhaustive, demonstrate the necessity to offer the premature baby another relationship between his body and environment that is not an aggressive experience. Approaching the infant's body with touching or massage offers an opening towards a positive and warm relationship.

As far as massage is concerned, we were inspired by "loving touch," a technique perfected by Eva Reich and Ruth Rice (1985). This is a sensory stimulation technique, adapted for the treatment of premature babies. During a stay in France, their therapists came to our hospital to show us how, when faced with the sensory disorientation experienced by a premature baby, enveloping the baby with our touch, our voice and massage can help the baby to calm itself and give it a sense of security.

This massage consists of firm and light touches to the baby's body. The arms, the legs, the back, the chest and the stomach, followed by the face and head are massaged. Then overall movements from the head to the feet help to recreate a reassuring cocoon around the baby.

By means of this massage, which we offer to teach the parents, a new means can be established to aid the communication between parents and baby. When a mother sees her baby, relax from the massage and its body unstiffen, open its eyes, make little smiles and enjoy a bond with her - we believe that this can contribute to the mother regaining her self-esteem. Fathers can also massage their babies. However, touching or massaging one's baby isn't always a matter of course. Some parents are afraid of touching their baby, particularly during the first few days. It is necessary to respect this apprehension and help the parents to start step by step. Alternatively, the parents can gently and at their own pace initiate this sensory relationship with their infant. This aversion to touch or massage may also come from the premature baby. Some babies may have been handled too much and thus turn away from this form of communication. In such cases, speech and music may be other means of cocooning and reassuring the infant.

Moreover, the staff pays particular attention to the daily comfort of the infants. Mattresses stuffed with polystyrene granules are placed in the incubators so that the premature baby can nestle and form it according to the shape and size of its body. We use specially adapted mittens, which stops us from having to tie the babies' hands. In the cribs, there are rolled-up flannel blankets in case the baby needs them.

Once the premature baby is ready to be taken out of the incubator we suggest that it meets its brothers and sisters. For the siblings, particularly if they are young, long-term hospitalization of the last-born infant is experienced as a disruptive element. "Is the baby always going to be in hospital?" This baby is demanding a lot of time, love and concern from their parents. Other children are not always happy about this new arrival. One or more encounters enable the siblings to get used to the reality of this baby, to touch it, to express their ambivalence and/or love and to better deal with the wait for its home-coming.

Parent Groups

Meetings among parents are regularly organized in the department. This is a means of bringing them together. They often find themselves feeling very isolated and alone in their infant's room, not daring to go and talk to the other parents. During these meetings, which are opened with a slide film about the department, parents ask many different questions, ranging from the problem of blood transfusions to how to prepare the family cat for the new baby's arrival. However, the foundation of these meetings is built on each parent being able to share the account of the story of their premature baby, to share their experiences and anguish which they have gone through. They feel less alone, discover that others experience feelings almost the same as theirs and can provide each other with mutual comfort. Parents whose babies are soon to be released by the department can explain, to those whose baby has just been born, their emotional turmoil and medical development during their baby's hospitalization.

In such moments, a lot of emotions, tears and doubts rise to the surface. On the other hand, the quality of the exchange enables many parents to leave the meeting feeling much more self-confident.

The premature baby's arrival home doesn't always imply a happy ending. The infant may still be suffering from the after-effects of its birth, or the parents are still feeling very vulnerable. Therefore, the possibility of subsequent pediatric and psychological support may arise. It sometimes takes several months before the parents feel sufficiently happy and competent regarding their infant. A future pregnancy, which renews the memory of the former birth, may also require several consultations.

CONCLUSION

A Neonatal Department is a place of high-strung emotions, where the infant's future is in the balance every day. Nevertheless, it is the beginning of life, when psychological moments or transformations are possible and when new links are forged. We are deeply concerned about supporting this relationship between parents and infant and enabling it to flourish. It is a time of psychological transformations for the parents, who have apprehensively become mothers and fathers, which can change their outlook to life. However, this emotional upheaval can also enable the forging of new links. Our goal is to support this parent–infant relationship and to enable it to flourish.

Chapter 10

FAMILY-CENTERED MUSIC THERAPY FOR INFANTS WITH COMPLEX MEDICAL AND SURGICAL NEEDS

Helen Shoemark

INTRODUCTION

The development of surgical and management techniques has ensured the physical survival of newborn infants with complex surgical needs during the first weeks of life. However, the cost of survival is the negative and pervasive experience of this care. The Neonatal Unit (NNU) is not a normal environment for a growing infant and his/her family. Apart from the experiences of pain and discomfort associated with medicals conditions, sensory experiences are altered by physically restrictive conditions, prohibitive monitoring, and intrusive care. The procedures and sensory environment of the NICU (Neonatal Intensive Care Unit) have been shown to have a negative impact on the immediate and long-term neurological development of the infant (Long, et al., 1980; Philbin, et al., 1994; Vimpani; 1999). For the family, the experience of the NNU is highly stressful and profoundly difficult to deal with. Yet parents remain the pivotal source of nurturing, comfort and learning for the infant. It is the intention of the hospital team that the infant will be discharged with a family that is ready to cope and move forward. The hospital experience will hopefully be only a small part of the child's life. Thus the hospital team's focus is on helping the family deal with the immediate situation and prepare for the future. Underlying any early intervention is the premise that the intervention is not for the child alone, but the entire family.

For those infants whose hospital stay is of a long duration, there is a need to introduce formal intervention to maximize all potential for development. While there is a rapidly growing body of literature to give evidence to music as an effective reinforcer (Standley, 1996), we do not have a music therapy literature base for the inclusion of music therapy as early intervention for the long term development of hospitalized infants. More specifically, there is a need for research and documentation of the role of music therapy in supporting the family as the intervention unit, rather than the infant alone.

This chapter will outline clinical insights, philosophy, and research bases for applying music therapy as a family-intervention with hospitalized infants.

Case studies will illuminate the musical material, significant elements of the approach and the connection between theory and practice.

THE UNIT

The following are examples of the clinical application of music therapy in the tertiary Neonatal Unit of the Royal Children's Hospital, Melbourne, Australia. This state-wide service provides 22 beds for infants with complex medical and surgical needs. Eleven beds are Intensive Care, and the other 11 are Special Nursery beds for infants maturing in anticipation of surgery or establishing feeding prior to discharge. All infants are transferred from their delivery hospital. Seven to eight hundred babies in the neonatal stage are admitted annually from Victoria and surrounding states. Care is based on the principle of family-centered care. The staff implement family-care through two professional constructs: case management and primary nursing. Case management is provided by a senior nurse, coordinating all elements of treatment and care, including diagnosis, surgery, pharmacological treatment, nursing care, allied health intervention and family interaction and education. The Case Manager monitors and expedites the scheduling of procedures, information sharing between team members and the family, and timely inclusion of such aspects as parent education and transition to the community in preparation for discharge. Case management offers the family one key person to whom they can refer for consistent and factual information, and gives an assurance that the most efficient and effective treatment/care pathway is being pursued. The Case Manager provides the music therapist with a consistent, dependable source of information when arriving for work on the unit. These benefits are also available from, or strengthened by, a Primary Nursing Team (PNT). A PNT is a small group of nurses who work together to care for the family and infant, ensuring that one of them will be caring for the infant on each shift.

Family-care promotes the empowerment of families in caring and nurturing the infant throughout the admission. The professional team seeks to provide containment for the family and the infant during hospitalization (Paul, 2000). As the stay progresses, this relationship will also include input about practical and developmental matters.

The inclusion of music therapy services on this NNU was originally based upon the request of one parent and the nurses' general premise that music held the promise of psychological benefit for individual infants. Support for the first family's strong desire to provide positive sensory experiences led the nursing team to pursue the possibility of regular service from the Music Therapy Unit. Since that initial request, education and first-hand experience of music therapy has increased the nursing and medical staff's understanding of auditory stimulation. It has also ensured the inclusion of music therapy alongside other interventions.

Specifically prepared music experiences are now understood to be a safe, predictable addition in the care of the most fragile infants (Cassidy & Standley, 1995), therefore forming a reasonable early intervention. The nursing staff makes more than 80% of referrals, and report that music therapy provides a positive starting point—particularly for those families whose infants will remain in hospital for extended periods.

Long Hospitalization

Infants who will be in the NNU for a period of more than 4 weeks form the largest group of referrals for the Music Therapy Unit and are thus the focus for this chapter. The clinical pathway for these infants is highly individual and complex, and as such they are often omitted from research studies. The range of literature on non-medical interventions is not yet well developed. Writing about such work in case study format is intended as a useful starting point for documentation of clinical work with these at–risk infants.

CLINICAL INSIGHTS

The Family

The infant's connection to the family is severed by his transportation from the delivery hospital to the NNU at RCH, Melbourne. By the time they arrive at RCH, infants have already survived invasive medical intervention to sustain life, transportation from the delivery hospital, extensive monitoring, and the commencement of diagnostic tests and standard preparations for immediate surgery. This highly technological and intrusive beginning maximizes the infant's chances for physical survival, but minimizes the opportunity for bonding and nurturing. Parents must contend with the pragmatic reality of administrative procedures, transport arrangements, keeping family members informed and at the same time trying to understand what is happening to their baby.

    The parents' experience of the NICU can cause feelings of disappointment, guilt, sadness and depression, hostility and anger, anxiety, helplessness, grief and loss of self-esteem (Wereszczak, 1997). There may be inner conflicts because this is not the baby they had fantasized about when s/he was in utero (Warren, 2000). The experience of the parent, and particularly the mother, who is still usually the primary caregiver, must be closely monitored. Amidst myriad emotions, the mother is faced with the challenge of learning how to be a mother to this sick newborn (Scharer, 1994). The parents do not know their child as well as the staff seems to due to all the new and strange requirements (Warren, 2000).

Miles & Holditch-Davis (1995) found that maternal recall of the NICU experience was still painful when the child was three and that it had some impact on the parenting of the child. Thompson, et al. (1994) reported that the psychosocial stress of the mother was a more potent influence on developmental outcome than the biological risk experienced by the infant. Therefore, this NNU has instituted parent support and education programs that commence within the first 24 hours and continue throughout the admission.

The aim of professional intervention is to promote family coping strategies by supporting healthy interactions and practical care. The professional team seeks to recognize family strengths and tailor their input to the family's needs and preferences. The role of the music therapist is to encourage existing skills for empowering the parents to nurture the baby through appropriate auditory and tactile stimulation. As the infants' medical condition stabilizes, the parents' gravest fear that the baby may die is diminished. However, it is increasingly accompanied by the practical difficulties of hospitalization over an extended period and concerns about the infant's long-term development.

Family Centered Practice

Dunst, Trivette and Deal advocate that "Families are the critical element in the rearing of healthy, competent, and caring children." (Dunst, Trivette & Deal, 1988). From a survey of Canadian families, Mustard (1999) reported that parenting was a key factor in early child development at all socio-economic levels and that supportive initiatives should commence as soon as possible after birth. The family, as a group of people connected to the infant, should be offered support designed to strengthen their ability to care for each other and successfully move forward. The role of any intervention is to enhance the resources and insights of the family, upon which they base decisions and choices. This approach to intervention strengthens the sustaining and adaptive of the family (Dunst, et al., 1988) and assists them to work through immediate and future situations.

The hospital context can inhibit the creation of more normal support systems (family, friends, mothers' groups etc.), and can even minimize normal contact within the immediate family. When intervention seeks to accommodate this loss, the team is cognizant of various levels of "helping." The principles for intervention have thus been defined:

> 1. To promote positive child, parent and family functioning base intervention efforts on family-identified needs, aspirations, and personal objects.
> 2. To enhance successful efforts towards meeting needs, use existing family functioning style (strength and capabilities) as a basis for promoting the family's ability to mobilize resources.
> 3. To ensure the availability and adequacy of resources for meeting

needs, placing major emphasis on strengthening the family's personal social network as well as promoting of untapped potential sources of informational aid and assistance.

4. To enhance a family's ability to become more self-sustaining with respect to meeting its needs, employ helping behaviors that promote the family's acquisition and use of competencies and skills necessary to mobilize and secure resources (Dunst,, 1988, pp 48).

In this model, the traditional paternalistic relationship in which the therapist "knows best" is replaced by an active partnership that preserves the central role of the parent/s as decision-maker and caregiver. Such a pivotal partnership comes at a key time. Nonetheless (if all goes well), at the time of discharge, the partnership is discarded in favor of more natural relationships with family, friends and the wider community.

Social Context for Early Intervention

Sufficient research has now clearly indicated that the cost of providing thorough, effective and systemic services for families with children under the age of three will reap huge economic savings for society as these children develop (Keating & Hertzmann, 1999). Governments of first world countries have recently begun to promote their "understanding" of this fact as a great social service to their communities. The World Bank states, "The challenge to care for society's youngest members is not just a challenge for a single country or continent; it is a challenge for the entire world community" (Young, 1997).

In Canada, key reports such as *The Early Years* (Mustard, 1999) and the work of the Canadian Institute for Advanced Research Program in Human Development (Keating & Hertzmann, 1999) have persuasively informed the structuring and financing of federal government programs. The Australian government is following suit with the national *Stronger Families and Community Strategy* (2000), advocating early intervention for families with young children. The Department of Family and Community Services states that a focus on prevention of problems in young children will, in the long-term, provide "better outcomes in the [areas of] health, education, employment, and mental health as well as lower crime rates" (Newman, 1999). Features of the *Stronger Families and Community* Strategy include supporting families through times of transition (such as having a baby) and helping them to find their own strengths. For the first time, early intervention is on the political agenda and receiving appropriate funding attention. Their efforts are informed by such organization as the National Investment For The Early Years (NIFTEY), which creates momentum within the community and gives excellent reporting and lobbying power for government action. NIFTEY makes excellent use of the Internet listserv (electronic newsletter with hyperlinks), to keep practitioners, families and decision-makers informed of key government decisions and major projects from around the world.

On the same basis of economic advantage, music therapists have been able to show that those infants receiving music will be discharged several days before their counterparts (Cassidy & Standley, 1995; Schwarz, 1998). These infants are, after all, some of the most expensive patients, costing more than $1400 per day.

Once an infant is discharged from hospital, families should have a much better chance of being linked into convenient effective programs. However, for those infants who are admitted for extended periods, early intervention must commence prior to discharge.

THE IMPACT OF EARLY EXPERIENCES IN LONG-TERM DEVELOPMENT

The "Medical Infant"

Common conditions treated in the NNU include tracheo-esophageal fistula and atresia, gastroschisis, exomphalus, diaphragmatic hernia, and bowel obstruction. In addition, infants born with suspected metabolic, endocrine or gastroenterological diseases are cared for alongside critically ill infants who require additional intensive care treatments with ventilation. Infants may experience pre-operative periods of wellness, crisis, post-operative states, and sometimes death.

The newborn exerts enormous amounts of energy establishing homeostasis of various body systems. Post-natal system balance relies on the achievement of three tasks: 1) establishing homeostasis through self-regulation of arousal (sleep/wake cycle), 2) processing, storing and organizing multiple stimuli, 3) establishing a reciprocal relationship with a primary caretaker and with the environment (Kaminski & Hall, 1996).

Unfortunately, the hospital environment does little to encourage any of these. Non-contingent intervention (e.g. repeated heel-pricks for blood, despite infant protest) denies any reciprocal relationship. Diurnal rhythms are defied by regular and routine care giving, and by the random auditory and visual stimuli of the NICU. The shift-work structure of nursing care means that often care and interaction is offered by an array of people with varying patterns of sensitivity to the infant's non-medical needs. Infants may also suffer from prolonged periods of discomfort or pain associated with wind, nausea, vomiting, or excessive secretions caused by the medical condition. These will cause prolonged or frequent periods in the "active alert" state (restless, agitated movements and grimaces) or "crying" state, which can magnify the energy expenditure of an infant by as much as 200%, and may cause an increase in an infant's basal metabolic rate (Rose & Mayer, 1968).

The energy exerted by a hospitalized infant in order to maintain physical homeostasis allows for very little energy to be expended on the normal development of other skills (e.g. head control). The basic skills that are developed, such as vocal production and head control, can be distorted by the impact of ventilator tubes or long naso-gastric tubes which restrict or impair muscle movement.

The "Developing Infant"

It is now understood that early experiences are not just the passive context for development, but have a decisive impact on the actual architecture of the brain (Vimpani, 1999). The mature organization of the brain will reflect the "quantity, quality and pattern of the somatosensory experiences of the first years of life" (p35, Perry, 1998). Mustard (1999) notes that the positive stimulation achieved through good nurturing helps to strengthen the brain's capacity in functions such as "cognitive development, stable emotions, attachment and normal balanced responses" (p31, Mustard, 1999). There are critical periods for neurological development that are use-dependent and unique to each infant. Synaptic connections that are stimulated will be strengthened, while those not used, are "pruned," based on the experiences of the infant (Cynader & Frost, 1999). Unfortunately, emerging evidence also suggests that those neurons most responsive in critical periods are also likely to be most responsive to stress hormones released during stressful periods.

What then is the impact of the NNU experience on an infant? It is likely that the invasive nature of neonatal care impedes neurological development at a number of levels within the brain because of the chronic and acute stress of the experience. At a neural level, the trauma of invasive procedures and monitoring evokes a response in molecular neurophysiology, creating memories (Perry, 1997). When the memory matches the current experience (e.g., for heel-pricks), the brain's stress-response systems are activated. A common example of NNU acute stress that becomes chronic is the clearing of esophageal secretions in the infant with Esophageal Atresia (EA).The EA infant has an esophagus that ends in a sack, rather than connecting to the stomach. Swallowed secretions pool in the bottom of the sack and must be removed with a small suctioning tube to prevent aspiration. During the procedure the infant cannot breathe, s/he often gags and responds with considerable physiological and behavioral distress. During the "quiet alert" state this may be done every 20 minutes. If the infant is unsettled or distressed it may be as often as every 5 minutes. It is completed less frequently during sleep. Infants develop protective strategies such as closing the mouth tightly to prevent access or putting a hand over the mouth to prevent the nurse from inserting the tube. The infant is not protected by these strategies, nor by the parent who must allow the procedure to be repeated despite the infant's protests. This brief but acutely invasive procedure continues to be part of the care regime until the infant is a suitable weight for surgery to repair the gap. The infant experiences the distress hundreds of times.

Such a procedure must be classified as traumatic as it overwhelms the infant and negatively disrupts homeostasis. Perry (1998) notes that trauma creates a persisting set of compensatory responses that in turn create a new but less flexible state of equilibrium.

The strongest hope available to the infant is that the family will be able to provide stimulation which by its positive and nurturing value, will counter-act the barrage of negative stimulation. Cynader and Frost (1999) conclude that the best strategies to prevent the impact of chronic stress are to create "sufficiently enriched environments so that critical period developments proceed optimally, or to diagnose problems early and attempt therapy promptly" (p184). The family, supported and informed by the professional team, provide habilitative stimulation, rather than waiting to provide rehabilitation services later in the infant's life.

Early intervention strategies begin then with a clear understanding of the infant's medical status and abilities, and the strengths and needs of the family. Music therapy is the first face–to–face allied health intervention offered to families because it is a simple, positive intervention which can empower families through the utilization of pre-existing strengths. Formal face–to–face intervention may be necessary where a parent is not available on a daily basis or not at a time when the baby can be stimulated (eg. during the day). As critical windows for development occur, formal intervention is employed to maximize the opportunities which, in normal circumstances, would be fulfilled by the incidental activity of everyday life.

Professional methods such as multi-modal stimulation (White-Traut, et al., 1999; Standley, 1998; Shoemark, 1999), infant-directed singing (Trainor, 1996) and programmed recorded music (Cassidy & Standley, 1996) maybe employed to ameliorate the effect of the immediate crisis and lay pathways for healthy development into the future.

RESEARCH BASIS

Live Music Making

The modality for face–to–face intervention is sung and spoken voice. The applications of infant-directed speech and singing have been described by the author elsewhere (Shoemark, 1998; 1999). In principle, infants and prefer their own mothers' voices (DeCasper & Fifer, 1980). The structure and content of the vocalizations is thus informed by principles of infant-directed singing (Trainor, 1996) and Communicative Musicality (Malloch, 1999). Fernald's (1989) pioneering recognition of maternal intonation patterns formed the basis for the formal recognition of maternal–infant communication in the Communicative

Musicality model (Malloch, 1999). Communicative Musicality articulates the successful patterns in timing, pitch contour and vocal timbre that occur within and between vocalization of the caregiver and the infant. It consists of the elements *pulse* (timing regularities in and between the caregiver's and infant's vocalization), *quality* (the pitch and timbre contours) and *narrative* (the combination of pulse and quality) (Malloch, 1999).

Malloch also notes that the rhythm, melody and timbre of a mother's voice are all regulated in predictable ways, matching the demonstrated preferences of the infant (Trehub, Unyk & Trainor, 1993), and are modified as the infant matures (Kitamura & Burnham, *under review*). The infant and parent listen to one another's sounds, creating co-operative patterns of vocalization. Malloch's micro-analyses of these vocalization reveal that beyond encouraging signals from his mother, the infant seeks signals that are appropriately timed and inflected (Nadel, et al., 1999). Indeed, in optimal communication, expressive phrases are precisely alternated or between the infant and the adult (Tronick et al., 1980). This attunement between mother and infant is critical. If it is lacking, as often occurs in maternal post-natal depression (Papousek & Papousek, 1997), both parties suffer.

In the production of vocal stimulation, the music therapist is vigilant in creating responses that respect such parameters. The therapeutic partnership accommodates the subtle alterations caused by the infant's status.

The physiological basis for using recorded music with preterm infants is well established in the American music therapy literature (Caine, 1992; Cassidy & Ditty, 1998; Cassidy & Standley, 1995; Schwarz & Ritchie, 1999; Standley, 1996). This research gives clear support for the safe use of recorded music with the most fragile infants, and its inclusion offers a source of external regulation in aiding homeostasis. Most of the recorded music used in the NNU is based on the principles of sedative music with a minimum of change and range in the elements (Shoemark, 1998).

Description of Musical Material

All live music created by the music therapist on the NNU is vocal and thus directed by infant-directed singing and musical communication. The simple personal philosophy of the unit's music therapist has long been that music comprises a "pool" of elements that may be more potently employed in isolation than in combination (Shoemark, 1994). A combination of these elements will evoke unique experiences for the therapist and the client, and thus the effect must be closely monitored.

Not surprisingly, the "pool" of elements includes melody, pulse, rhythm, harmony, tempo, pitch, timbre, attack, duration, register, dynamics, phrasing and silence. The author has found in her work with children with profound multiple disabilities and children in the pediatric wards at RCH, that they definitely favor one or two elements.

In the NNU, the employment and conscious manipulation of single musical elements allows the music therapist to assess those aspects of auditory stimulation that the infant can tolerate and enjoy. For instance, where an infant is easily over-stimulated by sudden sound, the exclusion of harsh vocal "attack" such as the sounds "p" and "ch" might enable the infant to tolerate more vocal stimulation than if that one element were included.

Phrasing is sometimes a contentious inclusion in the "pool" as it must rely upon other elements for its creation. It is included because it has often been observed to be the essence of a child's musical expression and we now know that phrasing is a fundamental attribute of mother-infant communication (Malloch, 1999). To emulate that element of communication in music therapy is to create a safe "environment" for self-expression. Further, the music therapist discerns the musical features of the mother's voice (such as register and timbre) and employs those features to provide a more accessible stimulus for the infant. The following case is a good example of this.

CHRISTOPHER - *The music therapist arrived on the ward to find Christopher, a recent referral, in a highly distressed state: howling, sweating and frantically moving his limbs. He was hungry, unable to be fed and his mother was not due at the hospital until later that morning. Strategies that had been previously successful—singing short phrases including open–vowels; making comforting sounds such as "sh–sh–sh" and "there–there;" singing his name; patting him lightly and rapidly, or slowly and with vigor; rocking him and shifting planes (from horizontal to vertical)—all had short-lived success. His "status" was modified to "unsettled" (no longer distressed) by the time his mother arrived. She immediately spoke to him in a high-pitched voice with exaggerated melodic intonation, to which he responded with smiles, gurgles and a rapid on-set of sleeping. Later that week, when the music therapist was again faced with Christopher in a highly distressed state, she spoke and then sang to him in a style which reflected his mother's high register and exaggerated melodic intonation. Christopher calmed and was in a quiet alert state by the time his mother arrived. It was evident that the imitation of the maternal voice made the formal intervention much more accessible and useful for the infant.*

Short improvised melodic phrases may be used to reflect the infant's breathing, muscle tone (if still), body movements and facial expressions. In the first instance, an open vowel or humming may be used as this offers the least forceful approach. An exception to this is the inclusion of the infant's name, which will usually be perceived as a familiar, sound and thus does not induce a stress response. The engagement using pre-determined patterns of maternal interaction, particularly specific intonation patterns require the music therapist to honestly address issues of transference and counter–transference. Professional supervision is undertaken so that the music therapist may keep her role and interaction clear.

SPECIFIC ELEMENTS OF APPROACH
Broadly defined, the role of the music therapist is to:
- counter-act the extraordinary environment and sensory experience base
- educate families to achieve long-term benefits
- provide appropriate developmental opportunities— particularly in self-expression and vocal interaction

This is achieved through a range of musically-informed methods that are described within the context of the case studies below.

CASE STUDIES

Counteracting the Environment

It is acknowledged that the in-utero auditory experience of the infant is also recognized after birth (DeCasper & Fifer, 1980). The full-term newborn can discriminate his own mother's voice reading as opposed to another woman reading and displays preference for stories heard in utero. The auditory pathway is commonly the most intact form of perception at birth, with perception discernable by 24 weeks and a consistent response to stimulation at about 28 weeks gestation. The music therapist is able to engage this experience and create early positive experiences to maximize homeostasis and learning, while monitoring and specific procedures may restrict other sensory systems.

As noted above, stressful procedures cannot be avoided, but positive associations with voices and music can be used to minimize the magnitude and duration of the stress response.

SANDRA — COUNTER-ACTING THE IMPACT OF REPEATED INVASIVE PROCEDURES. *Sandra was born at 27–weeks gestation, and was transferred on day one because of a bowel obstruction. Investigative surgery revealed a significant passage affected by necrotizing enterocolitis (NEC), which was removed. She was ventilated and endured other invasive handling and monitoring for further evaluation. Sandra's primary nursing team was concerned that all her sensory experiences were stressful and without counter-acting positive experiences. She did not protest about invasive procedures and thus the nurses reported that she seemed withdrawn.*

Her family was present only in the evenings when the procedures had concluded for the day. Sandra was referred at one week for the inclusion of recorded music in her care plan and was assessed for state organization via a simple observation format constructed from the key assessment points of

D'Apolito (1991), Als (1986), and Standley (1997). This tri-phase format (Standley, 1997) assessed physiological and behavioral stability across three 10–minute units, the first without intervention, the second during the intervention of playing recorded music, and the third post-music. The post-music phase is included to preclude a deregulating effect on heart or respiration once the music is discontinued (Standley & Moore, 1995). Sandra responded favorably to the music, with slightly improved oxygen saturation. She showed no signs of deregulation when the music was stopped.

A meeting with the parents revealed that they were pleased to know that some positive experience were planned for Sandra, and asked to be actively involved. During this first meeting various options were discussed and the underlying rationale explained. Two ideas were suggested: recorded sedative music to promote recovery following intrusive procedures and a tape of the family members talking to Sandra to be used at other times to promote a quiet alert state (preferred for feeding). The family chose to pursue both. The parameters given to them for the tape of voices were to sit in a comfortable place at home and discuss a positive experience, such as an all-expenses paid family holiday. The suggestion of a topic ensures that the tone of voice is predominantly positive (Lesley Tan, audiologist, personal communication, 1997). The tape was produced within the week, and a notice placed at Sandra's bedside to alert nursing staff not to use this tape at the time of procedures, but at any other time.

Within the family- practice model, the acknowledgement of family musical preferences is central in promoting the family's strengths. For the therapist to choose musical styles that are foreign to the family would deny the partnership, diminishing the family's sense of control in the nurturing care of the infant. It had also been found in the NNU, that when given a selection of stylistically familiar and unfamiliar music, families reported using only the familiar music.

In the case of Sandra's family, the preferences were for Celtic instrumental, Irish female vocalists, light modern orchestral and no classical music. The family was educated about a further parameter: the music must be sedative in quality (Lorch, Lorch, Diefendorf & Earl, 1994). Given the family preferences, the music therapist created compilation tapes. The family was then able to introduce the music to Sandra, thus promoting Sandra's positive association between her family's nurturing and the recorded music.

Sandra had become much more medically stable by 32 weeks. The recorded music was made available to her on an "as-needs" basis at the discretion of the nursing staff. The nurses were instructed that the music should not be played for more than 5 minutes per hour, in order to avoid over-stimulation (Standley, 1997) and retain maximum efficacy. The nurses did not strictly adhere to the short program as they became busy and forgot to turn off the tape at the appropriate time. Before resorting to re-taping the music into 5–minute segments, it was observed that Sandra was not adversely effected by the music, which continued for 30 minutes (one side of the tape). After discussion with the Primary Nurse Team, it was decided to change the instruction to a maximum of one side of the tape per hour. The clinical reality reflected the need for minimal intervention by the nursing staff beyond assessing her on-going behavioral response. The nurses did report that Sandra seemed "more relaxed" and quietly alerted to the sound of her brother's voice when he arrived on the unit.

The recorded music remained useful to Sandra throughout her 12–month hospitalization and on subsequent admissions, when she was placed on different wards where the staff did not know her. During her final admission at 13 months old, I visited her to find her obviously distressed, crying and straining her body. I held her, patted her and quietly sang the Brahms lullaby from her favorite tape. After I had sung this just a few times, she made eye-contact with me and emitted some small, harsh, plaintive cries. This evoked strong maternal feelings in me, as she seemed to plead with me for some kind of rescue. It seemed that she could no longer continue the battle for life. As I sang, she closed her eyes and slowly relaxed into a state of sleep. She was taken to Intensive Care two days later when her respiratory system had failed. At this point she was placed on ventilatory support and sedated. It seemed unlikely that she would survive. I sat and watched her assisted breathing for some time before singing the theme from two days earlier. The orienting response of a slight drop in her heart rate led me to believe that she was aware of the singing. I maintained the theme over a few minutes, allowing her to habituate to the stimulus, then departed. My final contact with her came on the morning before her death. Her parents had made the decision to turn off the ventilation support system the next day, and welcomed those people who knew her to come and say a private farewell. We recalled the way she had reacted to the sound of her 4–year old brother's voice on the family tape, and how she had become alert to the sound of his voice as he arrived on the NNU. We spoke of the relaxation she had experienced through her recorded music. I spoke of the courage and strength they had all shared. During ceremonies for staff, friends, and family to say farewell the next day, her music was played in acknowledgement of its importance in her life.

HILARY — CONSISTENCY OF COUNTER-ACTIVE SUPPORT THROUGH MULTIPLE ADMISSIONS. *Hilary was born at 36 weeks gestation with gastroschisis. She was transported from her interstate delivery hospital. Her mother, Margaret, requested music therapy, and at my arrival said, "I have 4 other children at home, but I just don't know what to do with this one. What can you suggest?" Hilary was unsettled and spending long periods in a distressed state when making the transition from wake to sleep. She had no self-soothing behaviors and while she engaged with her mother in other states, she was unable to make use of maternal stimulation to settle down. I decided to commence with recorded music, as Margaret was very accessible and otherwise working well with Hilary. Discussion revealed a maternal preference for classical and Celtic music. The main benefit of recorded music were explained thus: that the music could provide an external regulator to which her physiological system would entrain and she would readily fall asleep. Margaret agreed to commence with one tape containing slow movements of Mozart symphonies and another with instrumental Celtic lullabies.*

Margaret was shown how to use the music—placement of the player, volume, frequency of play and observation of the infant for signs of a stress response. The music was introduced during quiet alert and sleeping phases (Shoemark, 1998). Hilary showed a positive reaction to the music within a few days, responding with settling behaviors. Margaret was able to decide when to include the music in her care plan for periods of distress. After one week, she reported that the music evoked a release in muscle tone in Hilary's face and body. After a few more days, Margaret noted that Hilary sought to locate the tape player in her bed when the music commenced, and she would calm down and fall asleep.

As Hilary grew, she remained in hospital, becoming very aware of the cues of positive and negative stimulation. At the commencement of one interaction, I I had not washed my hands. As I moved to the basin I assured this happy and smiling infant I would "be right back." As I ripped the paper towel from the dispenser, I looked up to see her facial expression turn to one of fear and tears bursting forth. The cue of hand washing had come to mean a negative intervention. At this point I turned to her tape player and started her music, alerted the nurse to what had occurred, and departed. The music was a reassuring counter-active stimulus for Hilary in this situation. When I returned the next day, I washed my hands prior to entering her room.

At 4 months old, Hilary was transported back to the unit of her local metropolitan hospital with her tape collection. Her mother telephoned to tell me that the potentially negative impact of this foreign environment was ameliorated by the presence of her tape collection. Prior to discharge from RCH, the collection had grown in diversity of style to reflect Hilary's new found strengths and interaction. Her mother said that she had explained to the local nursing team how Hilary responded to her recorded music, asking them to play the music at the first signs of fatigue. She was delighted to report that regardless of which nurse cared for her, Hilary continued to respond favorably to her music.

At the age of 13 months, after several months at home, Hilary unexpectedly returned to the Intensive Care Unit of RCH with a respiratory infection. Though not admitted to the NNU, the family called me. I discovered that they had been transferred quickly, and I presumed that they were in need of duplicate tapes for Hilary. However, Margaret assured me they had brought their own copies and in fact they had a different request. Hilary's 12–year–old sister had made the journey with her sister and mother. The father and other siblings had all stayed at home. Shelley was her mother's companion and assistant on this journey with Hilary and she asked me if her siblings could have new tapes for Hilary. She noted that when Hilary had been very sick, the very serious music "matched" Hilary's state. But now that she was much better, they felt the music did not "fit" Hilary or them. She revealed that at home her mother placed a tape player in the hallway at bedtime so that they could all listen to the restful music.

Indeed, the slow Mozart movements now seemed to be a somber reminder of Hilary's difficult beginning. The siblings had discussed the music and wanted to keep the other "light orchestral" music and felt that "some singing" would be appropriate.

Over two sessions, Shelley and I listened to and talked about appropriate music. Shelley earnestly took the responsibility of choosing the music. Three categories were decided upon which reflected the level of "action" in the music and in the home: sleeping, resting and playing. We allocated her preferred music to these categories and I suggested that she and the others could produce covers for the tapes so that they might be used appropriately at home. The new tapes were prepared prior to Hilary's discharge. They included several "allegro" movements by Mozart, Irish female singing, modern lullabies sung by an American vocalist, and some children's artists, including Raffi (Canada) and The Wiggles (Australia). Shelley was very proud and delighted about the prospect of getting them home.

For this infant, recorded music had become a reliable source of comfort, associated with the nurturing context of her family. The use of the music was not bound by the hospital experience. It had become a source of relaxation for all family members. However, it was clear that specific music did have a limited life, and further music was needed to reflect the family's evolving hope about Hilary's life. The education of the sister about the characteristics of music enabled the family to actively choose the music themselves.

Educating Families to Achieve Long-Term Benefits

Sometimes the incredibly complex context of the NNU precludes the parent from accessing their pre-existing strengths to work through the experience with their child. Supported exploration of existing strengths may re-focus a parent's ability to bring a "healthy" part of her/himself to the infant. The music therapist may discuss the parent's musicality and where appropriate to the individual, model how to use that musicality with the infant.

DYLAN — UTILIZATION OF MOTHERS FORMER FRAME OF REFERENCE TO ENCOURAGE NURTURING. *Dylan was born just prior to full-term with a very rare gastrointestinal condition that caused frequent periods of great pain. He was understandably distressed and irritated by all manner of mild distraction. Dylan's mother Alison, was a professional woman in her mid-30s. This was her second pregnancy, but first birth. She was vigilant in her daily attention to him and in her pursuit of strategies to help him deal with his frequent pain. The referral for music therapy came about because Alison had expressed a love of music and noted that other infants were receiving recorded music. In early discussion with her, I discovered that she had been a member of a women's a cappella singing group prior to Dylan's birth, but had discontinued singing since his hospitalization. I explored with her the sensation of singing with others* and the repertoire of the group. Through singing small snippets of the repertoire, Alison visibly relaxed and recalled the joy in the physical act of singing. My suggestion that she could bring this to Dylan was met with initial uncertainty. In her role as mother there was little joy because of her inability to "save" Dylan from his pain. I singing to Dylan, who responded with calm interest. When we sang to him together, he rewarded Alison with a smile.

Because he could be disconnected from feeding tubes and monitoring equipment for several hours each day, Alison was able to take Dylan home for a few hours each afternoon. I suggested that during their home visits, she should sing to him. After a week she reported that she was singing every day and believed that Dylan was more relaxed. In desperation one day, she had sung to him in the car as he became unsettled. The singing distracted him until he fell asleep. After two weeks, Alison reported that she now sang improvised tunes to him everywhere about all activities of his day.

Dylan's prognosis—which took 6 months to determine—was that the condition would result in his death by the age of about two years. When he died unexpectedly at 10 months, Alison stated that the joy of their relationship began in the shared experience of music.

Providing Appropriate Developmental Opportunities

Despite all other restrictions on interaction, aural/oral interaction is usually possible. Significant support for the bonding process between mother and infant is achieved in the preservation and development of vocal interaction. The loss of positive vocal expression is common for infants with gastroschisis (who vomit repeatedly), infants with Bronchopulmonary Dysplasia who cannot tolerate mild stimulation, and infants who have been cannulated (tracheostomy) because of a compromised airway. Without an avenue for being heard, infants can become frustrated and resort to strong negative strategies such as sudden and immediate vigorous crying and body movements to obtain a response from caregivers. Such behavior consumes valuable energy which would otherwise be used to heal and grow.

JAMIE — CREATING A VOICE FOR THE CANNULATED INFANT. *Jamie was born at 41 weeks gestation to a Pacific Island family. An ultrasound during pregnancy had detected a giant exomphalus (an external sac containing organs). The large size of the exomphalus put significant strain on his heart and lungs necessitating ventilatory support. Jamie had a tracheostomy tube inserted as he was distressed by the intrusive and distressing nature of long-tube nasal CPAP (continuous pressure air pathway).*

Jamie could be a bright and happy infant despite his physical restrictions. However, he was referred because of frequent periods of distress resulting in sudden oxygen desaturation. He was unable to move his body because of the weight of the exomphalus and the restrictive ventilation regime. He would become frustrated, flailing his limbs about, perspiring and "howling" without voiced sound as the tracheostomy tube was situated below the vocal cords. The long-term impact of these frequent and repeated periods of distress remained very secondary to the immediate life-threatening drop in his oxygen level. I created a small selection of recorded music (light orchestral, female vocal lullabies) that was successful in preventing some episodes of distress if it was turned on when Jamie was unsettled but not yet distressed.

In a subsequent review of his treatment I noted that it was only during these periods of great distress, when Jamie protested vigorously, that he could make himself heard via the spluttering secretions of his tracheostomy tube. I felt that an alternate source of positive audible output was required to promote his positive presence in that environment. A set of variously sized bells was strung on one-inch wide elastic, and threaded across his cot in the vicinity of his feet. All members of his team were instructed to respond with clear vocal and facial expression each time he produced a sound by touching the bells with his feet. Within days, he had developed the skill to purposely strike the bells with his feet. Nurses would respond to him quickly with positive facial expressions and verbal reflections such as "Are you a happy boy today Jamie?" or "Who is making that lovely sound? Oh it's Jamie!" I observed that if they were not able to respond immediately, the nursing staff would call out to him from wherever they were in the room, saying such things as "I can hear you Jamie, I'll be there soon." His family and caregivers noted that while Jamie continued to have some periods of distress, he was able to initiate and respond to positive moments with his family and staff. It was the basis upon which further early intervention was begun.

Conclusion

There is so much for parents to do in surviving the experience of hospitalization of their newborn infant and yet—central to it all—is the need to feel that they can keep their baby safe. The purpose of early intervention is to give the family strength in mastering this fundamental role. While singing and playing recorded music are not of themselves profound acts, they can keep the thread of the infant-parent bond alive until such time as more normal sources of nurturing are available. As the infant matures and is more stable, the music becomes the positive space in which the parent–infant relationship is intact, and not governed by the medical and nursing care. It is a space that accommodates the experiences of hospitalization, but gives counteractive experiences to enrich development. To sing together, to express the shared joy, creates moments that form precious building blocks for neuronal development and cherished memories for everyone involved.

Chapter 11

A CLINICAL MODEL OF MUSIC THERAPY IN THE NICU

Joanne V. Loewy

INTRODUCTION

The following chapter addresses the institution of a music therapy program in the neonatal intensive care unit. Rationale for program development is based upon the premise that the therapeutic process of sound and awareness of the sound environment begins in the womb. As the fetus develops auditory perception, the synchronicity between mother and neonate is an essential aspect of development. As the infant enters the world, attention to the sound environment can be continually monitored. This is especially true for the premature infant, who is at risk in its growth and development. The implementation of a music therapy program requires prolonged observation, research review and presentation. This combination led to the development of an NICU Music Therapy Program in the NICU at Beth Israel Medical Center in the United States. This chapter discusses the implementation of a music therapy program including research and the presentation of areas of need; the development of a referral and assessment protocol, which includes private sessions with infants and parents; and specific interventions that address the detrimental noise levels through environmental music therapy. Clinical implications are highlighted as well as aspects of treatment that are necessary for on-going involvement of a music therapy team from a baby–parent–staff–environmental perspective. The model that is presented in the following pages is based on the NICU Music Therapy Program as developed by Andrew Stewart, Brian Abrams, Kristen Stewart, Ming-Chen Lu and Steve Schneider from 1999–2001.

LITERATURE REVIEW

The use of music and sound in treating neonates, infants and pregnant mothers has received significant attention in the past decade. The fields of medicine, music therapy, MusicMedicine, nursing, child life and music education have offered unique perspectives on how music, sound, music therapy and music psychotherapy can benefit both the developing fetus, the pregnant mother and the infant through both physiological and psychological parameters.

The pregnancy experience for the fetus involves primary sounds. The rhythm and meter of the mother's heart beat and the unique timbre of the womb sounds provide the initial overture for a physiological interplay of development that both mother and fetus experience for many months.

The importance of this relationship has been realized and the application of music in prenatal care is a growing area in the health arena (Lindquist, 1985; Liebman, 1989; McKinney, 1990). Schwartz (2000) noted that prenatal sound stimulation can increase newborn head circumference, a strong developmental indicator. It is important to consider his assertion that fetal hearing "...is probably the major component of learning dependant synaptic pruning and sprouting." This premise is supported by DeCasper and Spence (1986) whose research reflects the recognition of auditory stimulation presented to newborns in the prenatal phase. The importance of these physiological implications of sound and organized sound—music—are well warranted.

The fetus is part of a system, dependant upon the physical and emotional factors of another human being. From music therapy and MusicMedicine perspectives, working with meter and the rates of breath and heartbeats of both mother and fetus within the context of entrainment can have important synchronous medical implications. The life rhythm of the heart is the first sound that a developing fetus hears in the womb. The significance of a steady pulse has been noted as a primary means of awareness, as in the concept of basic beat (Nordoff-Robbins, 1975), and has been an indicant of neurological functioning in older adults (Clair, et al., 1995; Tomaino, 1999). Complementary medical programs have incorporated aspects of rhythm and breath work into a method of enhancing relaxation in pregnant women. Breath attunement has been effectively influenced through music therapy and MusicMedicine. Since the body actively uses breath to play wind instruments and to sing or tone, the use of these applications can be efficiently monitored and physiologically served through music therapy.

With the exception of Nöcker-Ribaupierre (1999), the developing relationship between mother and fetus has received little attention in the music therapy literature. McKinney (1990) has provided a review of music therapy used in obstetrics and has cited 3 studies, incorporating GIM (Linquist, 1985), music therapy using directed imagery and recorded music (Winslow, 1986), and progressive muscle relaxation using recorded music (Liebman, 1989). She has provided insight as how music therapy may be used. In addition, she has presented psychological rationale supporting the recognition that high anxiety and unresolved conflicts during pregnancy may have negative effects on the progress of labor and the incidence of obstetric complications.

When one considers implementing music therapy in the NICU, the environment cannot be overlooked. The sound environment needs to be nurturing and womb-like. The role of the parent/s and staff in enhancing growth for premature infants should reduce stress for the neonate and parent/s. Parent/s of premature babies often feel that their role is minimal. This may set-up feelings of guilt and inadequacy. Parents often feel powerless at a time when they thought they would have full control (pregnancy). Therefore, teaching ways to provide and nurture within the baby's sound environment may be medically advantageous while at the same time critical in the bonding process.

In the supplement of the *Journal of Perinatology* published through the American Academy of Pediatrics (December, 2000), 21 articles addressed the influence of auditory experience on the fetus, newborn and pre-term infant. This journal addresses the physiological responses of the fetus to sound and the acoustic environment of hospital nurseries, among other topics. Controlled studies cited in the journal demonstrate that the sound and language of mothers and their voices used during pregnancy are preferable to a foreign language, even if spoken by the same woman (Gebhardt & Abrams, 2000). Graven (2000), in writing about sound and the developing infant in the NICU, writes: "Recorded sound cannot replace interactive experience with another human, preferably a parent. They (earphones and other devices that deliver noise or music directly to the infant's ears) should never replace contingent human voice exposure." The rationale made against recording devices in a section following this statement warns that devices attached to the infant's ear cannot be easily monitored and therefore the decibel level may be threatening.

Fifer and Moon (2000) have cited a study (Hepper, et al., 1993) in this journal comparing fetus response to a recording of the mother's voice as compared to a stranger's illustrating little variance. Yet, as the mother's *live* voice was compared to a *recording* of her voice, a greater response was indicated by fewer movements. These authors set out to illustrate that 36 week old fetuses cannot seemingly discriminate between the mother's voice and a strange female voice. Emphasis is placed on the fact that auditory discrimination occurred more critically through the means of transmission. This has important implications for the music therapist. The elements of energy and attunement involved in creating live music provide the utmost vitality for the therapeutic encounter. One wonders why there is an abundance of tape-recorded music and studies involving sound recordings in NICUs in the United States. The greatest need for music therapy in the NICU is the challenge that addresses how the natural sounds of a neonates body function can be sustained (sucking, caloric intake, sleep enhancement, pain tolerance/avoidance) or altered (decrease heart rate, increase oxygen saturation, respiratory function, seizure) through implementing entrained toning, rhythm and breath with infants and also within the parent–infant relationship.

PROGRAM INSTITUTION

Music Therapy Consultation

The first aspect of building a program involves observation and team shadowing. The use of observation cannot be overestimated in the ICU environment. Prior to any program recommendations, the music therapy team at Beth Israel Medical Center spent 5 months attending rounds and approximately 2.5 hours per week observing the patients. It was important to learn and understand the disciplines involved in the care of the babies and parents. Each discipline provided a unique aspect of treatment. There are areas in which music therapy crosses into the team's domains, and areas that are specific to our discipline.

The observation period often involves asking questions that clarify policies and procedures already in place. Other concerns include how and if music therapy may be indicated. The therapist suggests how it may best be implemented. These kinds of questions create opportunities and provide a period of time in which the staff envisions how music therapy might compliment and/or expand the range of services that are provided.

Under observation, the medical needs and psychosocial issues of the babies and families become apparent. Though each case is unique, there are common aspects of care. Respiratory distress, meconium aspiration, neonatal abstinence syndrome, sepsis and intracranial hemorrhage are common syndromes along with a host of symptoms that can be addressed through team strategizing.

Program Proposal

The 2nd level of program development involves effective proposal development in a simple written document that is based on a complete review of the literature. There has been an increase in NICU music therapy research within the past 10 years. Ideally, the music therapist has compiled notation on the areas of need that have been presented in weekly rounds and through observation as well.

Supporting how the needs of the infants have been addressed through published documentation is a necessity. Music therapists such as Cassity and Ditty (1998), Collins and Kuck (1991), Nöcker-Ribaupierre (1998), Lenz (1998), Standley (1998), Shoemark (1998) and Burke et al. (1995) have laid the groundwork that has explicated convincing research and clinical practice in the effects of music therapy in the NICU. Doctors and nurses have interest in the fetus' hearing capacity and its effect upon development.

The following three postulates were developed as a means of providing rationale for the use of music therapy in the NICU. The postulates, presented to the Director of Neonatology and to the 5 attending neonatologists at Beth Israel Medical Center prior to program implementation, concern the significance of sound and music in the NICU. Each postulate features a particular area of the neonate's development, and is based upon available data, supporting significant areas. The postulates highlight particular aspects of how music therapy may serve the clinical (medical, emotional, psychosocial) needs of infants in the NICU; thus providing a basis for evaluating the effectiveness of music therapy with respect to a specific area of NICU care is imperative.

POSTULATE 1: The current level of noise in the NICU provides an inappropriate sensory environment for the premature infant.

a) Sustained noise above 45dB may result in cochlea damage (Stennert, et al., 1978; Zahr & Traversay, 1995, 1995; Nzama, et al: 1995).

b) This noise is usually produced by machinery in the NICU-specifically from ventilators and incubators.
100 dB—monitor alarms, telephones, cabinet doors
110 dB—closing incubator porthole
(American Academy of Pediatrics, 2000)

POSTULATE 2: Infants begin to hear at >19 weeks and can be provided with opportunities to organize and regulate their environment. Music can assist in this process.

a) Ultrasound studies reflect that at 16 weeks gestation, the fetus can respond to outside sound (Hepper & Shahidullah, 1994).

b) Music can be used to initiate states of relaxed awareness. This can be particularly effective in situations where music can mask noxious stimuli. A state of relaxation may facilitate the newborn's ability to regulate his behavioral state organization despite the noise levels in the hospital nursery. Sample size 20—one group pre-post design (Kaminski, J., & Hall, 1996).

c) Infants have a predisposition to musical consonance (ordered, predictable melodic and rhythmic structure) versus dissonance (noise, unordered sound). Dissonant sounds made infants "jumpy." Infants showed longer motoric attending behaviors when hearing the consonant vs. dissonant version of the same melody. Sample size 32 (4 months), 16 males, 16 females (Kagan & Zentner, 1996).

d) Stability of state organization appears to be an important characteristic of newborns. The inter-uterine music provides a means for the fetus to adapt and mature. The music within the womb is plentiful. The sounds of blood through the placenta are heard at a loud level—between 70–80dB (Gerhardt & Abrams, in: Schwartz & Ritchie, 1999).

POSTULATE 3: Music therapy can decrease the stress response and increase oxygen levels and weight gain in the neonate.

a) Increase in oxygen saturation and decrease levels of agitation. Sample size 17, 24–37 weeks. Compared 10 mins. music and breath sounds to 10 mins control (Collins & Kuck, 1991). Sample size 20 (Standley & Moore, 1995).

b) Lullabies used reflected fewer episodes of stress behaviors and oxygen desaturation. Sample size 52, 26–38 weeks; 22 males, 32 females (Caine, 1992). lso sample size 4 (Burke, et al., 1995 Suctioning and MT).

c) Music showed a 3–5 day earlier discharge (Caine, 1992; Coleman, Pratt, Stoddard, Gerstman, & Abel, 1998).

d) Weight–gain: infants in music group vs. mother's voice vs. control (NICU)–music group gained weight faster. 26–33 weeks gestational age. 153 infants (Chapman, 1978) 52 infants: mean weight loss 50% less for music group (Caine, 1992; Standley, 1998).

Results: Program Implementation

The postulates address the premise and rationale that is supported by literature citations. This provides a mechanism that calls upon the need for music therapy intervention. The Criteria for Referral correlates with the postulates and provides succinct areas of need and how music therapy might address medical, emotional and psychosocial aspects of care.

The Criteria for Referral was developed for purposes of clarity and explanation. Based on the literature and attending neonatologist's recommendations, the age of >32 weeks was established. Allowances for referrals prior to >32 weeks are made on a case by case basis.

The Criteria for Referral describes what a clinical music therapy intervention might look and/or sound like. The interventions that are used in the Armstrong Music Therapy Program primarily involve the use of live music. Therefore, simple descriptions of the instruments that are used, as well as the technique, its application and purpose provide rationale for staff. In this way, future skepticism is limited. Having a document that exemplifies the referral criteria has been useful to implement, especially in the hospital environment where nurses and other staff rotate and shifts change frequently.

Team members may have concerns about the amount of stimulation music therapy induces. It is important to use a sound meter, ensuring that the decibel level will not exceed 66dB. It is necessary to organize therapy time with the nurses in order that optimal cluster care can be provided. The nurses are aware of the infant's feeding schedule and may know particular times when the infants are prone to be irritable. Nurses know also when tests and procedures are scheduled and can assist in the implementation of music therapy at such times.

MUSIC THERAPY REFERRAL CRITERIA

Referrals may be made by the nurse practitioner, patient care manager and residents but must have the consent of the attending physician and the parent/caretaker.

Age: >32 weeks unless approved by the attending on a case by case basis.

I. BONDING:

Parents and infants (identified by the team) that are in need of collaborative experiences may be referred. Incorporating Brazelton's Neonatal Behavioral Assessment Scale, musical focus will emphasize infant–parent attachment. Music and soft singing with skin to skin contact will be encouraged. Melodic (3–5 note) vocalizations will be modeled and simple lullabies will be encouraged for use by mother/dad/caretaker. The parent–infant dynamic will be strengthened as the use of soft sounds (repeated sung phrases) will be patterned for use during times of sleep, transitions, and/or separations.

II. IRRITABILITY — CRYING (INTENSE HIGH PITCHED):

Music (lullabies and toning) will be offered as a means to contain the sound environment for the infant in distress. Toning will be provided as a blanket of steady sound to comfort and sustain a homeostatic environment. Tones enable the infant to trust his/her surroundings and offer an atmosphere of predictability. Human voice sounds made through vocal tones provide an atmosphere of safety which induces sleep and assists in relaxation.

III. RESPIRATORY DIFFICULTIES:

The Gato box (also called a tongue or slit drum) and breath sounds can be useful in helping the infant synchronize and regulate the rhythm of his/her breath. The Gato box provides a predictable rhythm that mimics the sound of a human heart. The infant can entrain to the provided rhythm which can lengthen and ease the meter of the breath. The breath voice is soothing and provides a flowing release of oxygen which can enhance the breathing process. The ocean drum is an inter-uterine sound environment that provides safety and familiarity, stimulating the infant's breathing process.

IV. FEEDING—SUCKING—WEIGHT GAIN:

Comfort sounds may be a catalyst for inducing gurgles and vegetative sucking. Soft, rhythmic sound scaping (mouth and vegetative clicking) prior to feeding may assist in the infant's coordination with sucking, swallowing and breathing. Nutritive sucking with rhythmic reinforcement may help infants maintain steady mouth motion which can be further sustained through melodic holding during feedings.

V. SEDATION—SLEEP—PAIN:

Music therapy can provide an environment of safety during painful procedures. Tonic tones that match the pitch of the infant's cry, entrained with the meter of the breath can ease and alter the experience/perception of pain. Using the Attia (et al., 1987) infant pain scale, the music therapist can assess the level of pain and distract the infant from focusing on the painful stimuli. Music can assist the infant in reconstitution at post procedure time. Music therapy can be used in conjunction with (complementary) or as an alternative pharmacological sedation, depending upon the MD order.

For the infant who appears over stimulated and/or is in need of sleep, simple lullabies containing <5 note melodies can provide an aural atmosphere of nurturance. Altering the tempo and meter of the lullaby can help the infant relax and shift gradually into a sleep state.

VI. SELF REGULATION:

Central to the infant's development is his/her ability to self regulate. Simple, consistent rhythms and melodies can help the infant organize and acclimate to the environment. Predictable, ordered aspects of music provide structure that assist in the development of self nurturing behavior, physiological organization and neurological pathways.

DOCUMENTATION OF REFERRALS

Intensive care units maintain procedures that include accountability and documentation of services. It is therefore useful to have a formal structure in the referral process. The following referral form accompanies the Criteria for Referral, and is especially useful at the beginning of music therapy program implementation. The form ensures that the infants will be seen and presents the music therapist with a clear idea regarding the area of greatest need from a medical and social perspective (see Attachment I).

As staff become more familiar with the kinds of interventions the music therapy team will be making, the Criteria for Referral is filed and the form is used as the primary mechanism for on-going case treatment.

It is recommended that the initial cases (at least 3) using music therapy in the NICU be "piloted" and summarized through leadership meetings. The music therapist may report the efforts taken with the team and how the music therapy interventions were effective or ineffective and modified based on the team member's referral. The techniques that were implemented can also be illustrated (e.g. singing AHH and using the ocean drum to demonstrate an inter-uterine environment with supportively toned breath sounds in the case of the infant referred for respiratory distress). It is useful to demonstrate case examples through the referral form (filled-out) and duplicated for the staff. In this way, the team efforts and contacts taken by the therapist are highlighted. Milieu care is a mainstay (Abrams, et al., 2000) for future referrals and illustrates the effectiveness of how music therapy complements aspects of care already effectively in place.

The referral form is filed in the chart and provides necessary support as to why music therapy is indicated. The following referral form was developed at Beth Israel Medical Center and correlates with the Criteria for Referral (see Attachment I).

ASSESSMENT

The assessment form is essential for the music therapist. It substantiates the work in terms of providing a baseline for treatment that will follow. It includes the collection of heart rate and respiratory rate, oxygen saturation levels and notations on this form outline the behavioral variances in the infant's sleep and awake states.

The infant's response to the therapist's choice of instruments is important to note. It is helpful for the music therapist to meet with the infant's parent/s. Tape recording the mother's voice for the purposes of learning her vocal (speaking) melodic range as well as her vocal timbre (nasal, hoarse, airy) can have positive implications for the use of toning and singing when she may be unavailable for sessions (see Attachment II).

DISCUSSION: ENVIRONMENTAL MUSIC THERAPY

There are many aspects to consider when developing a music therapy program in the NICU. The most obvious are the conditions under which music therapy can be offered. Upon observation of the activities in the NICU at several medical centers in the United States, the first, most pressing need that one cannot ignore is the level of constant sound that both babies and staff are affected by each and every day. From closing an incubator door to the staff relaying vital information to one another, the level of sound that the infants experience can be a hazard to their health. This hazard was recognized by the American Academy of Pediatrics in 1997 and was more vigorously addressed in three articles in the Journal of Perinatology (American Academy of Pediatrics, 2000), NICU Sound Environment and the Potential Problems for Caregivers (Thomas & Martin, 2000), Measuring Sound in Hospital Nurseries (Gray & Philbin, 2000), and Facility and Operations Planning for Quiet Hospital Nurseries (Evans & Philbin, 2000).

The sound environment in the NICU becomes an immediate issue for music therapists who work within the spectrum of live music. In actuality, it is an issue that faces those babies that wear earmuffs, ear cups, phonopad earphones and somatron as well. Although during music interventions, the noise of the sound field may be blocked out, the neonate must still face the noise when the intervention stops. In music therapy, intervening in the sound environment may provide specific ways of working with the sounds and silences which confront babies and staff on a day to day basis.

The intensive care unit calls the need for "environmental music therapy." Environmental music therapy is a term developed by the author and music therapist Steve Schneider (MT–BC, USA). It is a specific tract of music therapy in which the music therapist plays with the intention of lowering the amount of noise and stress in the environment. This is not accomplished by merely playing a particular kind of music at a specific tempo. The pitches of the machine beeps, the mood of the staff, and the rhythm of the chaos is assessed prior to initiating music therapy and is evaluated throughout the intervention.

Environmental music therapy has been effectively developed in the NICU as part of the Armstrong Music Therapy Program at Beth Israel Medical Center in New York City.

Prior to its inception, New York University Masters candidate and researcher Kristen Stewart surveyed the staff to learn about how and if they were influenced by the sounds in the NICU. As well, for 5 weeks, Ms. Stewart collected heart and respiratory rates several hours before, immediately prior to and after the environmental music therapy.

What is interesting to note about the results of this study (Stewart & Schneider, 2000) is that the majority of the babies who had been asleep prior to the music appeared to go into a deeper sleep state (heart rate decreased) with the environmental music therapy. The babies who were awake prior to the sleep, seemed to become more active and alert (heart rate increase) during the therapy. This reflects the impact that music therapy can provide. Specifically, to assist in stimulation, which has been noted (Standley, 1998; Shoemark, 1998) and to deepen a relaxed state, which is an essential need. Sleep helps the infant retain weight, and is important to the infant's overall growth and development.

The intensive care unit is remarkably different from other units in the hospital setting as the beds in ICUs have limited privacy. The environment is chaotic and noisy. The level of trauma often requires medical machines that are noisy and beeping sounds can be pervasive. The music therapist struggles to create a private, safe space in this setting. With noise being the major deterrent, environmental music therapy is an effective option.

The results of this study (Stewart & Schneider, 2000), a first of its kind, imply that both patients and staff seem to benefit from the intervention. The sound meter used before, during, and after the music therapy indicated that the noise level *can* be reduced. Music therapy purposefully organizes noise. As well, staff report that the music helps increase their awareness of one another, their voice level and assists them in being altogether quieter in their work activity.

The beeps of monitors are quieted at a quicker pace and staff tend to speak more softly when environmental music therapy is provided. At the present time, steps are being taken in program development working toward including environmental music therapy on a permanent basis in the NICU at Beth Israel Medical Center. There are succinct differences in the effect of environmental music therapy as compared to the effects of a music volunteer or taped music. The trained music therapist can shape and transform an atmosphere of tension and trauma. By playing with the environment rather than playing to it (Stewart & Schneider, 2000), the patients, staff and babies in the NICU are brought together and are no longer separate entities.

Attachment 1

MUSIC THERAPY NICU REFERRAL FORM:

BETH ISRAEL MEDICAL CENTER

Referrals may be made by the nurse practitioner, case manager and residents but must have the consent of the attending physician and the parent/caretaker. The age for referrals is >32 weeks unless approved on a case by case basis by the attending physician. If there are any questions or concerns, call Dr. Joanne Loewy at 420-3484 or beeper 15208.

Infant's name_____

Gestational age_____ Chronological age_____

Diagnosis_____

Name of consenting Attending Physician: _____ Beeper_____

Family informed by _____ Beeper_____

Reason for Referral: (Check all of the following that apply and write in any comments).

_____Bonding: Caretakers and infants that are in need of collaborative experiences.
         Comments: _____

_____

_____Psychosocial Issues: ACS hold, intrauterine exposure to drugs or alcohol, trauma, stress, violence, family illness, separation/divorce.

         Specify: _____

_____

_____Respiratory Difficulties: _____Crying/ Irritability:

_____   _____

____Feeding/Sucking/Weight Gain: ____ Sedation/Sleep/Pain:

_____   ___Difficulty sleeping
                               ___ Requires music
                               assistance for sedation
                               during procedure:
                               (date/time:)
_____Self Regulation:

_____   Beeper/extension:_____   Date:_____
Person referring

*Please place this form in music therapy referral box located at
the nursing station.*

Attachment 2

MUSIC THERAPY ASSESSMENT

Patient_____DOB_____

Average Heart Rate:

    Sleeping: _____bpm

    Awake: _____bpm

    Stress: _____bpm

Respiratory:

    Does infant become tachypeic: _____Yes   _____No

    Define stressors:

Crying/Comfort Sounds:

    Pitch: _____High _____Low _____Average

    Absence of cry: _____Yes _____No

    Colic: _____Yes _____No

    Irritable?   _____Yes _____No

    Feeding Noise:_____

Psychosocial Needs:

    ACS Hold: _____Yes _____No

    Intrauterine exposure to drugs/alcohol: _____Yes _____No

    If yes, specify: _____

    How music therapy can benefit the infant:_____

    _____

Name of family member who can help the infant benefit:

_____

Family's religious preference:

_____

Feeding/Intake/Weight Gain/Voiding:

_____Breast _____Gavage _____Bottle _____ Reflux

Is the infant's suck response in need of assistance? _____Yes

_____No

Is Physical or Occupational Therapy involved? _____Yes _____No

Can infant self-regulate? _____Yes _____No

Feed Schedule:

Sleep:

Irritable: _____Yes _____No

Stimulation:

Does baby respond to propreoceptive stimulus? _____Yes _____No

Pain:

Describe physiological indicators, location, and perceived level (1-10).

Ongoing procedures that may benefit from music therapy assessment:

Development: Indicate whether infant is organized in:

Sound: _____Yes _____No

Touch: _____Yes _____No

Movement: _____Yes _____No

Is the infant developing appropriate muscle tone? _____Yes _____No

Sedation:

    Is the infant on a sedative? _____Yes _____No

    Medication(s):_____

    Time(s): _____

Music Therapist_____

Date:_____Extension or beeper:_____

Chapter 12

A RESOURCE GUIDE FOR ESTABLISHING A NEONATAL MUSIC THERAPY PROGRAM

Deanna Hanson Abromeit

This chapter addresses the practical steps for establishing a neonatal music therapy program. It is modeled after the music therapy program in a Level III nursery (a state categorization system for the highest level of critical care for neonates) at the University of Iowa Hospitals and Clinics (UIHC), a tertiary care facility in the United States. The chapter is divided into two sections: program preparation and implementation of music therapy services.

INTRODUCTION

In utero, infants experience sounds that are mostly regular and patterned, but in the special care nursery environment, sounds are neither predictable nor organized (Glass, 1999). This chaotic auditory environment, in addition to the premature infant's unpredictable behavioral states, may perpetuate the deleterious effects of prematurity. Due to the organized structural characteristics of pitch, dynamics, timbre and harmony, music can provide positive sensory stimulation to counteract the adverse noisy environment of the special care nursery, contributing to a more ordered, positive auditory environment and potentially improving the premature infant's medical stability and ability to self-organize.

Caregivers are continually searching for methods to improve the quality of care for the premature infant while addressing cost effectiveness, better long-term outcomes for the infant and increased parent satisfaction. In support of relationship based family centered care, music therapy can enhance parental participation and provide normalization within the parent–infant relationship. Teaching parents how to read their infants' behavior cues and appropriate means of interaction may decrease the infant's stress responses and increase positive parental interactions (Whipple, 2000). Careful consideration for the infant's greatest potential and the well-being of the family unit make it necessary for medical institutions to examine all possibilities for improving neonatal outcomes.

LITERATURE REVIEW

The literature on the use of music with premature infants has demonstrated beneficial developmental outcomes. Music has been noted to decrease length of hospitalization (resulting in decreased costs), improve parent satisfaction and parent-infant bonding, improve nipple use (non-nutritive sucking), increase daily weight gain and decrease agitation. The majority of studies have used recorded music. There is also a growing body of knowledge addressing the use of live humming or singing within the context of multi-modal stimulation that involves auditory, tactile, visual, and vestibular stimulation (White-Traut & Tubeszeski, 1986; Caine, 1991; Collins & Kuck, 1991; Marchette, Main, Redick, & Shapiro, 1992; Leonard, 1993; Lorch, Lorch, Diefendorf, & Earl, 1994; Burns, Cunningham, White-Traut, Silvestri, & Nelson, 1994; Moore, Gladstone, & Standley, 1994; Burke, Walsh, Oehler, & Gingras, 1995; Cassidy & Standley, 1995; Standley & Moore, 1995; Kaminski & Hall, 1996; Standley, 1997, 1998, 2000; Shoemark, 1999; Whipple, 2000).

This collective body of literature supports the increased interest of neonatal nurseries and music therapists in using music to support the maximum development of premature infants. To date, relatively few clinical music therapy programs exist for the aforementioned purposes. A handful of music therapists across the globe are pioneering clinical programs with premature infants, working towards the best possible interventions with this population. The emergence of successful music therapy services within neonatal nurseries has encouraged the development of new programs. As clinical programs increase, music therapists will be responsible for developing standards of practice, conducting research and disseminating information to support the continued growth of clinical programs.

MUSIC THERAPY SERVICES IN A NEONATAL NURSERY

Nurses, neonatologists and families of premature infants are protective and responsible for the premature infant's well being. Gaining access to this population cannot be done without the full support of the medical staff. A well-executed program development plan for music therapy services is necessary in order to begin providing services. Program development is a cyclical process. Some aspects of program development occur in a linear fashion (e.g. reviewing background literature before proposing services) while other aspects take place simultaneously (e.g. refining observation skills while adapting to the unit). A program development plan contains two phases: preparation for services and implementation.

Program Preparation

Preparation for a new clinical program in neonatal music therapy involves a working knowledge of the relevant literature, networking with music therapists and facility contacts, and submitting a written proposal to the facility. An extensive review of the relevant literature is critical to understanding the needs, trends and types of services being offered to premature infants. It includes music therapy literature as well as neonatology, nursing and psychology. In addition, written literature provided to the parents and popular media sources such as television programs, parenting magazines and the Internet are also helpful. Familiarizing one's self with a broad body of literature gives the music therapist an understanding of the needs of the premature infant and how to best incorporate music therapy practices (see Appendix).

Understanding the issues related to the premature infant's medical stability and development enables the music therapist to network effectively. Communicating with music therapists who have established programs in special care nurseries, or those who are attempting to, gives the novice program developer useful tips and information. Reciprocal sharing of information builds support and encouragement, and is an educational tool.

Communication between music therapists is important, but it can be very difficult to begin a new clinical program without the support of the facility's administration and medical team. Key facility contacts include the nurse manager and assistant nurse manager of the neonatal nursery, neonatologists, unit social worker, and the supervisor or director of the music therapy program. These individuals can help the music therapist determine how the neonatal nursery is identifying and addressing the needs of the premature infants. Music therapy interventions can then be integrated into the overall neonatology program. An efficacious program demonstrates a reciprocal acceptance of nursery limitations and staff requirements. It is based on identified patient needs, supported by research-based literature and can be shown to benefit the infants, the families, the nursery and the facility. These elements may provide the foundation for a formal written proposal.

A formal written proposal is a succinct, clearly written document, shared with the neonatology division, the medical director, nursing staff, music therapy administration and others. It provides the model with which to introduce services and guides the development of the music therapy program. The written proposal may be in two parts: the first, a review of literature, and the second, a description of the neonatal music therapy program specific to the facility. Table 1 provides an outline of the basic components of the written proposal.

A literature review begins with an introduction to the problem. (*For example, in the proposal at the University of Iowa Hospitals and Clinics (UIHC), the opening paragraph outlined the target concerns for premature infants and suggested music therapy as an appropriate intervention to address those concerns.)* Next, the overall environment of the neonatal nursery and philosophy of care relevant to the specific unit is addressed. (*At the time of the proposal at the UIHC, the nurseries were concerned about environmental noise, thus the second section in the review of literature is on the sound environment and complications from noise to premature infant development.*)

The final section of the literature review summarizes the music therapy literature, noting the beneficial outcomes established in the literature and how music therapy relates to the philosophy of care within the nursery. Therefore, the proposal for music therapy may recap the positive outcomes. (*The nurseries at UIHC had just introduced developmental care and they were making changes in the environment to reflect that philosophy. Therefore, the proposal for music therapy contained the positive outcomes from the music therapy literature as it related to the developmental care literature.)*

The second part of the proposal outlines the specific elements of the neonatal music therapy program. The introductory paragraph describes other programs, serving as models, as well as significant literature, supporting the program development. (*For example, the UIHC program was modeled after the program at the Royal Children's Hospital in Melbourne, Australia and in consultation with Helen Shoemark at the Royal Children's Hospital and Jayne Standley at Florida State University, Tallahassee, Florida. Both of these programs were mentioned in this section as a way to demonstrate that the proposed program was based on established clinical programs and was following the most current levels of practice for premature infants.)*

The remainder of the proposal outlines the goals, a description of the music therapy interventions, the role of the music therapist (i.e. as a consultant and/or therapist) the referral process, and parental involvement. Music therapy goals are always relevant to the needs of the client, but in this case should also consider the family and the philosophy of care within the nursery. Interventions are guided by the role of the music therapist in the nursery. The level of involvement the nursery desires and what the music therapist can work into his or her clinical schedule determines how the music therapist will fit into the setting and the type of music therapy interventions offered. For example, in some nurseries the music therapist may function as a consultant on the use of recorded music. In others they may actually be part of the developmental care team, participate in rounds and make suggestions to the developmental care plan.

Table 1: Neonatal Music Therapy Program Proposal Outline

A.   Proposal Title
        1. Music therapist's name, department or service affiliation
        2. Development team or others involved in the proposal development

B.   Review of literature
        1. Target concerns for the neonatal population
        2. Overview of relevant neonatal development literature
        3. Overview of neonatal music therapy literature — relate music
           therapy literature to the philosophy of care for the nursery

C.   Neonatal Music Therapy Protocol Proposal
        1. Program development credits (i.e. contributions made by other
           programs, music therapists and professionals)
        2. Role of the music therapist
           a. consultant — to staff and parents
           b. clinical therapist — providing individual interventions
        3. Music therapy goals
        4. Description of music therapy interventions
        5. Criteria for referrals
        6. Parental involvement
        7. Financial issues
           a. funding support
           b. costs for implementation
        8. Development description of implementation of services with target
           completion dates (e.g. acceptance of proposal, orientation of
           music therapist, staff education, start of services and future
           program development goals)

Financial Support

Finances are another component of the written proposal. Financial issues are typically facility specific and depend on how the music therapy program functions within the facility. Funding options may include grants and endowments. A budget outlines the costs for program implementation. Direct costs include music therapist or department compensation, playback equipment for recorded music, a CD collection and an appropriate accompaniment instrument. Finally, inclusion of a task outline of the program development illustrates target completion dates for each step of program implementation.

Implementation of Music Therapy Services

The goal of any new clinical program is to begin providing music therapy services. The well-organized program development plan competently prepares the music therapist for clinical interventions. The first step to implementation of services is a thorough orientation to the neonatal unit. Developing an orientation schedule with the nurse manager can provide the music therapist with experience in the nursery environment prior to beginning services. For some facilities this may require more than one unit. (*At UIHC, the neonatal nurseries are collectively called the Special Care Nurseries, encompassing the Neonatal Intensive Care Nursery, and the Intermediate Care Nursery.*)

A general orientation involves a detailed tour of the unit to familiarize the music therapist with the unit set–up and any particulars regarding general precautions (i.e. hand washing, masking or no contact due to illness, sterilization of instruments and equipment). In addition, observing nursing care gives the music therapist practical experience with the nurserys philosophy of care, opportunities to ask questions and to build rapport with the nurses. Observing or consulting other professionals such as social workers, dieticians, physical or occupational therapists, nurse practitioners and neonatologists may also be helpful. (*Because UIHC is a teaching hospital, there are regular rotations of nursing and medical students and resident physicians. Understanding when new staff will be rotating into the nurseries is useful so that the music therapist can have the opportunity to educate and interact with these individuals.*)

Independent time in the nursery environment, as part of the orientation process, allows the music therapist to familiarize himself or herself with the medical charts, improve observational skills of infant behaviors and responses to environmental stimuli. Throughout the orientation process the music therapist can be developing and refining assessment and documentation tools. Revisiting certain aspects of the orientation process (i.e. shadowing nurses, consulting with other professionals) at regular intervals provides a cyclical review process to encourage the music therapist to evaluate the clinical program.

Orientation to the nursery environment is important for a variety of reasons. First, it allows the music therapist to become comfortable within the environment. Premature infants are very small and medically involved, requiring a variety of tubes, wires and medical monitors. Someone who has not had experience in this environment, or with premature infants, may initially be emotionally overwhelmed. Understanding the role of the life support systems and monitors, how to handle the infants, and general standards of the environment (parent roles, use of lights, noise restrictions) supports the integration of the music therapist into the environment in the least disruptive manner possible. This information will also foster rapport with the staff and a higher level of confidence for the introduction of services.

Music therapy services are provided on a consultation and clinical level.

Consulting services can be varied, such as providing guidelines for appropriate sound stimulation, analyzing the environment for noise levels, or staff and parent training on the appropriate use of sound stimulation in the nursery environment. (*At UIHC the Special Care Nurseries had purchased, with grant money, tape players for each infant's bedside and a variety of recorded music. The first project for the music therapist was to be a consultant to a team of nurses in designing guidelines for the appropriate use of the tape players and recorded music in the nursery environment. Staff in-services, led by the music therapist, were provided to explain the guidelines and to answer questions.*) Consulting services can also include making presentations at other facilities or neonatal conferences, as well as training parents on the use of music therapy interventions.

Clinical services are guided by the description of music therapy goals and interventions in the written proposal. The number of referrals accepted by the music therapist is dependent on his or her other clinical responsibilities and availability. Discussion with the medical staff determines the criteria for appropriate referrals. (*At UIHC, infants referred for music therapy services are greater than 29 weeks gestational age and are medically stable.*) Other criteria for referrals includes any one of the following: frequent irritability or agitated behaviors, difficulty transitioning into or out of a sleep state, potential benefit from developmental stimulation due to extended length of stay, parents unavailable for long intervals, or parents having difficulties bonding with infant.

Upon referral for music therapy services an initial assessment is made. At this time there are no standard assessment tools for music therapy interventions with premature infants, however, careful observation of the infant and consultation with the infant's nurse provide valuable information for service evaluation. The basic format of an observational assessment includes a baseline observation period, an intervention period and a post intervention observation period. Criteria to evaluate the infant's response in these three periods are heart rate, respiration rate, oxygen saturation levels, amount of supplemental oxygen, and the infant's stress and self-regulatory behavior responses. Through careful observation, the music therapist can use this information to assess the infant's ability to handle the sensory stimulation, the types of stress behaviors they exhibit, the infant's self-regulatory behaviors and the overall appropriateness for music therapy interventions.

The length and number of music therapy sessions is determined on an individual basis based on the premature infant's medical stability, developmental growth, gestational age at birth, family involvement, and response to music therapy. Prior to any session, it is important to consult with the infant's nurse to determine the appropriateness for music therapy at that time. Communicating with the nurse after the session provides verbal documentation of the therapist's observations and the infant's responses.

Documentation allows the music therapist to track changes, demonstrate outcomes and promote program support. Documenting sessions in the infant's medical charts, as appropriate or required by the facility, provide the music therapist the opportunity to educate other professionals in the nature and outcomes of music therapy interventions, as well as track the amount of services being offered. The music therapist's personal notes provide documentation that facilitates adaptations of interventions. Describing the music therapy experiences and the infant's responses to the parent is another important form of documentation. Family friendly notes posted at the bedside provide the therapist with an opportunity to communicate with the parents. *(Some parents, at UIHC, kept these notes as keepsakes to document their infant's hospitalization. Others have requested that the music therapist write directly to the infant in their personal journal.)*

A more non-traditional form of documentation is videotaping. With parental and staff permission, these tapes provide a vivid description of the music therapy program and individual infant's responses during a session. Videotapes can be used for staff education, music therapist training, conference presentations and in–services. They provide a visual documentation, offering another valuable tool to evaluate the music therapy program. Program evaluation supports the evolution of the neonatal music therapy program. Continuing development is fostered through ongoing education of music therapy and premature infant development theories and techniques, reciprocal relationships between nursery staff and the music therapist, and clinical experience.

CONCLUSION

The beneficial outcomes of such programs for premature infants is well documented. Neonatal music therapy programs, developed and managed by music therapists, can ensure the competent and appropriate use of music as a valid intervention for these fragile infants. Providing such services to the neonatal nurseries begins with music therapists who are willing to learn about the medical needs and development of premature infants and take the initiative to expand neonatal music therapy programs to their full, clinical potential.

Launching a new program with any population requires time and patience. New neonatal music therapy programs may require the music therapist to demonstrate the efficacy of music therapy to the nursery medical staff and facility administration. An articulate, research-supported and facility-specific development plan will aid the music therapist interested in developing a clinical practice with this population.

A successful program is built upon the shared experiences of other therapists, a thorough review of the literature, supporting the philosophy of the facility's neonatal unit and focusing on the clinical strengths of the music therapist. An established program continues and develops as the music therapist, nursery staff, other music therapists and related disciplines collaborate and work toward the vision of neonatal music therapy.

(The neonatal music therapy program at UIHC continues to flourish due to a number of factors. The program began in a conservative manner, concentrating on consultative services that allowed music therapy to fit into the philosophy and function of the neonatal unit. The music therapist used music therapy language within the context of the unit terminology and philosophy. The music therapist's involvement grew within the context of current clinical responsibilities in order to be manageable for the therapist and to ensure successful implementation of neonatal music therapy interventions.)

APPENDIX

BIBLIOGRAPHY OF NEONATAL MUSIC THERAPY
RELATED RESOURCES

This appendix is designed to be used as a beginning reference list for the music therapist interested in developing programs in the neonatal nursery. It is not meant to be a comprehensive list of resources related to music therapy with premature infants.

Music Therapy Sources

Burke, M., Walsh, J., Oehler, J., Gingras, J. (1995). Music therapy following suctioning: four case studies. *Neonatal Network*, 14 (7), 41–49.

Caine, J. (1991). The effects of music on the selected stress behaviors, weight, caloric and formula intake, and length of hospital stay of premature and low birth weight neonates in a newborn intensive care unit. *Journal of Music Therapy*, 28 (4), 180–192.

Cassidy, J. W., Ditty, K. M. (1998). Presentation of aural stimuli to newborns and premature infants: an audiological perspective. *Journal of Music Therapy*, 35 (2), 70–87.

Cassidy, J.W., Standley, J.M. (1995). The effect of music listening on physiological responses of premature infants in the NICU. *Journal of Music Therapy*, 32 (4), 208–227.

Coleman, J.M., Pratt, R.R., Stoddar, R.A., Gerstmann, D.R., Abel, H. (1998). The effects of male and female singing and speaking voices on selected physiological and behavioral measures of premature infants in the intensive care unit. *International Journal of Arts Medicine*, 5 (8), 4–11.

Collins, S.K., Kuck, K. (1991). Music therapy in the neonatal intensive care unit. *Neonatal Network*, 9 (6), 23–26.

Kaminski, J., Hall, W. (1996). The effect of soothing music on neonatal behavioral states in the hospital newborn nursery. *Neonatal Network*, 15 (1), 45–54.

Leonard, J.E. (1993). Music therapy: fertile ground for application of research in practice. *Neonatal Network*, 12 (2), 47–48.

Loewy, J.V. (Ed). (2000). *Music Therapy in the Neonatal Intensive Care Unit.* New York: Scatchnote-Armstrong Press.

Lorch, C.A., Lorch, V., Diefendorf, A.O., Earl, P.W. (1994). Effect of stimulative and sedative music on systolic blood pressure, heart rate, and respiratory rate in premature infants. *Journal of Music Therapy,* 31 (2), 105–118.

Marchette, L., Main, R., Redick, E., Shapiro, A. (1992). Pain reduction during neonatal circumcision. In: Spintge, R., Droh, R. (Eds.). *Music Medicine.* St. Louis, MO: MMB, Inc., 131–141.

Nöcker-Ribaupierre, M. (1999). Premature Birth and Music Therapy. In: Wigram, T., De Backer, J. (Eds). *Clinical Applications of Music Therapy in Developmental Disability, Pediatrics and Neurology.* London: Jessica Kingsley Publishers, 47–65.

Owens, L.D. (1979). The effects of music on the weight loss, crying, and physical movement of newborns. *Journal of Music Therapy,* 26 (2), 83–90.

Shoemark, H. (1999). Indications for the inclusion of music therapy in the care of infants with bronchopulmonary dysplasia. In: Wigram, T., De Backer, J. (Eds.). *Clinical Applications of Music Therapy in Developmental Disability, Paidiatrics and Neurology,* London: Jessica Kingsley Publishers, 32-46.

Standley, J.M., Madsen, C.K. (1990). Comparison of infant preferences and responses to auditory stimuli: music, mother, and other female voice. *Journal of Music Therapy,* 27 (2), 54–97.

Standley, J.M., Moore, R.S. (1995). Therapeutic effects of music and mother's voice on premature infants. *Pediatric Nursing,* 21 (6), 509–512.

Standley, J.M. (1998). The effect of music and multimodal stimulation on responses of premature infants in neonatal intensive care. *Pediatric Nursing,* 24 (6), 532–538.

Standley, J.M. (2000). The effect of contingent music to increase non–nutritive sucking of premature infants. *Pediatric Nursing,* 26 (5), 494–499.

Standley, J.M. (2001). Music therapy for the neonate. *Newborn and Infant Nursing Reviews,* 1 (4), 211–216.

Whipple, J. (2000). The effect of parent training in music and multimodal stimulation on parent–neonate interactions in the neonatal intensive care unit. *Journal of Music Therapy,* 37 (4), 250–268.

Premature Infant Development Resources

Als, H. (1982). Toward a synactive theory of development: promise for the assessment and support of infant individuality. *Infant Mental Health Journal,* 3 (4), 229–243.

Als, H. (1986). A synactive model of neonatal behavioral organization: framework for the assessment of neurobehavioral development in the premature infant and for support of infants and parents in the neonatal intensive care environment. In: Sweeney, J.K. (Ed.). The High–Risk Neonate: Developmental Therapy Perspectives. *Physical and*

Occupational Therapy in Pediatrics, 6 (3/4), 3–55.

Als, H., Gilkerson, L. (1997). The role of relationship–based developmentally supportive newborn intensive care in strengthening outcome of preterm infants. *Seminars in Perinatology, 21 (*3), 178–189.

Avery, G.B., Fletcher, M.A., & McDonald, M.G. (Eds.). (1999*). Neonatology: Pathophysiology and Management of the Newborn,* 5th ed., Philadelphia: JB Lippincott.

Brown, L.D., Heermann, J.A. (1997). The effect of developmental care on preterm infant outcome. *Applied Nursing Research,* 10 (4), 190–197.

Burns, K., Cunningham, N., White-Traut, R., Silbestri, J., & Nelson, M.N. (1994). Infant stimulation: modification of an intervention based on physiologic and behavioral cues. *Journal of Obstetric, Gynecologic, and Neonatal Nursing,* 23 (7), 581–589.

D'Apolito, K. (1991). What is an organized infant? *Neonatal Network,* 10 (1), 23–29.

Koch, S. (1999). Developmental Support in the Neonatal Intensive Care Unit. In: Deacon, J., O'Neill, P. (Eds). *Core Curriculum for Neonatal Intensive Care Nursing.* W.B. Saunders Company, Philadelphia, PA., 522–539.

Leib, S.A., Benfield, D.G., Guidubaldi, J. (1980). Effects of early intervention and stimulation on the preterm infant. *Pediatrics,* 66 (1), 83–90.

Merenstein, G.B., Gardner, S.L. (Eds.). (1998). *Handbook of Neonatal Intensive Care* (4th edition). St. Louis: Mosby.

White-Traut, R., Nelson, M., Silvestri, J., Patel, M., Vasan, U., Han, B., et al. (1999). Developmental intervention for preterm infants diagnosed with periventricular leukomalacia. *Research in Nursing and Health,* 22, 131–143.

White-Traut, R., Tubeszewski, K. (1986). Multimodal stimulation of the premature infant. *Journal of Pediatric Nursing,* 1 (2), 90–95.

Wolke, D. (1998). Psychological development of prematurely born children. *Arch Dis Child,* 78, 567–570.

Other Relevant Resources

Fernald, A. (1989). Intonation and communicative intent in mothers' speech to infants: is the melody the message? *Child Development,* 60, 1497–1510.

Kurihara, H., Chiba, H., Shimizu, U., Tanaihara, T., Takeda, M., Kkawakami, K., et al. (1996). Behavioral and adrenocortical responses to stress in neonates and the stabilizing effects of maternal heartbeat on them. *Early Human Development,* 46, 117–127.

Papousek, M., Papousek, H. (1991). The meanings of melodies in motherese in tone and stress languages. *Infant Behavior and Development,* 14, 415–

550.

Rock, A., Trainor, L., Addison, T. (1999). Distinctive messages in infant-directed lullabies and play songs. *Developmental Psychology,* 35 (2), 527–534.

Rubel, E. (1984). Special topic: Advances in the physiology of auditory information processing. *Ontogeny of the Auditory System Review of Physiology,* 46, 213–229.

Shahidullah, S., Hepper, P.G. (1993). The developmental origins of fetal responsiveness to an acoustic stimulus. *Journal of Reproductive and Infant Psychology,* 11, 135–142.

Trainor, L.J. (1996). Infant preferences for infant-directed versus noninfant-directed playsongs and lullabies. *Infant Behavior and Development,* 19, 83–92.

Trehub, S., Bull, D., Thorpe, L.A. (1984). Infants' perception of melodies: the role of melodic contour. *Child Development,* 55, 821–830.

Trehub, S., Thorpe, L. (1989). Infants' perception of rhythm: categorization of auditory sequences by temporal structure. *Canadian Journal of Psychology,* 43 (2), 217–229.

Trehub, S., Unyk, A., Trainor, L. (1993a). Adults identify infant-directed music across cultures. *Infant Behavior and Development,* 16, 193–211.

Trehub, S., Unyk, A., Trainor, L. (1993b). Maternal singing in cross-cultural perspective. *Infant Behavior and Development,* 16, 285–295.

Trehub, S., Unyk, A., Kamenetskyk, S., Hill, D., Trainor, L., Henderson, J., et al.(1997). Mothers' and fathers' singing to infants. *Developmental Psychology,* 33 (3), 500–507.

Unyk, A., Trehub, S., Trainor, L., Schellenberg, E.G. (1992). Lullabies and simplicity: a cross-cultural perspective. *Psychology of Music,* 20, 15–28.

Websites

Touchpoints	www.touchpoints.org
Zero to Three	www.zerotothree.org
Int'l Society on Infant Studies	www.isisweb.org
Neurobehavioral Assessment of the Preterm Infant	www.med.stanford.edu/school/pediatrics/NAPI
Premature Infants	www.familyvillage.wisc.edu/lib_prem.htm www.premature-infant.com

BIBLIOGRAPHY

Abrams, B., Dassler, A.M., Lee, S., Loewy, J., Silvermann, F., & Telesy, A. (2000). Instituting music therapy in the NICU. In J.V. Loewy (Ed.), *Music Therapy in the Neonatal Intensive Care Unit.* (pp.21–38). New York: Satchnote-Armstrong Press.

Abrams, R.M., Gerhardt, K.J., Rosa, C., & Peters, A.J.M. (1995). Fetal acoustical stimulation test: Stimulus features of three artificial larynges recorded in sheep. *American Journal of Obstetrics and Gynecology* 173: 1372–1376.

Abrams, R.M., Griffiths, S.K., Huang, X., Sain, J., Langford, G., & Gerhardt, K.J. (1998). Fetal music perception: The role of sound transmission. *Music Perception* 15: 307–317.

Achenbach, T.M., Howell, M S., Aoki, M.F., & Rauh, V.A. (1993). Nine–year outcome of the Vermont intervention program for low birth weight infants. *Pediatrics* 91 (1): 45–55.

Adolph, K.E., Eppler, M.A., & Gibson, E.J. (1993). Development of perception of affordances. In C. Rovee-Collier, & L.P. Lipsitt (Eds.), *Advances of Infancy Research*. Vol. 8. (pp.51–98). Norwood, N.J.: Ablex.

Ainsworth, M., D. S., & Wittig, B.A. (1969). Attachment and exploratory behaviour of one–year–olds in a strange situation. In B.M. Foss (Ed.), *Determinants of Infant Behaviour*. (Vol.4). London: Methuen.

Ainsworth, M.D.S. (1976). Attachment as related to mother–infant interaction. In J. Rosenblatt, R. Beer, & M.C. Busnel (Eds.), *Advances in the Study of Behavior*. Vol. 8: 1–51. New York: Academic Press.

Ainsworth, M.D.S. (1977). Feinfühligkeit versus Unempfindlichkeit gegenüber Signalen des Babys. In K.E. Grossmann (Ed.), *Entwicklung der Lernfähigkeit in der Sozialen Umwelt*. München: Kindler.

Ainsworth, M.D.S., Blehar, M.C., & Waters, E.W.S. (1978). *Patterns of Attachment: A psychological study of the strange situation*. Hillsdale, N.J.: Erlbaum.

Albrecht, K., & Zimmer, M.-L. (2000). Auditive Stimulation bei Frühgeborenen. In A.E. Lison, H.A. Diehl (Eds.), *Medizinische Forschung und Gesundheitswissenschaften in Bremen*. Lengerich: Pabst.

Als, H. (1982). Toward a synactive theory of development: Promise for the assessment and support of infant individuality. *Infant Mental Health Journal* 3/4: 229–243.

Als, H. (1986). A synactive model of neonatal behavioral organization: Framework for the assessment of neurobehavioral development in the premature infant and for support of infants and parents in the neonatal intensive care environment. In J.K. Sweeney (Ed.), The High-Risk Neonate: Developmental Therapy Perspectives. *Physical and*

Occupational Therapy in Pediatrics 6 (3/4): 3–55.

Als, H. (1995). The preterm infant: A model for the study of fetal brain expectation. In J.P. Lecanuet, W.P. Fifer, W.P. Smotherman, & N.A. Krasnegor (Eds.), *Fetal Development: A Psychobiological Perspective* (pp. 439–471). Hillsdale, N.J.: Erlbaum.

Als, H. (1998). Developmental care in the newborn intensive care unit. *Curr. Opin. Pediatr.* 10: 138–42.

Als, H. (1999). Reading the preterm infant. In: E. Goldson (Ed.), *Nurturing the Premature Infant: Developmental Interventions in Newborn Intensive Care* (pp.18–85). London: Oxford University Press.

Als, H., Duffy, F.H., McAnulfy, G.B., Badian, N. (1989). Continuity of neobehavioral functioning in preterm and fullterm newborns. In M.H. Bornstein u. N.A. Krasnegor (Eds.). Stability and continuity in mental development, (pp. 3–28).

Als, H. & Gilkerson L. (1995). Developmentally supportive care in the newborn intensive care unit. *Zero to Three* 15: 2–10.

Als, H., Gilkerson, L. (1997). The role of relationship–based developmentally supportive new-born intensive care in strengthening outcome of preterm infants. *Seminars in Perinatology* 21 (3): 178–189.

Als, H., Lawhon, G., Brown, E., Gibes, R., Duffy, F.H., McAnulty, G.B., & Blickman, J.G. (1986). Individualized behavioral and environmental care for the very low birth weight infant at high risk for bronchopulmonary dysplasia: Neonatal intensive care unit and developmental outcome. *Pediatrics* 78: 1123–1132.

Als, H., Lawhon, G., Duffy, F.H., McNulty, G.B., Gibes-Grossman, R., & Blickman, J.G. (1994). Individualized developmental care for the very low birthweight preterm infant. *Journal of the American Medical Association* 272 (11): 853–858.

Als, H., Lester, B., Tronick, E.Z., & Brazelton, B. (1982). Manual for the assessment of preterm infants' behavior (APIB). In H.E. Fitzgerald, B.M. Lester, & M.W. Yogman (Eds.), *Theory and Research in Behavioral Pediatrics*. New York: Plenum Press.

Als, H., Mcanulty, G.B. (2000). Developmental Care Guidelines for Use in the Newborn Intensive Care Unit. *Children's Medical Center Corporation* (unpublished manuscript).

Alvarez, A. (1992). *Live Company*. London: Routledge.

Alvarez, A. (1998). Failures to link: Attacks or defects? *J. Child Psychotherapy* 24, 2.

American Academy of Pediatrics (2000). The influence of auditory experience on the foetus, newborn, and preterm infant: Report of the Sound Study Group of the National Resource Centre: *The Physical and Developmental Environment of the High Risk Infant* 20 (8), Part 2: 2–142.

American Academy of Pediatrics, Committee on Environmental Health (1997).

Noise: A hazard for the fetus and newborn. *Pediatrics* 100; 4: 724–727.

Ammon, G. (1982). Zur Psychosomatik von Frühgeburt und psychosomatischer Erkrankung. In T.F. Hau, & S. Schindler (Eds.), *Pränatale und Perinatale Psychosomatik*. Stuttgart: Hippokrates.

Anand, K.J.S., Scalzo, F.M. (2000). Can adverse neonatal experiences alter brain development and subsequent behavior? *Biology Neonate* 77: 2: 69–82.

Anderson, G.C. (1991). Current knowledge about skin–to–skin (kangaroo) care for preterm infants. *Journal of Perinatology* 11 (3): 216–226.

Anderson, G.C. (1995). Touch and the kangaroo care method. In T.M. Field (Ed.), *Touch in Early Development*. Mahwah, N.J.: Erlbaum.

Anzieu, D. (1988): *Le Moi-Peau*. Paris: Bordas.

Anzieu, D., Houzel, D., & Lecourt, E. (1988). *Les Enveloppes Psychiques*. Paris: Dunod.

Armitage, S.E., Baldwin, B.A., & Vince, M.A. (1980). The fetal sound environment of sheep. *Science* 208: 1173–1174.

Arnand, K.J., & Hickey, P.R. (1987). Pain and its Effects in the Human Neonate and Fetus. *New England Journal of Medicine* 317: 1322–1329.

Atkinson, J., & Braddick, O. (1989). Development of basic visual functions. In A. Slater, & G. Bremner (Eds.), *Infant Development* (pp.7–41). Hillsdale, N.J.: Erlbaum.

Attia, J.,Amiel-Tison, C., Mayer, N., Shnider, S., & Barrier, G. (1987). Measurement of postoperative pain and narcotic administration in infants using a new clinical scoring system. *Anesthesiology* 67: A 532.

Avery, G.B., Fletcher, M.A., & McDonald, M.G. (Eds.) (1999). *Neonatology: Pathophysiology and Management of the Newborn*. 5th ed. Philadelphia: Lippincott, Williams, & Wilkins.

Balconi, M. (1994). Presentazione. In R. Negri, *Il Neonato in Terapia Intensiva – un Modello Neuropsicoanalitico di Prevenzione*. Milano: Raffaelo Cortina.

Barker, D., & Rutter, N. (1995). Exposure to invasive procedures in neonatal intensive care unit admissions. *Arch. Dis. Child* 72: F47–F48.

Barnett, R.C., & Baruch, G.K. (1985). Women's involvement in multiple roles and psychological distress. *J. Personality Soc. Psychol.* 49: 135–145.

Basch, M. (1994). Psychoanalysis and developmental processes. Infant research and the changing practice of psychoanalysis. *Symposium der R. Spitz-Gesellschaft*/Köhler-Stiftung, Köln.

Bates, J.E., &. Bayles, K (1988). Attachment and the development of behaviour problems. In J. Belky, & T. Nezworski (Eds.), *Clinical Implications of Attachment* (pp. 253–299). Hillsdale, N. J.: Erlbaum.

Bates, J.E., Maslin, C.A. & Frankel, K.A. (1985). Attachment security, mother–child interaction, and temperament as predictors of behaviour-problem ratings at age three years. In I. Bretherton, & E. Waters (Eds.), *Growing Points of Attachment Theory and Research. Monographs of the Society for the Research of Child Development* 50, 1–2, Serial No. 209: 67–193.

Becker, P.T., Grunwald, P.C., Moorman, J., & Stuhr, S. (1991). Outcomes of developmentally supportive nursing care for very low birthweight infants. *Nurs. Res.* 40: 150–155.

Beckwith, L., & Cohen, S.E. (1989). Maternal responsiveness with preterm infants and later competency. In M.H. Bornstein (Ed.), *Maternal Responsiveness: Characteristics and Consequences. New Directions for Child Development* (Vol. 43: 75–87). San Francisco: Jossey-Bass.

Beebe, B., Jaffe, J., & Lachman, F. (1992). A dyadic systems view of communication. In N. Skolnick, S. Warshaw (Eds.), Relational Perspectives in Psychoanalysis. Hillsdale, N.J.:Analytic Press.

Beebe, B., & Lachman, F. (2002). *Infant Research and Adult Treatment: Co-Constructing Interactions.* Analytic Press.

Belsky, J., & Rovine, M. (1987). Temperament and attachment security in the strange situation: An empirical rapprochement. *Child Development* 58: 787–795.

Bick, E. (1964). Notes on infant observation in psychoanalytic training. *Int. J. Psycho-analysis* 45.

Bick, E. (1968). The experience of the skin in early object relations. *Int. J. Psycho-analysis* 49.

Bion, W. R. (1962a). A theory of thinking. *Int. J. Psycho-analysis* 53.

Bion, W. R. (1962b). *Learning from Experience.* London: Karnac Books.

Bion, W. R. (1963). Elements of Psychoanalysis. London: Karnac Books.

Birnholz, J. C. (1988). On observing the human fetus. In W. P. Smotherman & S.R. Robinson (Eds.), *Behavior of the Fetus* (pp.47–60). New Jersey: Telford.

Birnholz, J.C., & Benacerraf, B.R. (1983). The development of the human fetal hearing. *Science* 222: 516–518.

Bo, L.K., & Callaghan, P. (2000). Soothing pain elicited distress in Chinese neonates. *Pediatrics* 105 (4): 49–56.

Bolton, B. (2000). Music alive: Pathway to communication. In J.V. Loewy (Ed.), *Music Therapy in the Neonatal Intensive Care Unit* (pp.81–84). New York: Satchnote-Armstrong Press.

Boom, D. van den (1988). Neonatal Irritability and the Development of Attachment: Observation and Intervention. *Unpublished Doctorate Thesis*, University of Leiden.

Boom, D. van den (1994). The influence of temperament and mothering on attachment and exploration: An experimental manipulation of sensitive responsiveness among lower-class mothers with irritable infants. *Child Development* 65: 1457–1477.

Boom, D. van den, & Hoeksma, J.B. (1994). The effect of infant irritability and mother–infant–interaction. A growth–curve analysis. *Developmental Psychology* 30: 581–590.

Botting, N., Powls, A., Cooke, R.W.I., & Marlow, N. (1997). Attention deficit hyperactivity disorders and other psychiatric outcomes in very low birthweight children at 12 years. *Journal of Child Psychology and Psychiatry and Allied Disciplines* 38 (8): 931–941.

Bowlby, J. (1969). *Attachment and Loss*. New York: Basic Books.

Bowlby, J. (1988). *A Secure Base: Clinical Implications of Attachment Theory*. London: Routledge.

Brachfeld, S., Goldberg, S., & Sloman, J. (1980). Parent–infant interaction in free play at 8 and 12 months: effects of prematurity and immaturity. *Infant Behavior and Development* 3: 289–305.

Brandt, R. (1983). *Griffiths Entwicklungsskalen (GES) zur Beurteilung der Entwicklung in den Ersten Beiden Lebensjahren*. Weinheim: Beltz.

Bray, P.F., Shields, W.D., Wolcott, G.J. & Madsen, J.A. (1969). Occipitofrontal head circumference: An accurate measure of intracranial volume. *The Journal of Pediatrics* 75 (2): 303–305.

Brazelton, B.T., Koslowski, B. & Main, M. (1974). Origins of reciprocity. The early mother-infant interaction. In M. Lewis, & L.A. Rosenblum (Eds.), *The Effect of the Infant on its Caregiver* (p.49). New York: Wiley Interscience.

Brazelton, T.B. (1981): A new model of assessing the behavioral organization in preterm and fullterm infants: two case studies. *J. Amer. Acad. Child Psychiat.* 20: 239.

Brazelton, T.B., & Nugent, J.K. (1995). *Neonatal Behavioral Assessment Scale*. 3rd ed. Cambridge: Cambridge University Press.

Bremner, G. (1989). Development of special awareness in infancy. In A. Slater, G. Bremner (Eds.), *Infant Development*, 123–141. Hillsdale, N.J.: Erlbaum.

Brown, J.V., & Bakeman, R. (1980). Relationships of human mothers with their infants during the first year of life: Effect of prematurity. In R.W. Bell, & W.P. Smotherman (Eds.), *Maternal Influences and Early Behavior*, 353–373. Jamaica, NY: Spectrum.

Brown, L.D., & Heermann, J.A. (1997). The effect of developmental care on preterm infant outcome. *Applied Nursing Research* 10 (4): 190–197.

Buehler, D.M., Als, H., Duffy, F.H., McAnulty, G.B., & Liederman, J. (1995). Effectiveness of individualized developmental care for low-risk preterm infants: Behavioral and electrophysiological evidence. *Pediatrics* 96: 923–932.

Burke, M., Walsh, J., Oehler, J., & Gingras, J. (1995). Music therapy following suctioning: Four case studies. *Neonatal Network* 14 (7): 41–49.

Burns, K., Cunningham, N., White-Traut, R., Silbestri, J., & Nelson, M.N. (1994). Infant stimulation: Modification of an intervention based on physiologic and behavioral cues. *Journal of Obstetric, Gynecologic, and Neonatal Nursing* 23 (7): 581–589.

Busnel, M.C., Mosser, Ch., & Relier, J.P. (1986). Preliminary results on the effect of acoustic stimulations on premature infants. *Pediatric Research* 20: 1056.

Caine, J. (1991). The effects of music on the selected stress behaviors, weight, caloric and formula intake, and length of hospital stay of premature and low birth weight neonates in a newborn intensive care unit. *Journal of Music Therapy* 28 (4): 180–192.

Caplan, G. (1960). Patterns of parental response to the crisis of premature birth. *Psychiatry* 23: 365–374.

Caplan, G., Manson, E., & Kaplan, D.M. (1965). Four studies of crisis in parents of prematures. *Community Mental Health Journal* 1: 149–161.

Capps, L., Sigman, M., & Mundy, P. (1994). Attachment security in children with autism. *Development and Psychopathology* 6: 249–261.

Carlson, E. (1998). A prospective longitudinal study of attachment disorganisation/disorientation. *Child Development* 69: 1107–1128.

Casaer, P., & Eggermont, E. (1985). Neonatal clinical neurological assessment. In S. Harel, & N.J. Nicholas (Eds.), *The At-Risk Infant: Psycho/Social/Medical Aspects,* (pp.197–220). Baltimore: Brookes.

Cassidy, J.W., & Ditty, K.M. (1998a). Gender differences among newborns on a transient otoacoustic emissions test for hearing. Paper presented at the *National Convention of the American Music Therapy Association,* Cleveland, OH.

Cassidy, J.W., & Ditty, K.M. (1998b). Presentation of aural stimuli to newborns and premature infants: an audiological perspective. *Journal of Music Therapy* 35 (2): 70–87.

Cassidy, J.W., & Standley, J.M. (1995). The effect of music listening on physiological responses of premature infants in the NICU. *Journal of Music Therapy* 32 (4): 208–227.

Castarede, M. F. (1987). *La Voix et les Sortilèges.* Paris: Les Belles Lettres.

Chapman, J. S. (1978). The relationship between auditory stimulation and gross motor activity of short gestation infants. *Research in Nursing and Health* 1 (1): 29–36.

Chapman, J.S. (1979). Influence of varied stimuli on development of motor patterns in the premature infant. In G. Anderson, & B. Raff (Eds.), Newborn Behavioral Organization: *Nurs. Res. and Impl.,* New York: 61–80.

Cheek, D.B. (1995). Early use of psychotherapy in prevention of preterm labor: The application of hypnosis and ideomotor techniques with women carrying twin pregnancies. *Pre- and Perinatal Journal* 10 (1): 5–19.

Chomsky, N. (1972). *Language and Mind.* New York: Harcourt Brace Jovanovich.

Clair, A.A., Bernstein, B., & Johnson, G. (1995). Rhythm playing characteristics in persons with severe dementia including those with probable Alzheimer's type. *Journal of Music Therapy* 3(2): 113–131.

Clark, M.E., McCorkle, R.R., & Williams, S.B. (1981). Music therapy assisted labor and delivery. *Journal of Music Therapy*, 18/2: 88–100.

Clements, A. (1996). New sense out of old sense. In R Pratt. Music and infant well-being (101-119) in R. Pratt, & D. Grocke (Eds) (1999). *MusicMedicine3: Expanding Horizons.* Melbourne: University of Melbourne.

Cohen, M. (1995). Premature twins on a neonatal intensive care unit. *J. Child Psychotherapy* 21: 2.

Cohn, J.F., Campbell, S.B., & Ross, S. (1991). Infant response in the still-face paradigm at 6 months predicts avoidant and secure attachment at 12 months. *Development and Psychopathology* 3: 367–376.

Coleman, J.M., Pratt, R.R., Stoddard, R.A., Gerstmann, D.R., & Abel, H.H. (1998). The effects of male and female singing and speaking voices on selected physiological and behavioral measures of premature infants in the intensive care unit. *International Journal of Arts Medicine* 5 (8): 4–11.

Collins, S.K. (1996). Music therapy and nursing in the neonatal intensive care unit. In M.R. Froehlich (Ed.), *Music Therapy with Hospitalized Children*, 73–76. New York: Jeffrey Books.

Collins, S.K., & Kuck, K. (1991). Music therapy in the neonatal intensive care unit. *Neonatal Network* 9 (6): 23–26.

Cowan, M.W. (1979). The development of the brain. *Scientific American* 113: 113–133.

Crade, M., & Lovett, S. (1988). Fetal response to sound stimulation: Preliminary report exploring use of sound stimulation in routine obstetrical ultrasound examinations. *Journal of Ultrasound Medicine* 7: 499–503.

Cramer, B. (1976). A mother's reaction to premature birth. In M.K. Klaus, & J.H. Kennell (1976): *Mother-Infant-Bonding.* St.Louis: C.V. Mosby.

Cramer, F. (1998): *Symphonie des Lebendigen. Versuch einer Allgemeinen Resonanztheorie.* Frankfurt a. M: Insel

Cynader, M., & Frost, B. (1999). Mechanisms of brain development: Neuronal sculpting by the physical and social environment. In D. Keating, & C. Hertzman (Eds.), *Developmental Health and Wealth of Nations: Social, Biological and Educational Dynamics.* 153–184. New York: Guilford Press.

Damasio, A.R. (1999). *The Feeling of What Happens. Body and Emotion in the Making of Consciousness.* New York: Harcourt Brace Comp.

D'Apolito, K. (1991). What is an organized infant? *Neonatal Network* 10 (1): 23–29.

Daniel, T., & Laciak, J. (1982). Observations cliniques et experiences concernant l'etat de l'appareil cochleovestibulaire des sujets exposes au bruit durant la vie foetale. *Revue of Laryngologie* 103: 313–318.

DeCasper, A.J., & Fifer, W.P. (1980). Of human bonding: Newborns prefer their mother's voice. *Science* 208: 1174–1176.

DeCasper, A.J., & Spence, M.J. (1986). Prenatal maternal speech influences newborns' perception of speech sound. *Infant Behavior and Development* 9: 133–150.

DeCasper, A.J., & Spence, M.J. (1986). Newborns prefer a familiar story over an unfamiliar one. *Infant Behavior and Development* 9: 133–150.

Decker-Voigt, H.H., & Maetzel, F.K. (1997). *Cardiovascular Complaints Music and Health. The Scientific-Medical Music Program* (book and CDs). Hamburg: Energon.

deSchonen, S., & Deruelle, C. (1994). Pattern and face recognition in infancy. In A.Vyt, H. Bloch, & M.H. Bornstein (Eds.), Early Child Development in the French Tradition. Contributions from Current Research. Hillsdale, N.J.: Erlbaum.

deWolff, M.S., & van Ilzendoorn, M.H. (1997). Sensitivity and attachment: A meta-analysis on parental antecedents of infant attachment. *Child Development* 68 (4): 571.

Department of Family and Community Services (2000). *Stronger Families and Communities Strategy, Department of Family and Community Services*—fact sheet. http://www.facs.gov.au/internet/facsinternet.nsf/aboutfacs/programs/fa milies-StrongFam-CommStrategy.htm.

Devlin, B., Daniels, M., & Roeder, K. (1997). The heritability of IQ. *Nature* 388: 468–471.

Dornes, M. (1993). *Der Kompetente Säugling. Die Präverbale Entwicklung des Menschen.* Frankfurt a. M.: Fischer.

Dornes, M. (1999). *Die Frühe Kindheit. Entwicklungspsychologie der Ersten Lebensjahre.* Frankfurt a. M.: Fischer.

Duffy, F.H., Als, H., & McAnulty, G.B. (1990). Behavioral and electro-physiological evidence for gestational age effects in healthy preterm and fullterm infants studied 2 weeks after expected due date. *Child Dev.* 61: 1271–1286.

Duffy, F.H., Mower, G.D., Jensen, F., & Als, H. (1984). Neural plasticity: A new frontier for infant development. In H.E. Fitzgerald, B.M. Lester, & M.W. Yogman (Eds.), *Theory and Research in Behavioral Pediatrics.* Vol. 2. .pp. 67–96. New York: Plenum Press.

Dunst, C., Trivette, C., & Deal, A. (1988). *Enabling and Empowering Families: Principles and Guidelines for Practice.* Cambridge, MA.: Brookline Books.

Dusick, A.M. (1997). Medical outcomes in preterm infants. *Seminars in Perinatology*, 21(3):164–177.

Eagle, M. N. (1984). *Recent Developments in Psychoanalysis. A Critical Evaluation.* New York: McGraw-Hill Inc.

Easterbrooks, A. (1989). Quality of attachment to mother and to father: Effects of perinatal risk status. *Child Development* 60: 825–831.

Emde, R., Biringen, Z., Clyman, R., & Oppenheim, D. (1991). The moral self in infancy: Affective core and procedural knowledge. *Developmental*

Review 11.

Erikson, E. H. (1950). *Childhood and Society*. New York: W. W. Norton.

Evans, J. B., & Philbin, K. M. (2000). Facilities and operations planning for quiet hospital nurseries. *Journal of Perinatology, American Academy of Pediatrics*, Dez. 2000: 105–112.

Fedor-Feyberg, P. G. (1987). *Pränatale und Perinatale Psychologie und Medizin*. Alsvjö: Saphir.

Feldman, R., & Eidelman, A.I. (1998). Intervention programs for premature infants. How and do they affect development? *Clin. Perinatol.* 25: 613–626.

Fernald, A. (1982). Acoustic Determinants of Infant Preferences for Motherese. *Unpubl. Doct. Thesis*, Oregon.

Fernald, A. (1989). Intonation and communicative intent in mothers' speech to infants: Is the melody the message? *Child Development* 60: 1497–1510.

Field, T. (1987). Interaction and attachment in normal and atypical infants. *Journal of Consulting and Clinical Psychology* 55 (6): 853–859.

Field, T., Dempsey, J.R., & Shuman, H.H. (1981). Developmental follow-up of pre- and post-term infants. In S.L. Friedman, & M. Sigman (Eds.), *Preterm Birth and Psychological Development*. Vol. 1. New York: Academic Press.

Fielder, A. (2000). Neonatal environment—light measurement/visual injury. *Lecture Presentation*, The Physical and Developmental Environment of the High Risk Infant. Florida.

Fifer, W.P., & Moon, C. (1988). Auditory experience in the fetus. In W. Smotherman, S. Robinson (Eds.), *Behavior in the Fetus*, 175–188. New York: Telford.

Fifer, W.P., & Moon, C.M. (1994). The role of the mother's voice in the organization of brain function in the newborn. *Acta Paediatr.* Supp. 397: 86–93.

Fleisher, B.E., Van den Berg, K., Constantinou, J., Heller, C., Benitz, W.E., Johnson, A., Rosenthal, A., & Stevenson, D.K. (1995). Individualized developmental care for very-low-birthweight premature infants. *Clin. Pediatr.* 34: 523–529.

Freeman, W. (1994). *Societies of Brain*. Hillsdale N.J.: Erlbaum.

Freud, A. (1965). *Normality and Pathology in Childhood*. London: Hogarth Press.

Freud, S. (1926). *Inhibitions, Symptoms and Anxiety*. Standard Edition Vol.20. London: Hogarth Press.

Frodi, A. (1983). Attachment behavior and sociability with strangers in premature and fullterm infants. *Infant Mental Health Journal* 4 (1): 13–22.

Gagnon, R., Benzaquen, S., & Hunse, C. (1992). The fetal sound environment during vibroacoustic stimulation in labour: Effect on fetal heart rate response. *Obstetrics and Gynecology* 79: 550–555.

Gelman, S.R., Wood, S., Spellacy, W.N., & Abrams, R.M. (1982). Fetal movements in response to sound stimulation. *American Journal of Obstetrics and Gynecology* 143: 484–485.

George, C., Kaplan, N., & Main, M. (1985). *The Adult Attachment Interview.* Unpublished manuscript.

Gerhardt, K.J. (1989). Characteristics of the fetal sheep sound environment. *Seminars in Perinatology* 13: 362–370.

Gerhardt, K.J., & Abrams, R. M. (1994). Fetal hearing: Characterization of the stimulus and response. *Seminars in Perinatology* 20 (1): 11–20.

Gerhardt, K.J., & Abrams, R.M. (2000). Foetal exposure to sound and VAS. *Journal of Perinatology,* 20: 21–30.

Gerhardt, K.J., Abrams, R.M., Kovas, B.M., Gomez, K.J., & Conlon, M. (1988). Intrauterine noise levels produced in pregnant ewes by sound applied to the abdomen. *American Journal of Obstetrics and Gynecology* 159: 228–232.

Gerhardt, K.J., Abrams, R.M., & Oliver, C.C. (1990): Sound environment of the fetal sheep. *American Journal of Obstetrics and Gynecology* 162: 282–287.

Gerhardt, K.J., Huang, X., Arrington, K.E., Meixner, K., Abrams, R.M., & Antonelli, P.J. (1996), Fetal sheep hear through bone conduction. *American Journal of Otolaryngology* 17: 374–379.

Gerhardt, K.J., Otto, R., Abrams, R.M., Colle, J.J., Burchfield, D.J., & Peters, A.J.M. (1992), Cochlear microphonics recorded from fetal and newborn sheep. *American Journal of Otolaryngology* 13: 226–233.

Gerhardt, K.J., Pierson, L.L., Huang, X., Abrams, R.M., & Rarey, K.E. (1999). Effects of intense noise exposure on fetal sheep auditory brainstem response and inner ear histology. *Ear and Hearing* 20: 21–32.

Glass, P. (1999). The vulnerable neonate and the neonatal intensive care environment. In G.B. Avery, M.A. Fletcher, & M.G. McDonald (Eds.), *Neonatology: Pathophysiology and Management of the Newborn* (pp.77–945). 5th Ed. Philadelphia: J.B. Lippincott.

Goldberg, S., Gotowiec, A., & Simmons, R.J. (1995). Infant–mother attachment and behaviour problems in healthy and chronically ill preschoolers. *Development and Psychopathology* 7: 267–282.

Goldberg, S., Perrotta, M., Minde, K., & Corter, C. (1986). Maternal behavior and attachment in low birthweight twins and singletons. *Child Development* 57: 34–46.

Goldsmith, H.H., Alansky, J.A. (1987). Maternal and infant temperamental predictors of attachment: A meta-analytic review. *Journal of Consulting and Clinical Psychology* 55 (6): 805–816.

Gorski, P.A., Huntington, L., & Lewkovicz, D.J. (1990). Handling preterm infants in hospitals: Stimulating controversy about timing of stimulation. *Clin. Perinatol.* 17 (1): 103–112.

Gottfried, A.W. (1985). Environment of newborn infants in special care units. In

A.W. Gottfried, & J.L. Gaiter (Eds.), *Infant Stress under Intensive Care*, 23–54. Baltimore: University Park Press.

Graber, G. (Ed.) (1974). *Pränatale Psychologie*. München: Kindler.

Graven, S. (2000). The full-term and premature newborn: Sound and the developing infant in the NICU: Conclusions and recommendations for care. *Journal of Perinatology* 20: 88–93.

Graven, S.N. (2001). Early visual development. *Lecture Presentation*, The Physical and Developmental Environment of the High Risk Infant. Florida.

Greenberg, M.T., & Crnic, K.A. (1988). Longitudinal predictors of developmental status and social interaction in premature and full-term infants at age two. *Child Development* 59: 554–570.

Griffiths, S.K., Brown, W.S., Gerhardt, K.J., Abrams, R.M., & Morris, R.J. (1994a). The perception of speech sounds recorded within the uterus of a pregnant sheep. *Journal of the Acoustical Society of America* 96: 2055–2063.

Griffiths, S.K., Pierson, L.L., Gerhardt, K.J., Abrams, R.M., & Peters, A.J.M. (1994b). Noise induced hearing loss in fetal sheep. *Hearing Research* 4: 221–230.

Grimm, H.; Schöler, H. (1991). *Heidelberger Sprachentwicklungstest— Handanweisung*. 2nd ed. Göttingen: Hogrefe.

Gutbrod, T., St. John, K., Rust, L., & Wolke, D. (2000). Very preterm infants' responses to structured and perturbed (still face) interactions at 3 months post term: The influence of maternal sensitivity and infant irritability. Paper presented at the *World Associaton for Infant Mental Health,* 7th Congress, Montreal, Canada.

Hack, M., Breslau, N., Weissman, B., Aram, D., Klein, M., & Borawski, E. (1991). Effect of very low birthweight and subnormal head size on cognitive abilities at school age. *The New England Journal of Medicine* 325 (4): 231–237.

Hack, M., Klein, N.K., & Taylor, H.G. (1995). Long-term developmental outcomes of low birth weight infants. *The Future of Children* 5: 171–96.

Hanser, S.B., Larson, S.C., & O'Connell, A.S. (1983). The effect of music on relaxation of expectant mothers during labor. *Journal of Music Therapy* 20 (2): 50–58.

Hau, T.F., & Schindler, S. (Hg.) (1982). *Pränatale und Perinatale Psychosomatik*. Stuttgart: Hippokrates.

Henderson, R.V., Subramaniam, M., & Boettcher, F.A. (1993). Individual susceptibility to noise-induced hearing loss: An old topic revisited. *Ear and Hearing* 14: 152–168.

Hepper, P.G. (1989). Foetal learning: Implications for psychiatry? *British Journal of Psychiatry* 155: 289–293.

Hepper, P.G., & Shahidullah, S.B. (1994a). Development of fetal hearing.

Archives of the Diseases of Children 71: 81–87.

Hepper, P.G., & Shahidullah, S.B. (1994b). The development of fetal hearing. *Fetal Maternal Medicine Review* 6: 167–179.

Hepper, P.G., & Shahidullah, S.B. (1992). Abnormal fetal behavior in Down's syndrome fetuses. *Q. J. Clin. Psych.* 44: 305–317.

Hepper, P.G., Scott, D, & Shaidullah, S.B. (1993). Newborn and foetal response to maternal voice. Journal of Reprod. *Infant Psychol.* 11: 147–155.

Herbinet, E., & Busnel, M.C. (1991): *L'aube des Sens.* Les cahiers du nouveau-né Nr 5. Paris: Stock.

Hipwell, A.E., & Kumar, R.C. (1997). The impact of postpartum affective psychosis on the child. In L. Murray, & P.J. Cooper (Eds.), Postpartum Depression and Child Development. New York: Guilford Press.

Hofer, M.A. (1988). On the nature and functioning of prenatal behavior. In W.P. Smotherman, & S.R. Robinson (Eds.), *Behavior of the Fetus* (pp.3–18). New Jersey: Telford.

Holditch Davis, D., & Thoman, E.B. (1988). The early social environment of premature and full-term infants. *Early Human Development* 17: 221–232.

Huang, X., Gerhardt, K.J., Abrams, R.M., & Antonelli, P.J. (1997). Temporary threshold shifts induced by low-pass and high-pass filtered noises in fetal sheep in utero. *Hearing Research* 113: 173–181.

Hubbard, F.O.A., & van Ijzendoorn, M.H. (1991). Maternal unresponsiveness and infant crying across the first 9 months: A naturalistic longitudinal study. *Infant Behavior and Development* 14: 299–312.

Huddy, C.L.J., Johnson, A., & Hope, P.L. (2001). Educational and behavioural problems in babies of 32–35 weeks gestation. *Arch. Dis. Child Fetal Neonatal.* Ed. 85: F23–F28.

Hüppi, P.S., Maier, S.E., Peled, S., Zientara, G.P., Barnes, P.D., Jolesz, F.A., & Volpe, J.J. (1998). Microstructural development of human newborn cerebral white matter assessed in vivo by diffusion tensor imaging. *Pediatr. Res.* 44: 584–590.

Hüppi, P.S., Schuknecht, B., Boesch, C., Bossi, E., Felblinger, J., Fusch, C., & Herschkowitz, N. (1996). Structural and neurobehavioral delay in postnatal brain development of preterm infants. *Pediatr. Res.* 39: 895–901.

Hüther, G. (2001). Die Bedeutung emotionaler Sicherheit für die Entwicklung des kindlichen Gehirns. In H. Gebauer, & G. Hüther (Eds.), *Kinder Brauchen Wurzeln. Neue Perspektiven für eine Gelingende Entwicklung.* Düsseldorf: Walter.

Ijzendoorn, M.H. van (1995). Adult attachment representations, parental responsiveness, and infant attachment: A meta-analysis on the predictive validity of the adult attachment interview. *Psychological Bulletin* 117 (3): 387–403.

Ijzendoorn, M.H. van, Dijkstra, J., & Bus, A.G. (1995). Attachment, intelligence, and language: A meta-analysis. *Social Development* 4(2): 115–128.

Ijzendoorn, M.H. van, Goldberg, S., Kroonenberg, P.M., & Frenkel, O.J. (1992). The relative effects of maternal and child problems on the quality of attachment: A meta-analysis of attachment in clinical samples. *Child Development* 63: 840–858.

Ijzendoorn, M.H. van, Schuengel, C., & Bakermans-Kranenburg, M. (1999). Disorganised attachment in early childhood: Meta-analysis of precursors, concomitants, and sequelae. *Development and Psychopathology* 11: 225–249.

Isabella, R.A., & Belsky, J. (1991). Interactional synchrony and the origins of infant–mother attachment: A replication study. *Child Development* 62: 373–384.

Jacobsen, T., Gronvall, J., Petersen, S., & Andersen G.E. (1993). Minitouch treatment of very-low-birthweight infants. *Acta Pediatr.* 82: 934.

Janus, L. (1997). *Wie die Seele Entsteht.* Heidelberg: Hoffmann & Campe.

Johansson, B., Wedenberg, E., & Westen, B. (1964). Measurement of tone response by the human foetus: a preliminary report. *Acta Otolaryngology* 57: 188–192.

Johnston, M.V. (1995). Neurotransmitters and vulnerability of the developing brain. *Brain and Development* 17: 301–306.

Kaës, R. (2000). Rêve et utopie dans la cure d'une adolescente. Paper presented at 4e *Congrès Intern—Le Rêve Cent Ans Après*. Metz.

Kagan, J. (1982). *Psychological Research on the Human Infant: An Evaluative Summary.* New York: W.T. Grant Foundation.

Kagan, J., & Zentner, M. (1996). Infant's perception of consonance and dissonance in music. *Infant Behavior and Development* 21: 483–492.

Kaminski, J., & Hall, W. (1996). The effect of soothing music on neonatal behavioral states in the hospital newborn nursery. *Neonatal Network* 15 (1): 45–54.

Kast, V. (1982): *Trauern.* Stuttgart: Kreuz.

Katz, V. (1971). Auditory stimulation and developmental behaviour of the premature infant. *Nursing Research* 20 (3): 196–201.

Keating, D., & Hertzman, C. (1999). *Developmental Health and Wealth of Nations: Social, Biological and Educational Dynamics.* New York: The Gilford Press.

Kemper, K.J., Martin, K., Block, S.M., Shoaf, R., & Woods, C. (2004). Attitudes and expectations about music therapy for premature infants among staff in a neonatal intensive care unit. *Alternative Therapies in Health and Medicine,* 10(2): 50-54.

Kersting, N.G.A., & Arolt, V. (2000). Psychosomatische Störungen bei Müttern. *Psychotherapeut* 45: 10–17.

Kiese, C., & Kozielski, P.M. (1979). *Aktiver Wortschatz für Drei– Bis Sechsjährige Kinder.* AWST 3–6. Weinheim: Beltz.

Kitamura, C., & Burnham, D. (under review). The perception of communicative intent in mother's speech: adjustments for age and sex in the first year. *Infancy.*

Klaus, M.H. (1995). Touching during and after childbirth. In T.M. Field (Ed.), *Touch in Early Development.* Mahwah, N.J.: L. Erlbaum.

Klaus, M.H., & Fanaroff, A.A. (1976). Bach, Beethoven or Rock—and how much? *J. Pediatr.* 88 (2): 300.

Klaus, M.H., & Kennell, J.H. (1971). Care of the mother of the high-risk infant. *Clinical Obstetrics and Gynecology* 14.

Klaus, M.H., & Kennell, J.H. (1976). *Maternal-Infant-Bonding.* St. Louis: C.V. Mosby.

Klaus, M., &; Kennell, J. (1982). *Parent-Infant Bonding.* St. Louis: C.V. Mosby.

Klein, M. (1952). Some theoretical conclusions regarding the emotional life of the infant. In M. Klein, *The Writings of Melanie.* Vol. 3. London: Hogarth Press.

Koch, S. (1999). Developmental Support in the Neonatal Intensive Care Unit. In J. Deacon, & P. O'Neill (Eds.), *Core Curriculum for Neonatal Intensive Care Nursing* (pp. 522–539). Philadelphia, PA: Saunders Company.

Kohnstamm, G.A., Bates, J.E., & Rothbart, M.K. (1989). *Temperament in Childhood.* New York:Wiley.

Kübler-Ross, E. (1975). *On Death and Dying.* New York: The Macmillan Company.

Kurihara, H., Chiba, H., Shimizu, U., Tanaihara, T., Takeda, M., Kkawakami, K., & Takai-Kawakami, K. (1996). Behavioral and adrenocortical responses to stress in neonates and the stabilizing effects of maternal heartbeat on them. *Early Human Development* 46: 117–127.

Lalande, N.M., Hetu, R., & Lambert, J. (1986). Is occupational noise exposure during pregnancy a high risk factor of damage to the auditory system of the fetus? *American Journal of Industrial Medicine* 10: 427–435.

Latmiral, S., & Lombardo, C. (2000). *Pensieri Prematuri—Uno Sguardo alla Vita Mentale del Bambino Nato Pretermine.* Roma: Borla.

Lazar, R.A., Röpke, C., & Ermann, G. (1998). Learning to be: On the observation of a premature baby. *Int. J. Infant Observation* 2, 1.

Lecanuet, J.-P. (1996). The Fetal Stage. In I. Deliege, & J. Sloboda (Eds.), *Musical Beginnings. Origins and Development of Musical Competence.* (pp.3–36). Oxford: Oxford University Press.

Lecanuet, J.-P., & Schaal, B. (1996). Fetal sensory competencies. *Europ. J. Obs. Gyn. Reprod. Biol.* 68: 1–23.

LeDoux, J. (1999): *The Emotional Brain.* London: Phoenix.

Leib, S.A., Benfield, D.G., & Guidubaldi, J. (1980). Effects of early intervention and stimulation on the preterm infant. *Pediatrics* 66 (1): 83–90.

Lenz, G.M. (1998). Music therapy and early interactional disorders between mothers and infants. In R.R. Pratt, & D. Grocke (Eds.), *MusicMedicine*

3: Expanding Horizons (pp.162–177), Melbourne: University of Melbourne.

Lenz, G.M. (2000). Musiktherapie bei Schrei-Babys. Eine Pilotstudie zu frühen Interaktionsstörungen zwischen Mutter und Kind. *Musiktherapeutische Umschau* 21: 126–140.

Leonard, J.E. (1993). Music therapy: Fertile ground for application of research in practice. *Neonatal Network* 12 (2): 47–48.

Lewit, E.M., Baker, L.S., Corman, H., & Shiono, P.H. (1995). The Direct Cost of Low Birth Weight. Chapter 3, Low Birth Weight: The Future of Children, *The David and Lucille Packard Foundation* 5(1): 35–56.

Lickliter, R. (2000). Atypical perinatal sensory stimulation and early perceptual development: Insights from developmental psychobiology. *J. Perinatol.* 20: 45–54.

Liebman, S.S. (1989). The Effects of Music and Relaxation on Third Trimester Anxiety in Adolescent Pregnancy. *Unpublished Doctoral Thesis*, Miami.

Liebman, S.S., & MacLaren, A. (1991). The effects of music and relaxation on third trimester anxiety in adolescent pregnancy. *Journal of Music Therapy* 28 (2): 89–100.

Lind, J. (1980). Music and the small human being. *Acta Paediatrica Scandinavia* 69: 131–136.

Lindquist, R. (1985). The Role of GIM in the Birthing Process. *Unpublished Fellow's Paper, Institute for Consciousness and Music,* Port Townsend, WA.

Linn, P.L., Horowitz, F.D., & Fox, H.A, (1985). Stimulation in the NICU: Is more necessarily better? *Clin. Perinatol.* 12 (2): 407–422.

Lipton, B.H. (1998). Nature, nurture, and the power of love. *Journal of Prenatal and Perinatal Psychology and Health* 13 (1): 3–10.

Loewy, J.V. (Ed.) (2000). *Music Therapy in the Neonatal Intensive Care Unit.* Boston, MA: The Louis & Lucille Armstrong Music Therapy Program, Beth Israel Medical Center.

Logan, B. (1991). Infant Outcomes of a Prenatal Stimulation Pilot Study. *Prenatal and Perinatal Psychology Journal* 6 (1): 7–31.

Long, J.G., Lucey, J.F., & Philip, A.G.S. (1980). Noise and hypoxemia in the intensive care nursery. *Pediatrics* 65: 143–145.

Lorch, C.A., Lorch, V., Diefendorf, A.O., & Earl, P.W. (1994). Effect of stimulative and sedative music on systolic blood pressure, heart rate, and respiratory rate in premature infants. *Journal of Music Therapy* 31 (2): 105–118.

Lynam, L. (1995). Developmental care in the intensive care nursery: Putting prevention into practice. *Neonatal Intensive Care*, Sept-Oct, S. 37–41.

Lyons-Ruth, K. (1998). Implicit relational knowing: Its role in development and psychoanalytic treatment. *Infant Mental Health J.* 19: 3.

Macey, T.J., Harmon, R.J., & Easterbrooks, M.A. (1987). Impact of premature birth on the development of the infant in the family. *Journal of Consulting and Clinical Psychology* 55 (6): 846–852.

Macfarlane, A. (1977): *The Psychology of Childbirth*. London: Open Books Publ. Ltd.

Maiello, S. (1995). The sound-object: A hypothesis about prenatal auditory experience and memory. *J. Child Psychotherapy* 21, 1.

Maiello, S. (1997a). Interplay—sound aspects in mother–infant observation. In S. Reid (Ed.), *Developments in Infant Observation—The Tavistock Model*. London: Routledge.

Maiello, S. (1997b). Going beyond: Notes on the beginning of object relations in the light of the perpetuation of an error. In J. Mitrani, & T. Mitrani (Eds.), *Encounters with Autistic States*. New York: Jason Arouson Linc.

Maiello, S. (1999). The Premature Infant and the Maternal Voice. *Unpublished.*

Maiello, S. (2000). Broken links: Attack or breakdown? Notes on the origins of violence. *J. Child Psychotherapy* 26, 1.

Maiello, S. (2001). Prenatal trauma and autism. *J. Child Psychotherapy* 27, 2.

Main, M., Kaplan, N., & Cassidy, J. (1985). Security in infancy, childhood, and adulthood: A move to the level of representation. *Monographs of the Society for Research in Child Development*, 50.

Malatesta, C.Z., Culver, C., Tesman, J., & Shepard, B. (1989). The development of emotion expression during the first two years of life: Normative trends and patterns of individual differences. *Monographs of the Society for Research in Child Development* 1–2, Serial No. 219.

Malloch, S. (1999). Mothers and infants and communicative musicality. Rhythm, musical narrative and origins of human communication. *Special Issue of Musicae Scientiae*: 29–57.

Mancia, M. (1981). On the beginning of mental life in the foetus. *Int. J. Psycho-Analysis* 62.

Mangelsdorf, S.C., Plunkett, J.W., Dedrick, C.F., Berlin, M., Meisels, S.J., McHale, J.L., & Dichtellmiller, M. (1996). Attachment security in very low birth weight infants. *Development Psychology* 32(5): 914–920.

Marchette, L., Main, R., Redick, E., & Shapiro, A. (1992) Pain reduction during neonatal circumcision. In R. Spintge, & R. Droh (Eds.), *Music Medicine* (pp.131–141). St. Louis: MMB.

Marin-Padilla, M. (1993). Pathogenesis of late-acquired leptomeningeal heterotopias and secondary cortical alterations: A Golgi study. In A.M. Galaburda (Ed.), *Dyslexia and Development*. Cambridge: Harvard University Press.

Masakowski, Y., & Fifer, W.P. (1994). The effects of maternal speech on foetal behavior. *Intern. Conf. Infant Studies*, Paris.

Mathelin, C. (1998): *Le Sourire de la Joconde, Clinique Psychoanalytique avec les Bébés Prématurés*. Paris: Denoel.

McCarton, C.M., Wallace, I.F., & Bennett, F.C. (1995). Preventive interventions with low birth weight premature infants: An evaluation of their success. *Seminars in Perinatology* 19(4): 330–340.

McCormick, M.C. (1997). The outcomes of very low birth weight infants: Are we asking the right questions? *Pediatrics* 99: 869–876.

McCormick, M.C., McCarton, C., Brooks-Gunn, J., Belt, P., & Gross, R.T. (1998). The infant health and development program: Interim summary. *J. Dev. Behav. Ped.* 19: 359–70.

McCormick, M.C., Workman-Daniels, K., & Brooks-Gunn, J. (1996). The behavioural and emotional well-being of school-age children with different birth weights. *Pediatrics* 97: 18–25.

McKinney, C.H. (1990). Music therapy in obstetrics: A review. *Music Therapy Perspectives* 8: 57–60.

McKinney, C.H., Tims, F.C., Kumar, A.M., & Kumar, M. (1997). The effect of selected classical music and spontaneous imagery on plasma beta-endorphin. *Journal of Behavioral Medicine* 20 (1): 85–99.

Medoff-Cooper, B. (1986). Temperament in very low birth weight infants. *Nursing Research* 35 (3): 139–143.

Meltzoff, A.N., & Moore, M.K. (1992). Early imitation within a functional framework: The importance of person identity, movement and development. *Infant Behavior and Development* 15: 479–505.

Mendelsohn, A. (1999). In the wrong place at the wrong time. Paper presented at *ACP 50th Anniversary Conference*, London.

Mennella, J.A., Jagnow, C.P., & Beauchamp, G.K. (2001). Prenatal and postnatal flavor learning by human infants. *Pediatrics* (6): 107. http://www.pediatrics.org/cgi/content/full/107/6/e88.

Merenstein, G.B., & Gardner, S.L. (Eds.) (1998). *Handbook of Neonatal Intensive Care*. 4. Aufl. St. Louis: C.V. Mosby.

Messer, D.J. (1999). Communication, bonding, attachment, and separation. In D.J. Messer & F.J. Jones (Eds.), *Psychology for Social Carers*. London: Jessica Kingsley.

Miethge, W. (1978). Auswirkungen spezieller medizinischer Interventionen auf die Entwicklung der Mutter–Kind–Beziehung in der Ontogenese. *Phil. Inaug. Diss.*, Tübingen.

Miles, M., & Holditch-David, D. (1995). Compensatory parenting: how mothers parent their three year old prematurely born children. *Journal of Pediatric Nursing* 10 (4): 243–253.

Minde, K. (1980). Bonding of parents to premature infants. Theory and practice. In P. Taylor (Ed.), *Monographs in Neonatology*. (pp.291–313). New York: Grune & Stratton.

Minde, K. (1984). The impact of prematurity on the later behavior of children and on their families. *Clinics in Perinatology* 11 (1): 227–244.

Minde, K., Goldberg, S., Perrotta, M., Washington, J., Lojkasek, M., & Parker, K. (1989). Continuities and discontinuities in the development of 64 very small premature infants to 4 years of age. *Journal of Child*

Psychology and Psychiatry 30(3): 391–404.

Minde, K., Whitelaw, A., Brown, J., & Fitzhardinge, P.(1983). The effects of neonatal complications in premature infants on early parent-infant interactions. *Developmental Medicine and Child Neurology* 25: 763–777.

Montague, A. (1979). *Le Peau et le Toucher, un Premier Language.* Paris: Seuil.

Moon, C., & Fifer, W.P. (1990). Newborns prefer a prenatal version of mother's voice. *Int. Society of Infant Studies,* Montreal.

Moon, C., & Fifer, W.P. (2000). Evidence of transnatal auditory learning. *J. Perinatol.* 20: 37–44.

Moore, R., Gladstone, I., & Standley, J.M. (1994). Effects of music, maternal voice, intrauterine sounds and white noise on the oxygen saturation levels of premature infants. Poster session presented at the *National Convention of the National Association for Music Therapy,* Orlando.

Morgan, A.C. (1998). Moving along to things left undone. *Infant Mental Health Journal* 19: 324–332.

Morton, J., & Johnson, M.H. (1991). Conspec and conlern: A two–process theory of infant face recognition. *Psychological Review* 98: 164–181.

Murdoch, D. R., & Darlow, B. A. (1984). Handling during neonatal intensive care. *Arch. Dis. Child* 59: 957–961.

Murray, A.D., & Hornbaker, A.V. (1997). Maternal directive and facilitative interaction styles: Association with language and cognitive development of low risk and high risk toddlers. *Development and Psychopathology* 9: 507–516.

Mustard, F. (1999). The Early Years Study: Reversing the Real Brain Drain. Toronto: *Ontario Children's Secretariat.* http://www.childsec.gov.on.ca/3_resources/early_years_study/early_ye ars.html.

Myers, R.E., & Myers, S.E. (1979). Use of sedative, analgesic, and anesthetic drugs during labor and delivery: Bane or boon? *Am. J. Obstet. Gynecol.* 133: 83–104.

Nadel, J., Carchon, I., Kervella, C., Marcelli, D., & Réserbat-Plantey, D. (1999). Expectancies for social contingency in 2-month-olds. *Developmental Science* 2 (2): 164–173.

Nathanielsz, P.W. (1995). The role of basic science in preventing low birth weight. The Future of Children, *The David and Lucille Packard Foundation* 5 (1): 57–70.

National Institutes of Health Consensus Report (1990). *Noise and hearing loss.* US Department of Health and Human Services, National Institutes of Health: Bethesda.

Negri, R. (1994). *The Newborn in the Intensive Care Unit—a Neuro-Psychoanalytic Prevention Model.* London: The Clunie Press.

Newman, J. (1999). *Opening Address of the Nat. Conference on Family Strengths.* Univ. of Newcastle, Australia.

Nöcker, M., Güntner, M., & Riegel, K.P. (1987). The effect of the mother's voice on the physical activity and the tcPO2 of very premature infants. *Pediatric Research* 22: 21.

Nöcker-Ribaupierre, M. (1994). Zur Entwicklung des subjektiven Erlebens: Ein musiktherapeutisches Konzept für die Behandlung frühgeborener Kinder. *Int. J. Prenatal and Perinatal Psychology and Medicine* 6, 2.

Nöcker-Ribaupierre, M. (1995). *Auditive Stimulation nach Frühgeburt. Ein Beitrag zur Musiktherapie.* Stuttgart: G. Fischer.

Nöcker-Ribaupierre, M. (1998). Short and longterm effects of the maternal voice on the behaviors of very low birth weight infants and their mothers as a basis for the bonding process. In R.R. Pratt, & D. Grocke (Eds.), *MusicMedicine 3: Expanding Horizons.* (pp.162–177). Melbourne: University of Melbourne.

Nöcker-Ribaupierre, M. (1999). Premature birth and music therapy. In T. Wigram, & J. De Backer (Eds.), *Clinical Application of Music Therapy in Developmental Disability, Pediatrics and Neurology.* (pp.47–68). London: Jessica Kingsley.

Nöcker-Ribaupierre, M. (2001). Entwicklung und Bedeutung des Hörens. In H.H. Decker-Voigt (Ed.), *Halbjahreszeitung für Musik in Therapie, Medizin und Beratung.* (pp.11–14). Lilienthal: Eres.

Nordoff, P., & Robbins, C. (1975). *Creative Music Therapy.* New York: Samuel Day.

Nyman, M., Arulkumaran, S., Hsu, T.S., Ratnam, S.S., Till, O., & Westgren, M. (1991). Vibroacoustic stimulation and intrauterine sound pressure levels. *Obstetrics and Gynecology* 78: 803–806.

Nzama, M., Nolte, A.G., & Dorfling, C.S. (1995). Noise in the neonatal unit: Guidelines for the reduction or prevention of noise. *Curationis* 18: 16–21.

Oberklaid, F., Prior, M., & Sanson, A. (1986). Temperament of preterm versus full-term infants. *Developmental and Behavioral Pediatrics* 7 (3): 159–162.

Ogden, T.H. (1989): *The Primitive Edge of Experience.* New York: Jason Arouson.

Oremland, J.D. (1987). Michelangelos' Sistina ceiling. In *A Psychoanalytic Study of Creativity.* New York: International Universities Press.

Owens, L.D. (1979). The effects of music on the weight loss, crying, and physical movement of newborns. *Journal of Music Therapy* 26 (2): 83–90.

Paneth, N. (1992). Neonatal care and patterns of disability in the community. *Clinics in Developmental Medicine* 124: 232–241.

Papoušek, H., & Papoušek, M. (1997. Fragile aspects of early social interaction. In L. Murray, & P.J. Cooper (Eds.), *Postpartum Depression and Child Development.* (pp.35–53). New York: Guilford Press.

Papoušek, M., & Papoušek, H. (1991). The meanings of melodies in motherese in tone and stress languages. *Infant Behavior and Development* 14: 415–550.

Papoušek, M. (1994). Die muttersprachliche Umwelt des Säuglings und ihre Bedeutung für die Entwicklung von Vokalisation und Sprache. In K.F. Wessel, & F. Naumann (Eds.), *Kommunikation und Humanontogenese.* Bielefeld: Kleine.

Papoušek, M. (1996): Intuitive parenting: A hidden source of musical stimulation in infancy. In I. Deliege, & J. Sloboda. (Eds.), *Musical Beginnings.* Oxford: Oxford University Press.

Papoušek, M. (2001): *Vom Ersten Schrei zum Ersten Wort.* Bern: Hans Huber.

Parker, S.J., Zahr, L.K., Cole, J.G., & Brecht, M. (1992). Outcome after developmental intervention in the neonatal intensive care unit for mothers of preterm infants with low socioeconomic status. *J. Pediatr.* 120: 780–785.

Paul, C. (2000). The experience of staff who work in neonatal intensive care. In N. Tracey (Ed.), *Parents of Premature Infants: Their Emotional World.* (pp.229–240). London: Whurr Publ.

Peltzam, P., Kitterman, J.A., Ostwald, P.F., Manchester, D., & Heath, L. (1970). Effects of incubator noise on human hearing. *The Journal of Auditory Research.*

Perry, B. (1997). Memories in fears: How the brains stores and retrieves physiologic states, feelings, behaviors and thoughts from traumatic events. In J. Goodwin, & R. Attias (Eds.), *Images of the Body in Trauma.* New York: Basic Books.

Perry, B., & Pollard, R. (1998). Homeostasis, stress, trauma, and adaptation: A neurodevelopmental view of childhood trauma. *Child and Adolescent Psychiatric Clinical of North America* 7 (1): 33–51.

Peters, A.J.M., Abrams, R.M., Gerhardt, K.J., & Longmate, J.A. (1991). Three-dimensional sound and vibration frequency responses of the sheep uterus. *Journal of Low Frequency Noise and Vibration* 10: 100–111.

Peters, A.J.M., Gerhardt, K.J., Abrams, R.M., & Longmate, J.A. (1993). Three-dimensional intra-abdominal sound pressures in sheep produced by airborne stimuli. *American Journal of Obstetrics and Gynecology* 169: 1304–1315.

Peterson, B., Vohr, B., Staib, L.H., Cannistraci, C.J., Dolberg, A., & Schneider, K.C. (2000). Regional brain volume abnormalities and long-term cognitive outcome in preterm infants. *JAMA* 284: 1939–1947.

Petryshen, P., Stevens, B., Hawkins, J., & Stewart, M. (1997). Comparing nursing costs for preterm infants receiving conventional vs. developmental care. *Nursing Economics* 15 (3): 138–150.

Pharooh, P.O.D., Stevenson, C.J., Cooke, R.W.I., & Stevenson, R.C. (1994a). Clinical and subclinical deficits in a geographically defined cohort of low birthweight infants. *Arch. Dis. Child* 70: 264–270.

Pharoah, P.O.D., Stevenson, C.J., Cooke, R.W.I., & Stevenson, R.C. (1994b).

Prevalence of behaviour disorders in low birthweight infants. *Arch. Dis. Child* 70: 271–274.

Philbin, K.M. (2000a). Sensory experience and the developing organism: A history of ideas and view to the future. *J. Perinatol.* 20: 2–5.

Philbin, K.M. (2000b). The influence of auditory experience on the behavior of preterm newborns. *J. Perinatol.* 20: 77–87.

Philbin, M.K., Ballweg, D.D., & Gray, L. (1994). The effect of an intensive care unit sound environment on the development of habituation in healthy avian neonates. *Developmental Psychobiology* 27 (1): 11–21.

Philbin, M.K., Robertson, A., & Hall, J.W. (1999). Recommended permissible noise criteria for occupied, newly constructed or renovated hospital nurseries. *Journal of Perinatology* 19 (8) Part I: 559–563.

Piontelli, A. (1992): *From Foetus to Child – An Observational and Psychoanalytic Study*. London: Routledge.

Pipp-Siegel, S., Siegel, C.H., & Dean, J. (1999). Neurological aspects of the disorganized/disoriented attachment classification system: differentiating quality for the attachment relationship from neurological impairment. *Monographs of the Society for Research in Child Development*: Serial No. 258, 64 (3): 25–44.

Plunkett, J., Meisels, S.J., Stiefel, G.S., Pasick, P.L., & Roloff, D.W. (1986). Patterns of attachment among preterm infants of varying biological risk. *Journal of the American Academy of Child Psychiatry* 25 (6): 794–800.

Pratt, R.R. (1999). Music and infant well-being. In R.R. Pratt, & D. Grocke (Eds.), *MusicMedicine 3—Expanding Horizons*. Melbourne: University of Melbourne.

Prechtl, H.F.R. (1989). Fetal behaviour. In A. Hill, & J. Volpe (Eds.), *Fetal Neurology*. New York: Raven Press.

Prechtl, H.F.R., & Beintema, D. (1974). *Neurobiological Examination of the Fullterm and Newborn Infant*. London: Heinemann.

Pujol, R., & Uziel, A. (1989). Auditory development: Peripheral aspects. In P.S. Timiras, & E. Meisami (Eds.), *Handbook of Human Biologic Development*. (pp.109–130). Boca Raton, FL: CRC Press.

Querleu, D., Renard, X., Boutteville, C., & Crepin, G. (1989). Hearing by the human fetus? *Seminars in Perinatology*, 13: S. 430–433.

Querleu, D., Renard, X., Versyp, F., Paris-Delrue, L., & Crepin, G. (1988). Fetal hearing. *European Journal of Obstetrics and Reproductive Biology* 29: 191–212.

Rakic, P. (1995). Corticogenesis in human and nonhuman primates. In M. Gazzaniga (Ed.), *The Cognitive Neurosciences*. (pp.127–146). Cambridge MA: MIT Press.

Rascovsky, A. (1977): *El Psichismo Fetal*. Buenos Aires: Paidos.

Rauscher, F.H., Shaw, G.L., Levine, L.J., Wright, E.L., Dennis, W.R., & Newcomb, R.L. (1997): Music training causes long-term enhancement of preschool children's spatial–temporal reasoning. *Neurological Research* 19(1): 218.

Richards, D.S., Frentzen, B., Gerhardt, K.J., McCann, M.E., & Abrams, R.M. (1992). Sound levels in the human uterus. *Obstetrics and Gynecology* 80: 186–190.

Richards, M.P.M. (1985). Bonding babies. *Archives of Disease in Childhood* 60: 293–294.

Riegel, K.P., Ohrt, B., & Wolke, D. (1985). *Die Entwicklung Gefährdet Geborener Kinder bis zum Fünften Lebensjahr.* Stuttgart: Enke.

Righetti, P.L. (1996). The emotional experience of the fetus: A preliminary report. *Pre- and Perinatal Psychology Journal* 11(1): 55–65.

Rock, A., Trainor, L., & Addison, T. (1999). Distinctive messages in infant-directed lullabies and play songs. *Developmental Psychology* 35 (2): 527–534.

Rode, S.S., Chang, P.-N., & Fisch, R.O.S. (1981). Attachment patterns of infants separated at birth. *Developmental Psychology* 17 (2): 188–191.

Rose, H., & Mayer, J. (1968). Activity, caloric intake, fat storage and the energy balance of infants. *Pediatrics* 41, 1: 18–29.

Roth, G. (2001). *Fühlen, Denken, Handeln. Wie das Gehirn Unser Verhalten Steuert.* Frankfurt a. M.: Suhrkamp.

Rubel, E.W. (1984). Ontogeny of auditory system function. *Annual Review Physiology* 46: 213.

Salk, L. (1973). The role of the heartbeat in the relationship between mother and infant. *Scientific American.*

Schindler, S., & Zimprich, H. (Eds.) (1983). *Ökologie der Perinatalzeit.* Stuttgart: Hippokrates.

Schölmerich, A., Fracasso, M.P., Lamb, M.E., & Broberg, A.G. (1995). Interactional harmony at 7 and 10 months of age predicts security of attachment as measured by q-sort ratings. *Social Development* 4 (1): 62–74.

Schuck, K.D., Eggert, D., & Raatz, U. (1975). *Columbia Skala als Gruppenintelligenz-Test für die Erste Bis Dritte Grundschulklasse,* CMM 1–3. Weinheim: Beltz.

Schwartz, F.J. (2000). Music and sound effect on perinatal brain development and the premature Baby. In J. V.Loewy (Ed.), *Music Therapy in the NICU.* (pp.9–20). New York: Satchnote-Armstrong Press.

Schwartz, F.J. (1997). Perinatal stress reduction, music, and medical cost savings. *Journal of Prenatal and Perinatal Psychology and Health* 12(1): 19–29.

Schwartz, F.J., & Ritchie, R. (1998). Perinatal stress reduction music, and medical cost savings. Paper presented at the *VIIth International Music and Medicine Symposium*, Melbourne.

Schwartz, F.J., & Ritchie, R. (1999). Music listening in neonatal intensive care units. In C. Dileo (Ed.), *Music Therapy and Medicine: Theoretical and*

Clinical Applications. (pp.13–22). Silver Spring, MD: American Music Therapy Association.

Seifer, R., & Schiller, M. (1995) The role of parenting sensitivity, infant temperament, and dyadic interaction in attachment theory and assessment. In E. Waters, B.E. Vaughn, G. Posada, & K. Kondo-Ikemura (Eds.), *Monographs of the Society for Research in Child Development*: Caregiving, Cultural and Cognitive Perspectives on Secure-Base Behavior and Working Models.

Shahidullah, S., &; Hepper, P.G. (1992). Hearing in the fetus: Prenatal detection of deafness. *International Journal of Prenatal and Perinatal Studies* 4 (3/4): 235–240.

Shahidullah, S., & Hepper, P.G. (1993). The developmental origins of fetal responsiveness to an acoustic stimulus. *Journal of Reproductive and Infant Psychology* 11: 135–142.

Shahidullah, S., & Hepper, P.G. (1994). Frequency discrimination by the fetus. *Early Human Development* 36: 13–26.

Shehan, C.L. (1996). Sociodemographic perspectives on pregnant women at work. *Seminar in Perinatology* 20: 2–10.

Sheth, R.D., Mullett, M.D., Bodensteiner, J.B., & Hobbs, G.R. (1995). Longitudinal head growth in developmentally normal preterm infants. *Archives of Pediatric Adolescent Medicine* 149: 1358–1361.

Shetler, D. J. (1989). The inquiry into prenatal musical experience: A report of The Eastman Project 1980–1987. *Pre- and Perinatal Psychology Journal* 3(3): 171–189.

Shoemark, H. (1994). The process of music therapy as it relates to the development of children with multiple disabilities. In A. Lem (Ed.), *Music Therapy Collection.* (pp.45–49) Canberra: Ausdane.

Shoemark, H. (1998). Singing as the foundation for multi-modal stimulation. In R.R. Pratt, & D. Grocke (Eds.), *MusicMedicine 3: Expanding Horizons.* (pp.140–153). Melbourne: University of Melbourne.

Shoemark, H. (1999). Indications for the inclusion of music therapy in the care of infants with bronchopulmonary dysplasia. In T. Wigram, & J. De Backer (Eds.), *Clinical Applications of Music Therapy in Developmental Disability, Paidiatrics and Neurology.* (pp.32–46). London: Jessica Kingsley.

Shonkoff, J.P., & Philipps, D.A. (Eds.) (2000). From neurons to neighborhoods. The science of early childhood development. *National Research Council. Institute of Medicine.* Washington DC.

Simkin, P.T. (1986). Stress, pain, and catecholamines in labor: Part 1. A review. *Birth* 13 (4): 227–233.

Singer, L.T., Salvator, A., Guo, S., Collin, M., Lilien, L., & Baley, J. (1999). Maternal psychological distress and parenting stress after the birth of a very low-birthweight infant. *Journal of the American Medical Association* 281 (9): 799–805.

Smotherman, W.P., & Robinson, S.R. (1988). Dimensions of fetal investigation. In W.P. Smotherman, & S.R. Robinson (Eds.), *Behavior of the Fetus.* (pp.19–34). New Jersey: The Telford Press.

Spangler, G., & Scheubeck, R. (1993). Behavioural organisation in newborns and its relation to adrenocortical and cardiac activity. *Child Development* 64: 622–633.

Spence, M.J., & DeCasper, A.J. (1987). Prenatal experience with low frequency maternal-voice sounds influence neonatal perception of maternal voice samples. *Infant Behavior and Development* 10: 133–142.

Spintge, R., & Droh, R. (1987). Effects of anxiolytic music on plasma levels of stress hormones in different medical specialties. In R.R. Pratt (Ed.), *The Fourth International Symposium on Music: Rehabilitation and Human Well-Being.* (pp.88–101).Lanham: University Press of America.

Spitz, R.A. (1945). Hospitalism: An inquiry into the genesis of psychiatric conditions in early childhood. *Psychoanalytic Study of the Child* 1: 153–172.

Sroufe, L.A. (1985). Attachment classification from the perspective of infant–caregiver relationships and infant temperament. *Child Development* 56: 1–14.

Standley, J.M. (1996a). Music research in medical/dental treatment: An update of a prior meta-analysis. In C.E. Furman (Ed.), *Effectiveness of Music Therapy Procedures: Documentation of Research and Clinical Practice* (pp.1–60). Silver Spring: NAMT.

Standley, J.M. (1996b). The effect of music and multimodal stimulation on physiologic and developmental responses of premature infants in neonatal intensive care. Presented at the *VIth International Society of Music in Medicine Symposium*, San Antonio, Texas.

Standley, J.M. (1997). The effect of contingent music to increase non-nutritive sucking of premature infants. Paper presented at *The Meeting of the National Association for Music Therapy,* Los Angeles.

Standley, J.M. (1998a). Effect of music intervention on head circumference of premature infants: A post-hoc analysis of music research in neonatal intensive care. Paper presented at the *National Convention of American Music Therapy Association.* Cleveland, OH.

Standley, J.M. (1998b). The effect of contingent music to increase non-nutritive sucking of premature infants. Presented at *the VIIth International Society of Music in Medicine Symposium*, Melbourne.

Standley, J.M. (1998c). The effect of music and multimodal stimulation on responses of premature infants in neonatal intensive care. *Pediatric Nursing* 24 (6): 532–538.

Standley, J.M. (1998d). The effect of music and multimodal stimulation on physiologic and developmental responses of premature infants in neonatal intensive care. *Pediatric Nursing* 21 (6): 509–512, 574.

Standley, J.M. (2000). The effect of contingent music to increase non-nutritive sucking of premature infants. *Pediatric Nursing* 26 (5): 494–499.

Standley, J.M. (2001). Music therapy for the neonate. *Newborn and Infant Nursing Reviews* 1 (4): 211–216.

Standley, J.M., & Madsen, C.K. (1990). Comparison of infant preferences and responses to auditory stimuli: Music, mother and other female voice. *Journal of Music Therapy* XXVII (2): 54–97.

Standley, J.M., & Moore, R. (1995). Therapeutic effects of music and mother's voice on premature infants. *Pediatric Nursing* 21 (6): 509–512, 574.

Stennert, E., Schulte, F.J., Vollrath, M., & Brunner, E. (1978). Etiology of neurosensory hearing defects in premies. *Arch. Otorhinolaryngol* 221: 171–182.

Stern, D. (1977). *The First Relationship: Infant and Mother.* London: Open Books.

Stern, D. (1985). *The Interpersonal World of the Infant.* New York: Basic Books.

Stern, D. (1990). *Diary of a Baby. What your Child Sees, Feels, and Experiences.* New York: Basic Books.

Stern, D. (1995). *The Motherhood Constellation.* New York: Basic Books.

Stern, D. (1997). The development of the self. The narrative. Presentation *Lindauer Psychotherapiewochen.*

Stern, D. (1998). The process of therapeutic change involving implicit knowledge: Some implications of developmental observations for adult psychotherapy. *Infant Mental Health Journal* 19: 300–308.

Stern, D. (1999). The development of the self. Presentation *Weltkongress Psychotherapie,* Wien.

Sternqvist, K. (1996). The birth of an extremely low birth weight infant (ELBW) < 901g: impact on the family after 1 and 4 years. *Journal of Reproductive and Infant Psychology* 14: 243–264.

Stevens, B., Petryshen, P., Hawkins, J., Smith, B., & Taylor, P. (1996). Developmental versus conventional care: A comparison of clinical outcomes for very low birth weight infants. *Canadian J. Nurs. Res.* 28: 97–113.

Stewart, K., & Schneider, S. (2000). The effects of music therapy on the sound environment in the NICU: A pilot study. In J. V. Loewy (Ed.), *Music Therapy in the NICU* (pp.85–100). New York: Satchnote-Armstrong Press.

Sticker, E.J., Brandt, I., & Hoecky, M. (1999). Resilience: Die Überwindung von Entwicklungsproblemen am Beispiel sehr kleiner Frühgeborener. *Monatsschr. Kinderheilkd.* 147: 676–685.

Stiefel, G.S., Plunkett, J.W., & Meisels, S.J. (1987). Affective expression among preterm infants of varying levels of biological risk. *Infant Behavior and Development* 10: 151–164.

Stjernqvist, K., Svenningsen, N.W. (1999). Ten-year follow up of children born before 29 gestational weeks: Health, cognitive development, behaviour and school achievement. *Acta Pediatr.* 88: 557–562.

Stork, J. (1986). Die Ergebnisse der Verhaltensforschung im psychoanalytischen Verständnis. In J. Stork (Ed.), *Zur Psychologie und Psychopathologie des Säuglings.* Stuttgart: Frommann-Holzboog.

Sudsuang, R., Chentanez, V., & Veluvan, K. (1991). Effect of Buddhist meditation on serum cortisol and total protein levels, blood pressure, pulse rate, lung volume and reaction time. *Physiology and Behavior* 50: 543–548.

Sumner, E. (1993). Pain: Its implications in the newborn and premature baby. Proceedings of *Conference Problemi Medici e Chirurgici in età Pediatrica.* Bergamo.

Szur, R. (1981). Children in hospital. *J. Child Psychotherapy* 7. 2.

Thompson, R., Goldstein, R., Oehler, J., Gustafson, K., Catlett, A., & Brazy, J. (1994). Developmental outcome of very low birth weight infants as a function of biological risk and psychosocial risk. *Developmental and Behavioral Pediatrics* 15: 232–238.

Tomaino, C. (1998). Music on Their Minds: A Qualitative Study of the Effects of Using Familiar Music to Stimulate Preserved Memory Function in Persons with Dementia. *Doctoral Thesis.* New York.

Tomatis, A.A. (1981). *La Nuit Utérine.* Paris: Stock.

Trainor, L.J. (1996). Infant preferences for infant–directed versus noninfant-directed playsongs and lullabies. *Infant Behavior and Development* 19: 83–92.

Trehub, S.E., Bull, D., & Thorpe, L.A. (1984). Infants' perception of melodies: the role of melodic contour. *Child Development* 55: 821–830.

Trehub, S., & Thorpe, L. (1989). Infants' perception of rhythm: categorization of auditory sequences by temporal structure. *Canadian Journal of Psychology* 43 (2): 217–229.

Trehub, S., Unyk, A., Kamenetskyk, S., Hill, D., Trainor, L., Henderson, J., & Saraza, M. (1997). Mothers' and fathers' singing to infants. *Developmental Psychology* 33 (3): 500–507.

Trehub, S., Unyk, A., & Trainor, L. (1993a). Adults identify infant-directed music across cultures. *Infant Behavior and Development* 16: 193–211.

Trehub, S., Unyk, A., & Trainor, L. (1993b). Maternal singing in cross-cultural perspective. *Infant Behavior and Development* 16: 285–295.

Trevarthen, C. (1979). Communication and cooperation in early infancy. A description of primary intersubjectivity. In M.M. Ullowa (Ed.), *Before Speech: The Beginning of Interpersonal Communication.* New York: Cambridge University Press.

Trevarthen, C. (1993). The functions of emotions in early infant communication and development. In J. Nadel, & L. Camaioni (Ed.), *New Perspectives in Early Communicative Development.* London: Routledge.

Trevarthen, C., Aitken, K., Papoudi, D., & Robarts, J. (1996). *Children with Autism.* London: Jessica Kingsley Pub.

Tronick, E. (1989). Emotions and emotional communication in infants. *American Psychologist* 44.

Tronick, E. (1995). Touch in mother-infant interaction. In T.M. Field (Ed.), *Touch in Early Development*. Mahwah, N.J.: J. Erlbaum.

Tronick, E.Z. (1989). Dyadically expanded states of consciousness and the process of therapeutic change. *Infant Mental Health Journal* 19: 290–299.

Tronick, E., Als, H., & Brazelton, T. (1980). Monadic phases: A structural descriptive analysis of infant-mother face–to–face interaction. *Merrill-Palmer Quarterly of Behaviour and Development* 26: 1–24.

Tustin, F. (1986). *Autistic Barriers in Neurotic Patients*. London: Karnac.

Tustin, F. (1990). *The Protective Shell in Children and Adults*. London: Karnac.

Unyk, A., Trehub, S., Trainor, L., & Schellenberg, E. G. (1992). Lullabies and simplicity: A cross-cultural perspective. *Psychology of Music* 20: 15–28.

Uvnäs-Moberg, K. (1997). Physiological and endocrine effects of social contact. *Annals New York Academy of Sciences* 807: 146–163.

Vimpani, G. (1999). The renaissance of early childhood. Keynote presentation to the *National Conference of the Association for the Welfare of Child Health*, Sydney.

Vince, M.A., Armitage, S.E., Baldwin, B.A., & Toner, J. (1982). The sound environment of the foetal sheep. *Behaviour* 81: 296–315.

Vince, M.A., Billing, A.E., Baldwin, B.A., Toner, J.N., & Weller, C. (1985). Maternal vocalizations and other sounds in the fetal lamb's sound environment. *Early Human Development* 11: 179–190.

Volpe, J. (2000). *Neurology of the Newborn*. 4th ed. Philadelphia PA:WB Saunders.

Walker, D.W., Grimwade, J.C., & Wood, C. (1971). Intrauterine noise: A component of the fetal environment. *American Journal of Obstetrics and Gynecology* 109: 91–95.

Warren, B. (2000). The premature infant in the mind of the mother. In N. Tracey (Ed.), *Parents of Premature Infants: Their Emotional World* (pp.67–84). London: Whurr.

Wartner, U.G., Grossmann, K., Fremmer-Bombik, E., & Suess, G. (1994). Attachment patterns at age six in south Germany: Predictability from infancy and implications for preschool behaviour. *Child Development* 65: 1014–1027.

Wereszczak, J., Shandor Miles, M., & Holditch-Davis, D. (1997). Maternal recall of the neonatal intensive care unit. *Neonatal Network16* (4), S. 33–40.

Werner, L.A., & Marean, G.C. (1996). *Human Auditory Development*. Boulder, CO, S. 20.

Westrup, B., Kleberg, A., von Eichwald, K., Stjernqvist, K., & Lagercrantz, H. (2000). A randomized, controlled trial to evaluate the effects of newborn individualized developmental care and assessment program in a swedish setting. *Pediatrics* 105: 66–72.

Wettstein, P. (1983): LSVT: *Logopädischer Sprachverständnistest.* Zürich: Heilpädagogisches Seminar.

Whipple, J. (2000). The efect of parent taining in music and multimodal stimulation on parent-neonate interactions in the neonatal intensive care unit. *Journal of Music Therapy* 37 (4): 250–268.

White-Traut, R., Nelson, M., Silvestri, J., Patel, M., Vasan, U., Han, B., Cunningham, N., Burns, K., Kopischke, K., & Bradford, L. (1999). Developmental intervention for preterm infants diagnosed with periventricular leukomalacia. *Research in Nursing and Health* 22: 131–143.

White-Traut, R., & Tubeszewski, K. (1986). Multimodal stimulation of the premature infant. *Journal of Pediatric Nursing* 1(2): 90–95.

Wille, D.E. (1991). Relation of preterm birth with quality of infant-mother attachment at one year. *Infant Behavior and Development* 14: 227–240.

Winick, M. (1969). Malnutrition and brain development. *The Journal of Pediatrics* 74 (5): 667–679.

Winnicott, D.W. (1965). *The Maturational Processes and the Facilitating Environment.* London: Tavistock.

Winnicott, D.W. (1971). *Playing and Reality.* London: Tavistock.

Winokur, M.A. (1984). The Use of Music as an Audio-Analgesia during Childbirth. *Unpublished Master's Thesis,* The Florida State University, Tallahassee.

Winslow, G. (1986). Music therapy in the treatment of anxiety in hospitalized high-risk mothers. *Music Therapy Perspectives* 3: 29–33.

Wolke, D. (1987). Environmental and developmental neonatology. *Journal of Reproductive and Infant Psychology* 5: 17–42.

Wolke, D. (1991). Annotation: Supporting the development of low birth weight infants. *Journal of Child Psychology and Psychiatry,* 32 No. 5: 723–741.

Wolke, D. (1998). The psychological development of prematurely born children. *Archives of Disease in Childhood* 78: 567–570.

Wolke, D., & Eldrige, T. (1991). Environmental care. In A.G.M. Campbell, & T. McIntosh (Eds.), *Forfar and Arneil's Testbook of Pediatrics.* Edinburgh: Churchill Livingstone.

Wolke, D., & Meyer, R. (1994). Psychologische Langzeitbefunde bei sehr früh geborenen. *Perinatal Medizin* 6: 121–123.

Wolke, D., & Meyer, R. (1999). Ergebnisse der Bayerischen Entwicklungsstudie: Implikationen für Theorie und Praxis. *Kindheit und Entwicklung* 8(1): 24–36.

Wolke, D., & Meyer, R. (2000). Ergebnisse der Bayerischen Entwicklungsstudie an neonatalen Risikokindern: Implikationen für Theorie und Praxis. In K.N. Franz Petermann, & H. Scheithauer (Eds.), *Risiken in der*

Frühkindlichen Entwicklung (pp.114–138). Göttingen: Hogrefe.

Wolke, D., Ratschinsk, G., Ohrt, B., & Riegel, K.P. (1994). The outcome of very preterm infants may be poorer than often reported: an empirical investigation of how methodological issues make a big difference. *European Journal of Pediatrics* 153: 906–915.

Wolke, D., Schulz, J., & Meyer, R. (1998). Identifying very low birthweight (VLBW) infants at high risk for longterm cognitive sequelae. In P. van den Hazel (Ed.), *XXII International Congress of Pediatrics* (IPA World Congress of Pediatrics). Amsterdam, 99.

Woodward, S.C., & Guidozzi, F. (1992). Intrauterine rhythm and blues? *British Journal of Obstetrics and Gynaecology* 199: 787–789.

Young, M. (Ed.) (1997). *Early Child Development: Investing in Our Children's Future.* New York: Elsevier.

Zahr, L.K., & Traversay, J.D. (1995). Premature infant responses to noise reduction by earmuffs: Effects on behavioral and physiologic measures. *Journal of Perinatology* 15(6): 448–455.

Zahr, L.K., & Balian, S. (1995). Responses of premature infants to routine nursing intervention and noise in the NICU. *Nurse Res.* 44: 179–185.

Zeanah, C.H., Boris, N.W., & Larrieu, J.A. (1997). Infant development and developmental risk: A review of the past ten years. *Journal of the American Academy of Child and Adolescent Psychiatry*, 36(2): 165–178.

INDEX